USING THE WORLD WIDE WEB AND CREATING HOME PAGES

A How-To-Do-It Manual

Ray E. Metz
Gail Junion-Metz

**HOW-TO-DO-IT MANUALS
FOR LIBRARIANS**

NUMBER 67

NEAL-SCHUMAN PUBLISHERS, INC.
New York, London

Published by Neal-Schuman Publishers, Inc.
100 Varick Street
New York, NY 10013

Printed and bound in the United States of America.

Library of Congress Cataloging-in-Publication Data

Metz, Ray E.
   Using the World Wide Web and creating home pages : A how-to-do-it
manual for librarians / by Ray E. Metz, Gail Junion-Metz.
     p.   cm.—(How-to-do-it manuals for libraries ; no. 67)
Includes bibliographical references and index.
ISBN 1-55570-241-4
1. World Wide Web (Information retrieval system)   2. Library information
networks. I. Junion-Metz, Gail, 1947-   II. Series.
Z675.75.W67M48   1996
025.04—dc20   96-20304

CONTENTS

ACKNOWLEDGMENTS

We would like to thank the following people who helped us produce this book. Tom Klingler, for his help in proofreading and text editing; Jim Nauer, for his help producing the screen images used in the book; and George Burgyan, for his help producing the original graphics used in the book. We would also like to thank the folks at Neal-Schuman, especially Charles Harmon and Judy Walters who patiently helped us through the creation and editing process. Finally we would like to thank Derrek, our inspiration always.

FIGURES

PREFACE

Using the World Wide Web and Creating Home Pages provides you with basic information about the Web so that you can

- understand why it is such an important information tool;
- choose and establish an Internet connection that supports Web access or upgrade your present Net connection;
- plan for and create a "starter" Web site; and
- train staff and patrons to use the Web.

Like other books in Neal-Schuman's "How To" and "Net-Guide" series, *Using the World Wide Web and Creating Home Pages* is designed for library administrators, professional and support staff, and interested patrons.

There are many Web books on the market focusing on how to use browser software or where to find Web resources. *Using the World Wide Web and Creating Home Pages* does take a broader approach to the topic, but focuses on the Web for libraries and for providing patrons with Web access. It explains a wide variety of Web concepts in a practical manner, so you understand enough to start making decisions about getting and using the Web. Our book is one of the first that discusses, in detail, the process of planning for and implementing a library/community Web site. We break down the planning process into clear and simple steps, discuss the decisions you need to make, and suggest who should be involved in making decisions at each step along the way.

Our practical approach to this complex subject is evident throughout the book. For instance, instead of writing about Internet connections and supplying you with every technical detail that you may or may not need, we provide you with just enough detail, in plain, non-technical English, so you can decide which Internet connection is best for your situation. You can also use our "plain language" approach to the Web and telecommunications to better understand your computer experts or consultants, who often speak "techie" rather than English.

When we agreed to write *Using the World Wide Web and Creating Home Pages* we knew that we wanted to provide you with basic information about the Web. We also knew that we had to, at the same time, keep abreast of the latest Web developments and hottest Web sites popping up on a daily basis, and incorporate them into each chapter. Thus this basic planning guide includes some of today's newest and best Web sites. More importantly, it provides you with an understanding of how to find the newest and best Web sites yourself.

This book grew out of our differing experiences with the Internet and the Web. When Ray, a university library director, planned, budgeted for, and oversaw his campus' Web page development, he had to answer the same kinds of questions and solve the same kinds of problems faced by every librarian who crosses the Internet threshold:

- How can I afford to do this?
- How can I provide Web access and publish information on the Web given my current staff?
- How can I convince my Board, my City Manager, or my principal that this is important and worth the cost?

While writing *Using the World Wide Web and Creating Home Pages*, Gail, a librarian and professional Internet trainer, kept in mind all the situations people have asked her about as she has helped them use the Web and create their home pages. The answers found here have been field-tested with school, public, academic, and special libraries.

Chapter 1 provides you with an overview of the basics of the Web in simple, non-technical language. **Chapter 2** gets you thinking about and discussing some of the big issues related to libraries and the Web before you start getting organized and making decisions. **Chapter 3** provides you with basic technical information you will need to select and budget for an Internet connection that will support the Web. If your library already has an Internet connection, it will provide you with the information you need to upgrade your connection. **Chapter 4** covers how to train staff and patrons and encourage them to become "Web-savvy." It also covers various types of training and great places to start exploring the Web. **Chapter 5** outlines the planning process we suggest you follow to create a Web presence for your library. **Chapter 6** describes how to design Web sites. It covers design principles common to a good Web site and realistically discusses how much control you have/don't have over how your Web pages look to others. **Chapter 7** provides you with a primer of basic HTML text and graphic tags, so you can either start writing your Web site or better understand what your HTML authors will be doing. It also provides you with basic information on HTML editors. **Chapter 8** describes how you can test your Web site once you have it designed and written. It suggests ways you can get staff and patrons to help you keep your Web site up-to-date. **Chapter 9** suggests how you can let patrons, community members, and the "Web-world" know that your Web site is available. **Chapter 10** is an easy-to-understand glossary of terms to help you learn about, and teach others about, the Web. **Chapter 11** provides you with lots of chances to "Lead More About It . . . " We include lots of informative print and Net-based resources.

By following the steps outlined in *Using the World Wide Web and Creating Home Pages: A How-to-Do-It Manual for Librarians*, you will be able to choose an appropriate Web Connection for your library, better facilitate staff exploration of the Web, and introduce it to patrons. We show you how to plan, design, and create a "starter" home page for your library as well as help you avoid the most commonly experienced setbacks when creating a home page.

While beginning to use and publish on the Web is challenging, it also opens a whole new world of information to your staff and your patrons and enables you literally to market your library to the whole wide world. We hope this book will make the experience easier and faster for you.

INTRODUCTION

The World Wide Web is part of the Internet. In order to fully understand how the Web works and why it is such an important tool, you first need to understand some basics about the Net and how it affects your library. As most librarians know, the Internet is a worldwide network of computers, connected together by telecommunication links, and all speaking a common computer language. The Internet is composed of the 3 Cs.

- **Computers**
  all makes and models, from the dumbest terminal to the smartest supercomputer
- **Communications**
  phone lines and modems, digital data-lines, fiber-optic cabling, Ethernet, LANs, microwave towers, and communication satellite uplinks, that connect computers to each other
- **Common language**
  a language (or more correctly protocol) called TCP/IP, that computers agree to speak so that they can share information with each other

The Internet connects millions of computers and people. It is estimated that 50 million people have some form of Internet access. Colleges small and large, libraries of all kinds, schools and school districts, companies, government agencies (U.S. and foreign), non-profit organizations, and a myriad of individuals make up the population of the Net. The Net is a diverse place where people—business people, senior citizens, government officials, experts in many fields, librarians, teachers and students—can communicate and share information as equals.

YOUR LIBRARY AND THE INTERNET

The Internet makes it possible for you to provide patrons with a direct link to computers and people worldwide and to discussions on just about any topic. The Internet makes it possible for you to provide patrons with information no matter where on the globe it is located. The Internet also makes it possible for you to deliver and publish information quickly and efficiently.

COMMUNICATING VIA ELECTRONIC MAIL

You probably already use the Internet to send and receive e-mail messages. Some of you also probably provide your patrons with e-mail access. With electronic mail, distances don't matter. Messages travel halfway around the world or around the block in seconds, and there is no additional cost for how far the message travels.

Some of you probably use e-mail to participate in electronic discussion groups. Discussions cover a galaxy of topics from the scholarly to the just plain fun and can be a way of connecting patrons to others who share similar interests. There are discussions for almost every kind of library service/resource, which can be an important part of your ongoing professional development.

LOCATING AND DELIVERING INFORMATION

Many of you have already used Gophers (and key word search tools like Veronica and Jughead) to find information for patrons. Gophers connected you to "virtual reference desks," helped you find large databases of government information, and located information on just about any other subject as well. Using Gopher e-mail, you could deliver text information directly to patrons. In late 1995, Gophers began phasing out and were replaced by the World Wide Web, which offers a greater variety of information and easier ways to do basic Internet functions.

You can also use the Internet function called file transfer protocol (FTP) to connect to a computer anywhere in the world, find a document, computer program, or statistical database and have the computer send a copy of it to your computer so you can use it locally.

PROVIDING LOCAL COMMUNITY INFORMATION

Through the Internet you can provide patrons with a wide variety of information about your community (however you define it).

- Your public library can provide patrons, community leaders, and civic groups with information about your city/county/state government, local schools, businesses, local and regional attractions, festivals, parks, and helpful tidbits such as local bus schedules and Red Cross bloodmobile dates and locations.
- Your college or university library can provide administrators, faculty, and students with information on courses and college services, local and regional research collections, and a wide variety of campus information (e.g.,

maps, schedules, and social activities) that students and faculty want and need.

- Your school library can provide students, teachers, and parents with information on local public library and college library collections and hours, information on school and district policies and deadlines, school activities (e.g., sports schedules, upcoming concerts/plays), and specific information such as school bus routes, weekly lunch menus, parent/teacher conference dates, and "virtual" galleries of student art and literature.

As the above examples demonstrate, the Web is the most global and user-friendly information tool yet invented. It has the potential for enabling even the smallest library to market its services worldwide as well as bringing text, video, and sound from anywhere in the world to its own patrons. Turn the page to begin learning how to connect your library to this revolutionary tool.

1 IN THE BEGINNING— WEB BASICS

INTRODUCTION

This section introduces the Web and provides you with a summary of how it is different from other Internet tools.

The World Wide Web has become a household word. Web addresses now appear on television commercials. The phenomenally fast popularization of the Web occurred for the following reasons:

Internet—An international network of computer networks that communicate with each other using a common communication language (protocol) called TCP/IP.

- The World Wide Web is the most popular <u>Internet</u> tool because it makes exploring the Internet and its resources easy. You don't have to be a computer expert to use the Web, all you need are some basic computer skills. You can connect to information all over the globe simply by clicking on a Web link. You can deliver any information you find back to your computer, printer, or e-mail box simply by pulling down menus and choosing easily-understandable options.
- The Web is popular because it makes exploring the Internet visually exciting. You can find a staggering variety of interesting textual information as well as lots of pictures (e.g., maps, artwork, cartoons, diagrams, photographs), sound bites (both musical and spoken words), and video clips (live, animated, and computer-generated).
- The Web is popular because it provides simplified access to other Internet navigation tools such as Gopher, Veronica, Jughead, Archie, and FTP which can help you find information. You can think of the Web as a well-stocked Internet toolbox containing all the tools you need to locate, view, and deliver a wide variety of information.
- The Web has made the Internet both attractive and easy to use thanks to some simple, but powerful, concepts. The Web is officially defined as a "distributed hypermedia system." That may not make much sense right now, but by the end of this chapter you will have a better sense of what the Web is, how it works, and the concepts behind it.

INTERESTING HIGHLIGHTS FROM WEB HISTORY

1989-1991

CERN (European Lab for Particle Physics)—Place where the World Wide Web project originated and the Web was developed.

Tim Berners-Lee of the European Lab for Particle Physics (CERN) in Switzerland, proposed a way of sharing information based on the concept of hypertext. CERN staff (including Berners-Lee) produced the first version of the Web and made it available to Internet users. A few people connected to CERN, tried out the Web for themselves, and saw the Web's potential. The Web was known mostly to scientists and academics.

1992–1993

The first text-based Web browser from CERN in Switzerland became available for Internet users to download and then load onto their own computers. The first graphical browser, Mosaic, was developed at the National Center for Supercomputing Applications (NCSA) at the University of Illinois. Lots of people reacted favorably to the graphical format and Mosaic quickly became the first Web browser most people heard about and used. Computer programmers started experimenting with Web client programs on their own, adding more "bells and whistles" to them. Web sites became common on college and university campuses and for most high-tech businesses. Some libraries started using the Web, began to see its potential, and started authoring Web sites. The first non-technical books about the Web were written and published. They were snapped up immediately by interested academics, librarians, and business people. The Web was known by a small segment of the general public.

1994-1995

Commercial Web browsers came on the market. The popular Netscape browser, developed by Marc Andreessen, competed with Mosaic for dominance. Media resources became common on the Web. Conferences for technical users furthered developments in Web client and server software. Lots of e-mail discussion groups and Usenet newsgroups related to the Web appeared. More people learned HTML and companies that create and house Web sites began to do a thriving business. Individuals, companies, libraries, schools, and non-profit organizations put up Web sites and began to see the Web as an integral part of their organizations. Businesses began to see the potential for customer service and commerce via the Web and soon everyone was jumping into this new business environment. Libraries began to provide Web access for patrons, planned how to integrate it with their traditional services, and began to look at ways of providing new information and services to patrons. Lots of books on the Web were published. You couldn't go anywhere without hearing about the Web.

INFORMATION YOU CAN FIND USING THE WEB

- you can locate and display text-based information on just about any topic and deliver this information to either yourself or patrons in a number of ways.
- you can view digitized pictures (e.g., works of art, weather maps), hear sound bites (e.g., historical speeches, the Brady Bunch theme), and watch short video clips (e.g., scientific experiments, cartoons) and deliver this information to either yourself or patrons in a number of ways.
- you can connect to and use Web indexes and search engines that help you locate information and connect to it.
- you can explore the text information available from Gophers and use key word search tools like Veronica and Jughead to speed search for specific information buried within Gopher menus. Although many Gophers are being phased out in favor of the Web, some still contain valuable information resources.
- you can connect to remote computers using telnet, view any text information you find, and then deliver this information to yourself or patrons.
- you can connect to library catalogs worldwide.
- you can connect to remote computers that contain software, statistical data, etc. When you find something you want, you can deliver it to your computer so you can use it locally.
- you can read Usenet news postings and participate in Usenet newsgroups without having to learn any of the complex commands associated with newsreader programs.
- you can use a helper program, like WAIS, to search for information. WAIS gives each document it finds a score and then puts all the information together into a list for you to browse.
- you can send e-mail messages to people, organizations, and businesses and participate in e-mail discussion groups.
- you can fill out Web-based forms to register for services, purchase items, and answer surveys or questionnaires.

HOW THE WEB IS DIFFERENT THAN OTHER INTERNET TOOLS

Web commands are non-technical and easy to use. This is not

Gophers—Tools developed at the University of Minnesota, that provides simple, menu-based access to Internet resources. Gophers access texts stored both locally and remotely. They enable you to search Gopher menus using keyword search tools named Veronica and Jughead.

FTP (File Transfer Protocol)—An Internet function that enables you to transfer files from one computer to another. File transfer is a simple function through the Web.

always the case with other Internet functions or tools (like FTP and Archie) that may present you with a daunting array of technical responses or assume that you know UNIX commands.

The Web provides you with a single method for accessing and exploring the Internet's resources. Once you learn how to navigate the Web, you can use the same commands to navigate Gophers, FTP sites, and Usenet newsgroups (something you couldn't do before the Web came along).

The Web provides you with both text and media resources. If you want to explore Web-based media you must have a computer that is powerful enough, and can run programs, to handle both text and graphics. For instance, to run a graphical Web browser like Netscape, your computer needs to have Windows (or MacOS 7+) loaded on it. You also need to use a fast modem (28.8kbps) or high-speed dedicated Internet connection (ISDN, 56K, or better). (For specific computer requirements for both Macintosh and PC computers see the box on p. 59.)

WEB CONCEPTS

This section provides you with brief, non-technical explanations of Web concepts. It explains concepts related to how the Web works as well as the hardware and software concepts that allow you to view and use the Web.

HYPERTEXT/HYPERMEDIA—WHERE IT ALL BEGINS

Hypertext (Hypermedia)—Text formatted with links that enable you to jump from one place on the Web to another.

Hyperlink—A place in a web document you can select using a pointing device, like a mouse, that will take you to a document stored either on your Web server or any other Web server on the Internet.

The concept unique to the Web is hypertext. Hypertext/hypermedia takes you in real time to other text or media resources on the Internet. For instance, by clicking with your mouse on a word or picture that is a hyperlink, you can connect to another Web document on your computer or on any computer in the world.

- Hypertext allows you to access information in a serendipitous and unstructured manner.
- Hypertext makes large amounts of information easy to sort through quickly, so you can get to the specific bit of information you need.
- Hypertext provides you with options for viewing information so that you control your research process.

> **FIGURE 1.1   Example of an HTML Document With a Hypertext Link**
>
> ```
> <HTML>
> <HEAD>
> <TITLE>Samler</TITLE>
> </HEAD>
> <BODY>
> <H1>Sample HTML File</H1>
> This shows you what an HTML document with <B>tags</B> looks like.
> <P>
> This sentence contains a <a HREF="hlink.html">hypertext link</a>
> to another document.
> </BODY>
> </HTML>
> ```

HTTP—HOW INFORMATION IS SHARED

<u>HTTP</u> stands for HyperText Transfer Protocol. HTTP is a set of rules that describes the steps that your computer and a Web server take to communicate and share information.

There are four steps to the HTTP process. When you want to connect to a Web site, your browser software gets in touch with the Web server where the Web site resides and gets connected to that computer. The Web site computer then sends the information you request to your computer. Your browser software retrieves the information and displays it for you. Your computer and the Web server then disconnect from each other. While you are viewing the contents of a Web page or selecting a link to click on, other people are able to access and view that same Web site.

When you finally decide to click on a link, your browser reconnects/connects to the appropriate Web server, gets and displays the information you request, and then disconnects again. Connecting in this fashion allows many more people to access the Web computer's resources and maximizes the use of each Web server's limited number of Internet connections.

<u>**HTTP (HyperText Transfer Protocol)**</u>—A function that enables your browser to communicate with a Web server, get a response from the server and transfer the data requested back to your computer.

FIGURE 1.2   How Web Clients and Servers Communicate

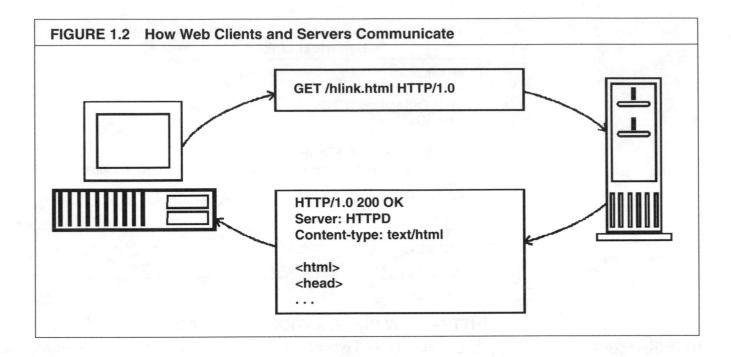

In contrast, when you are connecting to the Internet using telnet or FTP, you are continuously connected to the server you are using, whether you are actively using it at the moment or passively viewing the information that it supplied to you. While you are connected this way, you are taking up an Internet connection that no one can use but you. Connecting in this fashion limits the number of people who can connect to and use a particular computer's resources.

WEB SERVERS—WHERE INFORMATION IS STORED

Web servers are computers that house and store Web documents and information. They are one half of the pair of computers that share information via the Web. Web servers communicate with Web browsers, also called <u>clients</u>, by using HyperText Transfer Protocol.

Planning for and setting up a Web server, in the past, was a complex process that demanded many hours of "techie" work. There are now "servers-in-a box" that come with pre-loaded software and detailed instructions for setting them up. This has greatly simplified establishing a Web <u>server</u> and does not require that you have someone on your staff with a computer science degree. Keeping a Web server running, however, usually requires that someone with some level of computer expertise be assigned to backup files and troubleshoot problems.

Clients—Programs running on your computer that make it possible to connect to a Web, Gopher, e-mail, or FTP server. Clients customize the way these Internet tools both look and work.

Server—1) A computer that runs server software. 2) The software that allows one computer to offer services to another computer.

Why You May Not Be Able to Connect to a Web Site

The Web server is jammed with requests for connections.

This can happen when you attempt to connect to popular sites like Yahoo, or when lots of people are trying to get the newest browser software from NCSA or Netscape. It can also happen when you attempt to connect to undersized servers that for some reason are swamped. You may get a message "host contacted, waiting for reply" and then nothing happens. You can either wait (and wait) for the connection, or you can break the connection and try to connect at a low-use time.

The Web site may have moved a new server.

Many Web sites move from one server to another. Most leave "forwarding addresses" to where they will be moving and provide you with a link to the new URL. Like the Post Office, this "forwarding" message is temporary. If you miss it, use a Web search engine or index to locate the site's new URL.

The Web site may have been removed or the Web server may no longer be on the Net.

Many Web sites are created by college students. When they graduate, their Web sites will often be deleted. Many businesses and organizations create Web sites and then go out of business, or decide not to continue providing Web access for their company. If you try to connect to one of these sites your browser will display an "404 Not Found" message indicating that the URL no longer exists. Use a Web search engine or index to see if the site exists somewhere else or to search for alternative Web sites that can supply you with the information you seek.

The Web server is off the Net for routine maintenance.

This can occur very late in the evening, very early in the morning, or on weekends. Routine maintenance usually takes a Web server off the Net only for a couple of hours. When you attempt to connect to a Web server that is having maintenance done, you never get connected. You will see a status message on your browser that says "host contacted, waiting for reply" but nothing happens after that or you see an browser message that says "connection timed-out." Try connecting to the Web server in a couple of hours, it will probably be back up and available.

The Web server is off the Net for emergency repairs.

Repairs can take hours or days depending on what needs to be fixed. When you attempt to connect to a Web server that is being fixed, you will receive a "waiting for reply" or "connection timed-out" message from your browser, just like you do for a server that is having routine maintenance done. If you try for a number of days and are not successful in connecting to a Web server, you can contact the site's Webmaster to find out when the server will be available.

Your connection to your Internet provider is down or the connection from your Internet provider to the Net is down.

Unless the problem is very serious, your connection to the Net through your local network or Internet provider will be reestablished fairly quickly. Try connecting to the Net in a couple of hours. If the outage is longer than that, contact your local network administrator or Internet service provider for a status report.

WEB BROWSERS—HOW YOU SEE INFORMATION

Web browser programs loaded on your (or your Internet provider's) computer contact Web servers, request information, and display it for you. Computers running browsers comprise the other half of the pair of computers that share information via the Web.

Web browsers receive information from Web servers and translate it into a reader-friendly document. You can customize browsers so that you see information the way YOU want to see it. (e.g., big bold font or tiny little one, colored or white backgrounds, pictures or no pictures). You can also customize your browser to arrange the list of Web sites you feel are important enough to save and put into your bookmark list. (See pp. 29–30 for more information on bookmarks.)

Many text and graphical browsers are available as freeware on the Internet. There are also commercial versions of browsers available at your local computer store. (For more information on how browsers work see the section titled "Browser Basics" later in this chapter.)

FIGURE 1.3   A Web Page as Displayed by a Graphical Browser

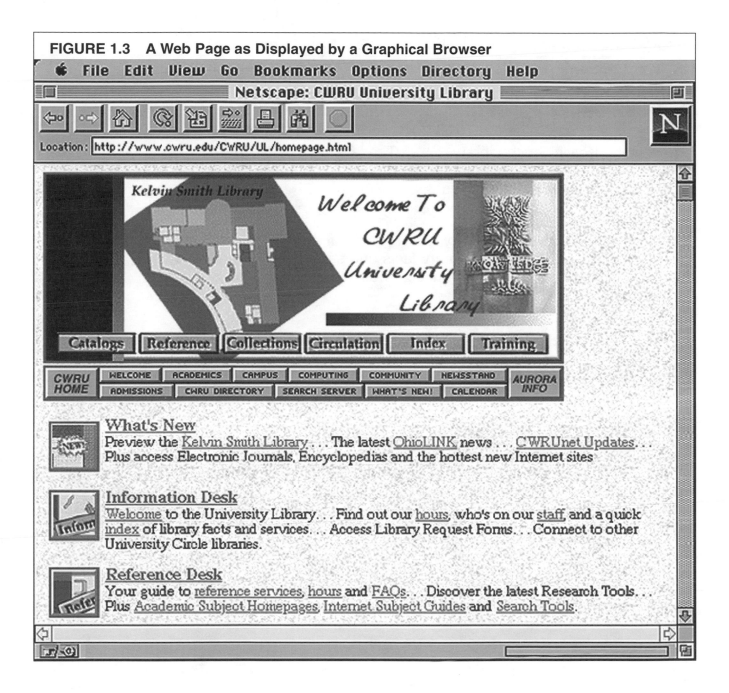

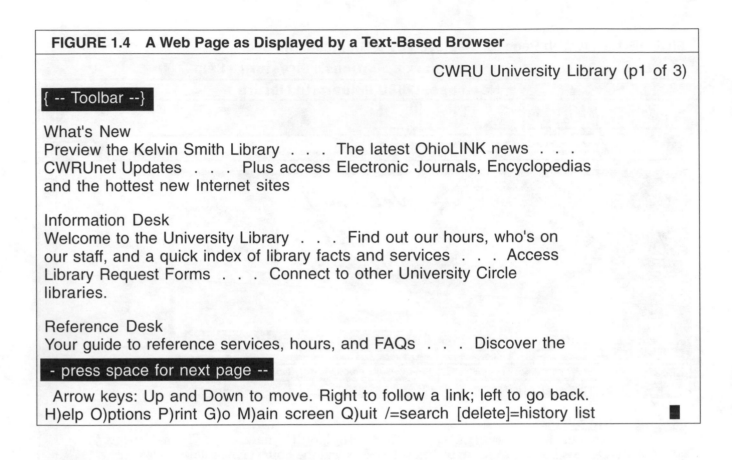

FIGURE 1.4   A Web Page as Displayed by a Text-Based Browser

CWRU University Library (p1 of 3)

{ -- Toolbar --}

What's New
Preview the Kelvin Smith Library . . . The latest OhioLINK news . . .
CWRUnet Updates . . . Plus access Electronic Journals, Encyclopedias
and the hottest new Internet sites

Information Desk
Welcome to the University Library . . . Find out our hours, who's on
our staff, and a quick index of library facts and services . . . Access
Library Request Forms . . . Connect to other University Circle
libraries.

Reference Desk
Your guide to reference services, hours, and FAQs . . . Discover the

- press space for next page --

 Arrow keys: Up and Down to move. Right to follow a link; left to go back.
H)elp O)ptions P)rint G)o M)ain screen Q)uit /=search [delete]=history list

HOME PAGES—WHERE INFORMATION IS ORGANIZED

Home page—1) The primary page of a Web site. 2) The place where you start exploring the Web when you start up your browser software.

A <u>home page</u> is the main (or starting) page for a series of other pages that makes up a Web site. Web sites exist for all types of businesses, universities, libraries, schools, and organizations, and most of them have a home page that give you a place to start searching for information.

FIGURE 1.5   Library Web Home Page Sample

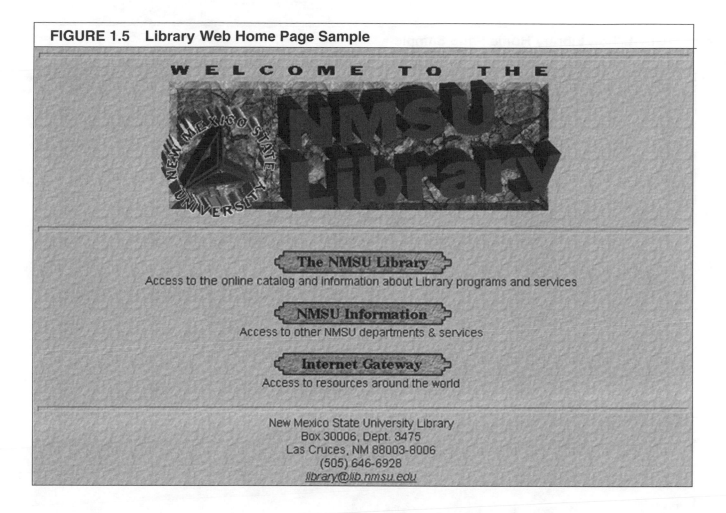

Your library home page represents your library to Internet patrons. It is like the first view of your building, or the staff member who answers the telephone. It may be the only contact with your library a patron may ever have. Your home page first identifies your library and gives essential information to patrons such as policies, services, and hours. It then usually lists all the other resources available through links to your more specific library Web pages or to Web resources anywhere in the world.

FIGURE 1.6   Library Home Page Sample

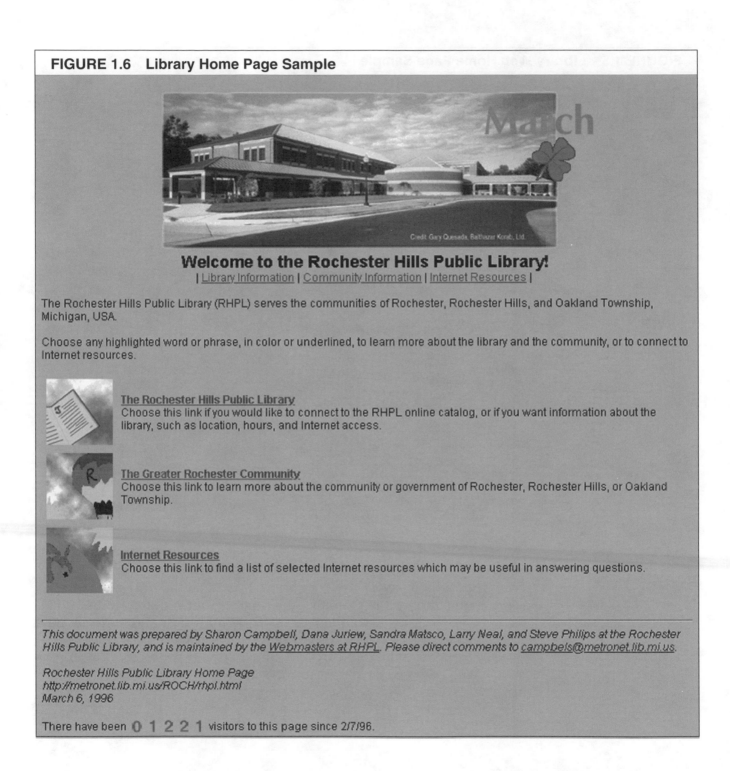

Welcome to the Rochester Hills Public Library!
| Library Information | Community Information | Internet Resources |

The Rochester Hills Public Library (RHPL) serves the communities of Rochester, Rochester Hills, and Oakland Township, Michigan, USA.

Choose any highlighted word or phrase, in color or underlined, to learn more about the library and the community, or to connect to Internet resources.

The Rochester Hills Public Library
Choose this link if you would like to connect to the RHPL online catalog, or if you want information about the library, such as location, hours, and Internet access.

The Greater Rochester Community
Choose this link to learn more about the community or government of Rochester, Rochester Hills, or Oakland Township.

Internet Resources
Choose this link to find a list of selected Internet resources which may be useful in answering questions.

This document was prepared by Sharon Campbell, Dana Juriew, Sandra Matsco, Larry Neal, and Steve Philips at the Rochester Hills Public Library, and is maintained by the Webmasters at RHPL. Please direct comments to campbels@metronet.lib.mi.us.

Rochester Hills Public Library Home Page
http://metronet.lib.mi.us/ROCH/rhpl.html
March 6, 1996

There have been 0 1 2 2 1 visitors to this page since 2/7/96.

A home page is also the page you first see when you start up your own browser. This page can be one you create and store locally on your own computer. It can list all the places you like to visit or it can be the home page of another site on the Internet (such as Yahoo) that you tell your browser to display for you when you start it up. In both cases, this type of home page serves as your own personal jumping-off place for exploring the Internet.

FIGURE 1.7   Personal Web Links Page

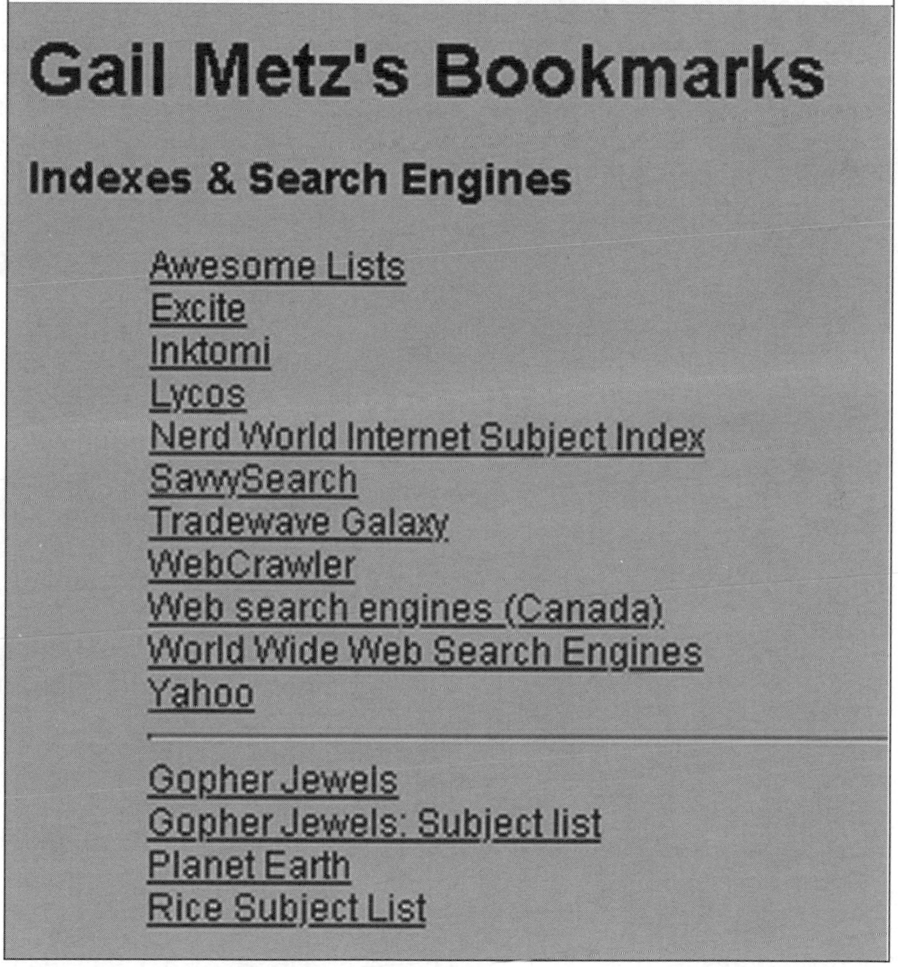

Gail Metz's Bookmarks

Indexes & Search Engines

Awesome Lists
Excite
Inktomi
Lycos
Nerd World Internet Subject Index
SavvySearch
Tradewave Galaxy
WebCrawler
Web search engines (Canada)
World Wide Web Search Engines
Yahoo

Gopher Jewels
Gopher Jewels: Subject list
Planet Earth
Rice Subject List

How to View Web Sites Faster

Get a faster connection, faster computer, or faster modem

Turn Off the Graphics

If you are connecting to a Web site that has lots of graphics and the page is slow loading (and doesn't provide you with a "text-only" option) you can use your graphical browser's options to turn off the graphics. You can then reload the page and you'll be able to view it much more quickly. Instead of the graphic you will see a word that represents the image. Most browsers let you click on the substitute text to display the image should you decide you want to view it.

Use Your Browser's History File

Another way to move quickly from one Web site to another (that you have already viewed) is to use your browser's "history" option. Your browser's memory reloads previously viewed Web pages from its stored memory so you don't have to reconnect to a Web server and wait for it to send you the document. You can use this when teaching the Web, especially in the afternoon and early evening when connecting to the popular Web sites can take some time.

UNIFORM RESOURCE LOCATORS—HOW TO CONNECT TO A SPECIFIC SITE

URL stands for Uniform Resource Locator. URLs have three main functions:

- They are a standardized way of expressing information to your browser software so that it can locate, retrieve, and display it for you.
- They are the directions embedded into HTML documents that make it possible for you to connect to and create links from one Web document (or other Internet resource) to another.
- They are a standard way of citing Internet information in bibliographies and footnotes.

How URLs are Structured

The first part of a URL (before the :// or :) indicates the kind of Internet resource your browser will be connecting to (in this case a Web site).

http://

The second part of a URL identifies the <u>Internet address</u>, and sometimes port number, of the computer you will be connecting to (in this case a computer at Rice University in Houston).

chico.rice.edu

The third part of a URL describes the specific directory or document you want to view once you are connected (in this case a K-

Internet Address—The address of a computer on the Internet. Internet addresses can be expressed as numerals, as an IP (Internet Protocol) address (e.g., 129.22.4.2), or as a series of letters, called a pseudonym address (e.g., po.cwru.edu).

12 Internet resources list). Many Web file URLs end with .html or .htm

/armadillo/Rice/k12resources.html

Sample URLs for Different Internet Tools

telnet

telnet://cal.ohlolink.edu

Gopher

gopher://riceinfo.rice.edu:70/11/Subject/Anth

File Transfer Protocol (FTP)

ftp://nis.nsf.net/resources/hitchhikers.guide
file://nis.nsf.net/resources/hitchhikers.guide

Usenet newsgroups

news:comp.infosystems.www.announce

URL Errors & How to Avoid Them

- Check to see that there are no spacing errors
  htt**p: //**www.clark.net/pub**/ j**ournalism/kids**. h**tml
- Check to see that there are no spelling errors
  http://www.**cl**rak.net/pub/jour**nl**ism/kids.html
- Check to see that all punctuation marks are correct
  htt**p;**//www.clark**,n**et/pub/journalism**\k**ids.html
- Check to see that letters or words are in the proper case
  http://www.cochran.com/theosite/**K**sites.html
- Check to see whether to use a hyphen (-) or underscore (_) in the URL
  http://ananse.lrv.uit.no/trade_law/nav/trade.html
  http://www.law.vill.edu/fed-agency/fedwebloc.html
- Check to see whether the URL contains a tilde (~)
  http://www.eskimo.com/~jlubin/disabled.html
- Check to see whether the URL ends in .html or .htm
  http://www.pixi.com/~skull/hr_graph**.htm**
  http://www.cit.gu.edu.au/images/Images**.html**
- Check to see that you included the correct port/path number
  gopher://riceinfo.rice.edu**:70/11**/Subject/Anth
  http://http://guaraldi.cs.colostate.edu**:2000**/form
- Check to make sure that there isn't a space before the URL
- When you type in a URL and you get an error message instead of a Web document, try typing shorter and shorter versions of the URL till you get connected, then search for the information you wanted.
  http://www.std.com/NE/usatour.html
  http://www.std.com/NE/
  http://www.std.com/

GRAPHICAL USER INTERFACES—MAKING THE WEB LOOK SIMPLE

A graphical user interface (GUI), pronounced "gooey," is a graphical program that takes complex computer tasks and turns them into simple graphical choices. Apple and Macintosh computers were the first to popularize graphical user interfaces. They made personal computing as simple as pointing at functions and files and clicking. Windows was developed for the same reason.

Web browsers that work in a Macintosh, Windows, or other graphical environment are GUIs. GUIs mask all the technical commands and make it simple for you to open up and use a software program or move a file from one place to another on your computer; they turn navigating the Web and other Internet tools into a point-and-click environment.

FIGURE 1.8   GUI Text and Matching HTML File

Sample HTML File

This shows you what an HTML document with **tags** looks like.

This sentence contains a <u>hypertext link</u> to another document.

```
<HTML>
<HEAD>
<TITLE>Sampler</TITLE>
</HEAD>
<BODY>
<H1>Sample HTML File</H1>
This shows you what an HTML document with <B>tags</B> looks like.
<P>
This sentence contains a <a HREF="hlink.html">hyptertext link</a>
to another document.
</BODY>
</HTML>
```

HTML—THE STRUCTURE BEHIND THE SCENES

<u>HTML</u> is short for Hypertext Markup Language. HTML describes the structure and content of Web documents, not their specific appearance. This is done on purpose so that your browser software has more control over how a Web site looks. Graphical User Interfaces cover up the HTML tags and links in a Web document so what you see looks like plain text. Basic HTML tags for creating a library Web site are covered in Chapter 7: Getting Down To It—Authoring Your Web Site.

HTML (Hypertext markup language)—A system of tags used to describe and create World Wide Web documents and display them using browser programs. HTML consists of text and tags that assign text special meanings, formatting instructions and hypertext links. HTML is a subset of SGML.

FIGURE 1.9   HTML Document Sample

```
<HTML>
<HEAD>
<TITLE>Sampler</TITLE>
</HEAD>
<BODY>
<H1>Sample HTML File</H1>
This shows you what an HTML document with <B>tags</B> looks like.
<P>
This sentence contains a <a HREF="hlink.html">hypertext link</a>
to another document.
</BODY>
</HTML>
```

TO LEARN MORE...

Also refer to Chapter 11 for additional print and Web resources. For full bibliographic information, see Chapter 11. For general Web information we recommend you read and connect to:

- *The World Wide Web Unleashed* 2nd. ed. by J. December & N. Randall
- *The World Wide Web Complete Reference* by R. Stout
- *Internet and the World Wide Web Simplified*
- *WWW FAQ* by T. Boutell http://www.boutell.com/faq/
- *Yahoo: Web* http://www.yahoo.com/Computers/ World_Wide_Web/

BROWSER BASICS

Browsers—Web client programs that access and display Web documents. Common Web browsers are Netscape, Mosaic, and Lynx.

Browsers connect to and communicate with Web servers. First they ask Web servers to send them the information you want to see, then they receive the information sent by the Web server and display it to you in the way you want to see it.

HOW BROWSERS INTERACT WITH WEB DOCUMENTS

Your browser requests a Web document from a Web server and what it receives is an HTML document full of tags and hypertext links. The tags indicate how your browser software should format and arrange the information in the document. The links provide "jumps" to documents and media.The options you set up locally on your browser affect how you view a Web page. What your browser does is take all the HTML tags, links, and browser options together, and displays the document as easy-to-read text and graphics.

FIGURE 1.10   How Browers, HTML files, and Web Servers Interact

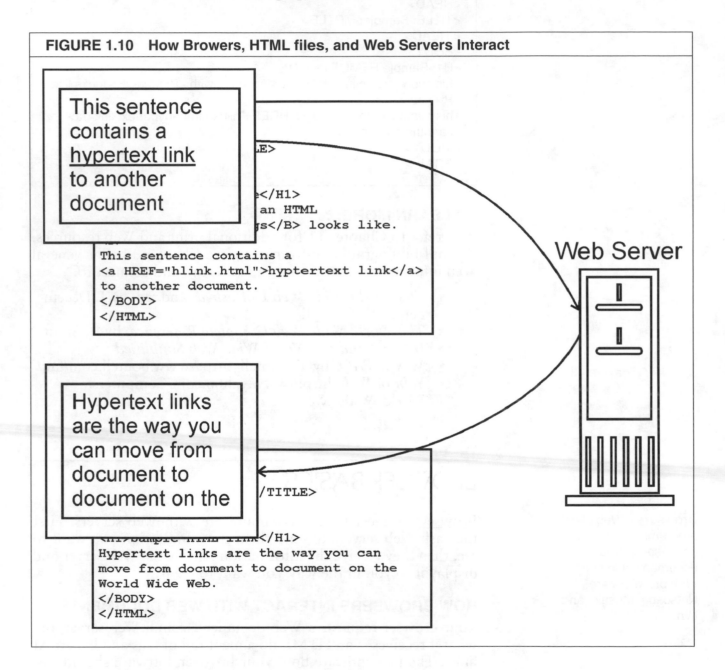

This sentence contains a <u>hypertext link</u> to another document

```
            LE>

          e</H1>
       an HTML
     s</B> looks like.

This sentence contains a
<a HREF="hlink.html">hyptertext link</a>
to another document.
</BODY>
</HTML>
```

Web Server

Hypertext links are the way you can move from document to document on the

```
          /TITLE>

<h1>Sample html link</H1>
Hypertext links are the way you can
move from document to document on the
World Wide Web.
</BODY>
</HTML>
```

INTERNET CONNECTIONS AND BROWSERS

The Web browser you use depends on the computer you are using. (If you are using a Mac, is it running System 7.0 or higher? If you are using an IBM-compatible computer, does it support Windows?) The browser you use also depends on the type of Internet connection you have.

If you have a dialup shell Internet connection, you are not directly connected to the Internet. You generally are restricted to a text-based browser. Software programs have been developed that make it possible for you to use a graphical browser with a dialup shell connection but many Internet providers do not encourage their use. In the future, the Web will be an increasingly unsatisfactory experience for those restricted to text-based access, as more sites rely on graphics and stop providing alternative pages for text-based browsers.

If you have a SLIP/PPP, ISDN, or dedicated Internet connection and a machine that is running Windows or Mac System7.0+, you can use graphical browser software. The most common freeware browsers are Netscape and Mosaic.

Graphical Browsers

The first graphical browser, <u>Mosaic</u>, was developed by Marc Andreessen at the Software Design Group at the National Center for Supercomputing Applications (NCSA) at the University of Illinois, Urbana-Champaign. Most graphical browsers make your computer look and act like they are running either Macintosh or Windows programs. You move around a graphical browser by pointing your mouse at something and clicking on it. Many of the things you normally do (e.g., saving files) using a Mac or Windows program are identical (or very similar) when using a graphical browser. (See p. 23 for a summary of Netscape commands.)

<u>Graphical browsers</u> require you either to have a SLIP/PPP Internet connection (or program to make a dialup shell connection act like a SLIP/PPP connection) or a dedicated Internet connection. Graphical browsers work best when connecting with a 28.8kbps modem.

Mosaic—The first Web browser to support graphics, sound, and video in addition to text. Mosaic requires that you have either a dedicated Internet connection, a SLIP/PPP/ISDN connection, or a program to make a dialup shell connection act like a SLIP/PPP connection

Graphical Browsers—Browser programs capable of displaying graphics, video, sounds, etc. in addition to text. Graphical browsers, such as Netscape, enable you to navigate the Web and the rest of the Internet using a mouse (or other pointing device).

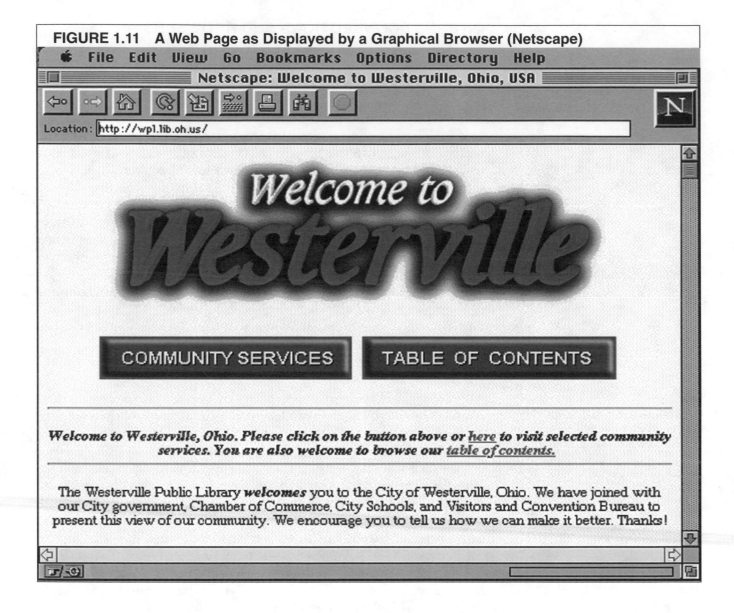

FIGURE 1.11   A Web Page as Displayed by a Graphical Browser (Netscape)

If your library has a connection that will support graphical browsers, you can offer patrons the full range of resources available from the Web: text, graphics, software, audio, and video. Many graphical browsers come in different versions for different kinds of computers. The good news is that different versions of graphical browsers are almost identical to each other, so it doesn't matter much what kind of computer you use; they all look and work pretty much the same way. This can be important in a library, campus, school environment where there may be different kinds of computers (e.g. Macs, PCs, UNIX) available.

If you are already familiar with Macintosh or Windows application software packages, most Web browsers will look familiar and you will find learning one a simple matter of picking up a few additional commands unique to the Web. On the other hand, if you are clueless about Mac or Windows basics, the Web pretty much requires that you learn Mac/Windows skills in addition to Web skills. Depending on your patrons' skills, you may be teaching either short courses on the Web or starting from scratch with basic Mac and Windows skills. (Plan to teach both.)

Graphical browsers offer an appealing view of the Internet, but there is a price to pay in terms of speed. Graphical browsers require a high-speed dedicated connection to the Net or at least a dialup connection with a 28.8kpbs modem. Even then, <u>multimedia</u> applications such as graphics, audio files, or video clips can take minutes or even hours to load and display.

Text-Based Browsers

As implied by their name, text-based browsers are limited to displaying text. Media resources on the Web are not accessible using a text-based browser. Text-based browsers use keyboard commands to follow links within a Web document. They don't require anything but a dialup shell connection and they can be used with slow modems (below 14.4kbps). You can also use text-based browsers to get dumb terminals connected to, and using, the Web.

The most common <u>text-based browser</u>, Lynx, developed at the University of Kansas, is available for free via FTP. Many Internet providers supply Lynx to their dialup shell account customers. If your Internet provider supplies it, all you have to do is choose the Lynx menu option or at your command line simply type "lynx". (See p. 25–26 for a summary of Lynx browser commands.)

Multimedia—A term that describes a resource, like a Web document, that integrates text, graphics, sound, video, etc.

Text-Based Browser—A browser program, such as Lynx, that does not display graphics or provide multimedia access. Typically text-based browsers are used mostly with dialup shell Internet connections.

FIGURE 1.12   A Web page as Displayed by a Text-Based Browser

Welcome to Westerville, Ohio, USA (p1 of 3)

Welcome to Westerville, Ohio, USA

Community Services Community Table of Contents

Welcome to Westerville, Ohio. Please click on the button above or **here** to visit selected community services. You are also welcome to browse our table of contents.

The Westerville Public Library welcomes you to the City of Westerville, Ohio. We have joined with our City government, Chamber of Commerce, City Schools, and Visitors and Convention Bureau to present this view of our community. We encourage you to tell us how we can make it better. Thanks!

For libraries that have limited Internet access and even those with a high-speed connection, text-based browsers can be a useful addition to your library's suite of Internet tools. A text-based browser is fast; it delivers information more quickly than a graphical browser can. Consider using one at your busy reference desk. Text-based browsers also provide you with most of the important browser tools (e.g., bookmarks, download capability, print, e-mail).

COMMON BROWSER COMMANDS

NETSCAPE COMMANDS

Navigation Commands

BACK [go menu]—back one page
FORWARD [go menu]—forward one page
HOME [go menu]—back to first/main page

Search Commands

FIND [search menu]—search word on a page
OPEN LOCATION [file menu]—opens a specific URL
VIEW HISTORY [go menu]—look at history file
GO TO NEWSGROUPS [directory menu]—connect to Usenet
newsgroups

Delivery Commands

MAIL DOCUMENT [file menu]—e-mail current document
PRINT [file menu]—print current document
SAVE AS [file menu]—download current document

Bookmark Commands

ADD BOOKMARK [bookmark menu]—add bookmark
VIEW BOOKMARK [bookmark menu]—arrange/edit bookmarks

Miscellaneous Commands

HELP [help menu]—help files
EXIT [file menu]—exit Netscape
SOURCE [view menu]—view the HTML document
STOP LOADING [go menu]—stop connection
RELOAD [view menu]—reload the document
PREFERENCES [options menu]—view options
AUTOLOAD IMAGES [options menu]—turns graphics on/off
OPEN FILE [file menu]—open a file on your computer

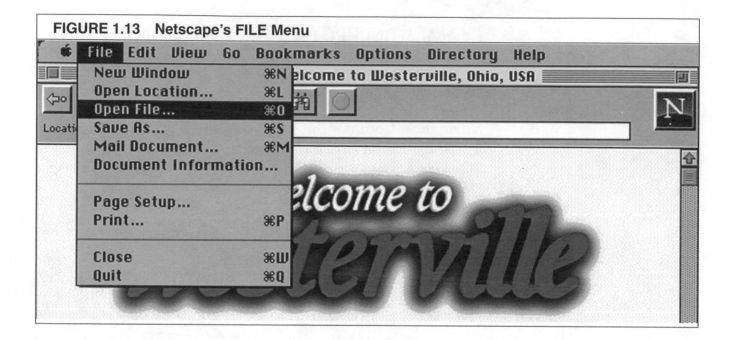

FIGURE 1.13 Netscape's FILE Menu

FIGURE 1.14 Netscape's GO Menu

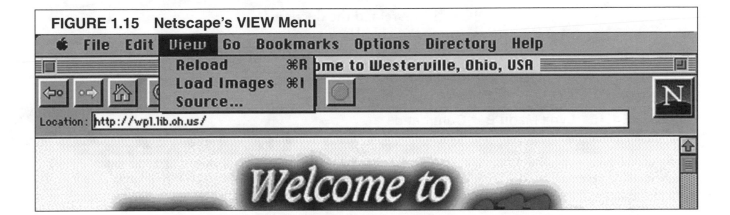

FIGURE 1.15   Netscape's VIEW Menu

LYNX COMMANDS

Navigation Commands
[UP ARROW]—back one link
[DOWN ARROW]—forward one link
[BACK ARROW]—back one page
[FORWARD ARROW]—select the link
[SPACE BAR]—next page
[MINUS KEY]—back one screen
[PLUS KEY]—forward one screen
B—top of page
M—back to first/main page

Search Commands
/—search word on a page
G—open up a specific URL
[BACKSPACE KEY]—look at history file

Delivery Commands
P—print, mail, save current file
D—download current file

Bookmark Commands
A—add bookmark
V—view bookmark list
R—remove bookmark

Miscellaneous Commands
? or H—help
Z—stop the connection
Q or q—exit Lynx

[CTRL] l—reload the document
\—view the HTML document
=—show the URL, host computer address
O—view the options menu

FIGURE 1.16 Lynx Menu Bar Commands

```
Commands: Use arrow keys to move, '?' for help, 'q' to quit, '<-' to go back
 Arrow keys: Up and Down to move. Right to follow a link; Left to go back.
H)elp O)ptions P)rint G)o M)ain screen Q)uit /=search [delete]=history list   ▮
```

FIGURE 1.17 Lynx Command Help File

```
                   +++ KEYSTROKE COMMANDS +++


  MOVEMENT:      Down arrow      - Highlight next topic
                 Up arrow        - Highlight previous topic
                 Right arrow,    - Jump to highlighted topic
                 Return, Enter
                 Left arrow      - Return to previous topic

  SCROLLING:     + (or space)    - Scroll down to next page
                 - (or b)        - Scroll up to previous page

  DIRED:         c               - Create a new file
                 d               - Download selected file
                 e               - Edit selected file
                 f               - Show a full menu of options for current file
                 m               - Modify the name or location of selected file
                 r               - Remove selected file
                 t               - Tag highlighted file
```

CERN LINE-MODE BROWSER COMMANDS

Navigation Commands
PREVIOUS—back one link
NEXT—forward one link
BACK—back one page
DOWN—down one screen
TOP—top of page
BOTTOM—bottom of page
UP—up one screen

HOME—back to first/main page

Search Commands

FIND—search word on a page
GO—open up a specific URL
RECALL—view the history list
[SPECIFIC NUMBER]—jump to a specific # link

Delivery Commands

>—saves current document
PRINT—prints current document

Miscellaneous Commands

HELP—help files
EXIT or QUIT—exit CERN browser

How to Connect to a Specific URL

- Using Netscape, locate the "Open Location" option in the menus or the "Open" button and type the specific URL.
- Using Lynx, find the "GO" option in the menu bar at the bottom of the screen. Type G and at the prompt that says "URL to open", type the specific URL.
- Using the CERN line-mode browser, type GO and then the specific URL.

IMPORTANT BROWSER FEATURES

This section explains in more detail some of the most important features common to many browsers.

Browsers, both text-based and graphical, supply you with various ways to deliver the information and images you find.

E-MAILING INFORMATION

Most browsers make it possible to mail text information to either your, or another person's, e-mail address. Sending a Web document via e-mail is simple (although some new Web users may find it confusing at first). You locate and display the desired information on your computer screen. Choosing your browser's e-mail option, you supply your browser with the e-mail address where the information should be sent, invoke your browser's command to start the mailing process, and your browser delivers a copy of the information to the correct e-mail address. You should plan for starting to use e-mail to deliver information, especially to those who request information via phone or fax.

E-mailing documents can:

- cut down your copying and printing costs.
- reduce the need for patrons to come into your library to pick up a paper document.
- save your library the cost of faxing information to patrons who need it immediately.
- deliver assigned readings to students in college/university and K-12 school environments.
- eliminate the need to rekey text in order to add it to a word-processed document.
- prove to be a valuable outreach service to local businesses, organizations, and professionals in your community.

PRINTING INFORMATION

You can deliver documents to patrons using the "print" option on all types of browsers. If you are using a graphical browser like Netscape or Mosaic, when you choose to print you will see the standard "print" window just like in any other Mac or Windows application. This option provides you with the ability to locate and deliver information directly to yourself or patrons.

You need to plan for covering the cost of paper and toner cartridges when planning for Web access. You might also consider charging patrons a nominal fee for printing in order to cover your ongoing costs.

Depending on the type of printer you purchase, printers can deliver either text or text and graphics. You should seriously consider purchasing black and white laser or inkjet printers that can handle 600 DPI graphics and PostScript documents, as well as at least one color laser printer.

TRANSFERRING/SAVING INFORMATION ON YOUR COMPUTER

Transferring and saving the information you find via the Web is also an important way of delivering information. You can transfer information (text, graphical, audio, and video) and save it to either a floppy disk or to your computer's hard drive. Transferring and saving information is relatively simple. Most browsers provide you with a transfer option. If you are using a graphical browser like Netscape, the "save as" feature will be identical to "save as" on either Mac or Windows applications. To transfer the information, you first locate and then view the text (or media resource) you wish to transfer. Using your browser you choose the drive (floppy or hard) you wish to save the information, image, or sound to, then you choose the folder or directory you wish to save it in. You then invoke the transfer process. In most cases you will be able to watch as the transfer process takes place in real time.

Before allowing staff or patrons to transfer information you must discuss policy issues and plan for appropriate training sessions. Issues that must be decided are:

- whether patrons will be able to transfer information themselves or whether it can be done only by staff. (Some libraries lock or disable the floppy drives of their public computers to discourage cracking and unauthorized loading/use of patron-supplied software.)
- whether you will allow patrons to insert their disks into your library computers, or whether your library will insist that patrons use library-supplied disks. (Some libraries do this to prevent virus contamination, others do it to ensure that all disks are formatted for their library machines.) Training sessions must teach about computer viruses and how to use antivirus software to avoid data loss.
- how much you will charge patrons for disks if they can only use library-supplied ones.

Transfering graphics, video, and audio files also brings up issues of copyright. Some of the media files on the Web are copyrighted and are on the Web in violation of the copyright law. You'll need to spend time training staff to check copyright status before they transfer and use resources for library purposes. You'll also need to post notices about the copyright law near Web computers capable of downloading information, in the same way you post notices about the copyright law near your photocopy machines.

BOOKMARKS

Most browsers allow you to create a "save" file of addresses for Web sites you visit often. This file is called a <u>bookmark</u> list. Browsers let you arrange bookmarks any way you wish. You can create subject folders and subfolders to organize your saved Web sites. You can also rename Web sites so that they are "memory-friendly." And of course, browsers make it easy for you to delete out-of-date or dead hypertext links from your bookmark list. Your bookmark list is uniquely yours and resides on your computer's hard drive. It will remain there until you specifically edit or delete it.

Bookmark—A Web site saved by your Web browser software that you can access again whenever you want.

FIGURE 1.18 A Graphical Browser (Netscape) Bookmark List

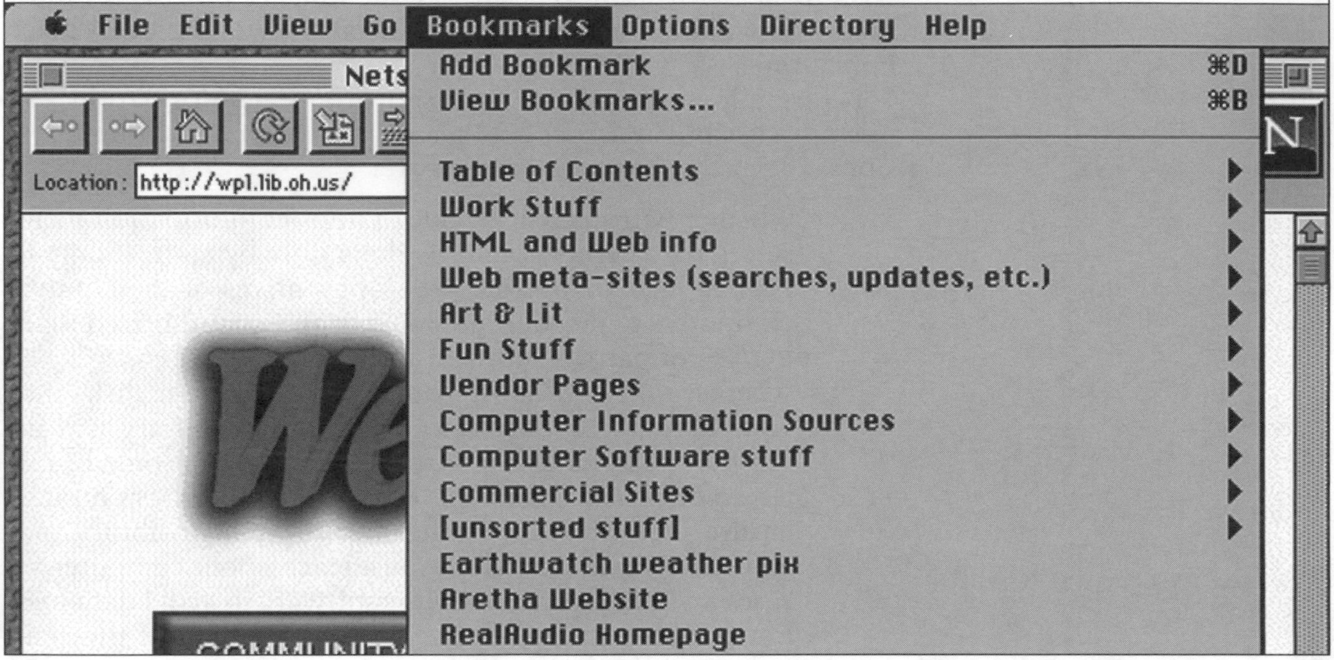

```
  File   Edit   View   Go   Bookmarks   Options   Directory   Help
                             Add Bookmark                        ⌘D
               Nets          View Bookmarks...                   ⌘B                    N

  Location: http://wpl.lib.oh.us/   Table of Contents                 ▶
                                    Work Stuff                        ▶
                                    HTML and Web info                 ▶
                                    Web meta-sites (searches, updates, etc.)  ▶
                                    Art & Lit                         ▶
          We                        Fun Stuff                         ▶
                                    Vendor Pages                      ▶
                                    Computer Information Sources      ▶
                                    Computer Software stuff           ▶
                                    Commercial Sites                  ▶
                                    [unsorted stuff]                  ▶
                                    Earthwatch weather pix
                                    Aretha Website
          COMMUNITY                 RealAudio Homepage
```

Most libraries create bookmarks for their in-house computers. Some browser developers offer "kiosk versions" of their software that make it difficult for patrons to modify your library's list of bookmarks once it is set up. Libraries not using browsers with this feature must look at other options (like making your library computer files "read only") to discourage patrons from adding or deleting items from your pre-set bookmarks.

Many library staff members use shared computers, especially at reference and circulation desks. You can get staff using who share computers to agree on often-referred-to resources and create shared bookmark lists. You can create bookmark folders by subject (e.g., government, business, education), by Internet resource type (e.g., Gopher, Web), or by media type (e.g., video, audio, graphics). You can also create bookmark folders for individuals so that they can store resources unique to their subject expertise or interests. You can also create a hypertext link to your library's bookmarks so that patrons can view and use them while connected to your Web site from home or office.

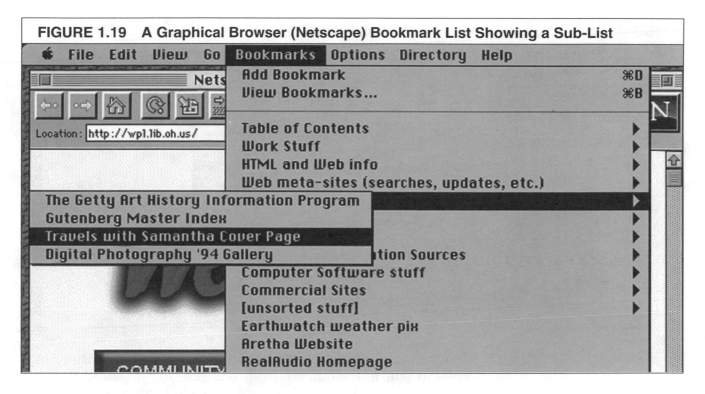

FIGURE 1.19   A Graphical Browser (Netscape) Bookmark List Showing a Sub-List

HISTORY LISTS

History Lists—Lists of Web sites you have visited during your current Web browser session.

History lists show you the places on the Web you have visited recently while using your browser. They are temporary and disappear when you close your browser window. History lists are limited in size. You can quickly move from Web site to Web site without having to wait for your browser to contact the Web server and reload the document, because the sites on your history list are stored in your browser's memory. History lists allow you to quickly backtrack to view a site you recently visited.

FIGURE 1.20 A Graphical Browser (Netscape) History List

File	Edit	View	**Go**	Bookmarks	Options	Directory	Help	

Back		⌘[
Forward		⌘]
Home		
Stop Loading		⌘.
View History...		⌘H
✓**Welcome to Westerville, Ohio, USA**		⌘0
CWRU University Library		⌘1
University Circle Libraries		⌘2
Case Western Reserve University		⌘3

Location: http://wp1.lib.oh.us/

When teaching people about the Web, you can use history lists to help you move quickly from one resource to another, especially if you are using a slower modem. (In fact you can pre-connect to Web sites, so they are stored in your browser's memory and more quickly accessible when it is time to do a demo of different Web sites.)

TO LEARN MORE...

See Chapter 11 for complete bibliographic citations. Also refer to Chapter 11 for additional print and Web resources. For more information about Web browsers we recommend you read and connect to:

- *Netscape Virtuoso* by E. Keeler & R. Miller
- *Ten Minute Guide to Netscape for Windows 95* by G. Grimes
- *Yahoo: Browsers* http://www.yahoo.com/Computers/World_Wide_Web/Browsers

MEDIA AND THE WEB

This section provides you with an overview of helper application software and the types of media that are part of the Web.

HELPER APPLICATION SOFTWARE

Web browsers are fairly large programs. In order to keep them as small and uncomplicated as possible, browsers don't include all the software you need to play/view all forms of media. In order to view, store, and replay Web media files, you often need to load what is called helper application software onto your computer. Most, but not all, graphical browsers include programs so you can view common types of graphic files. Most browsers don't include programs to let you hear audio files or view video clips. The helper programs that are included/not included with browsers vary from one brand to another and from one version to another.

It is easy to tell if you need to load "helper app" programs onto your computer to help out your browser. First, launch your graphical browser and connect to a site like Rob's Multimedia Lab, that has lots of media links. Select a sound, video, or graphic link and ask your browser to retrieve and display/play it for you. Your browser will load the file (which can take some time, depending on the media format and the file's size). If your browser has the necessary software, you will see the image, hear the sound, or view the video. If your browser doesn't have the necessary software (in other words needs "helper apps") it will tell as such, rather than displaying or playing the media file you request.

Media files come in various formats, for instance video files can come in either MPEG or QuickTime format. Be sure and test your browser against both file types, so you know if you have to load one or more "apps" (or find one helper program that handles multiple file formats). There are also different audio, video, and sound "apps" for Macintosh and Windows-based PCs. Knowing the specific kind of helper file you need and what computer it will run on will help you locate and download the right file the first time.

Once you know the types of helper programs you need to get, it's easy to find and transfer them to your computer. Most helper programs are available as freeware or shareware (which means that they are either free or very cheap). You can find them in Mac and PC software archive sites. (See the Chapter 11, p. 201–202 for URLs to some of the best archives.)

It's also easy to install helper programs. Many will come in compressed form which need to be uncompressed. Instructions on how to install and configure the software so it works with your browser are often included along with the program files. Be sure and read installation/configuration instructions carefully (and of course, virus check the software before using it the first time).

GRAPHIC IMAGES

When you visit a Web site you may see two types of graphics. The first type are inline graphics. Inline graphics display automatically when you connect to and view a Web site. The second type are external graphics. External graphics display only when you select a graphic hyperlink on a Web page. To view certain graphic files you may need to load helper software onto your computer. Other types of graphic files may load without helper software. This depends on both your computer and Web browser.

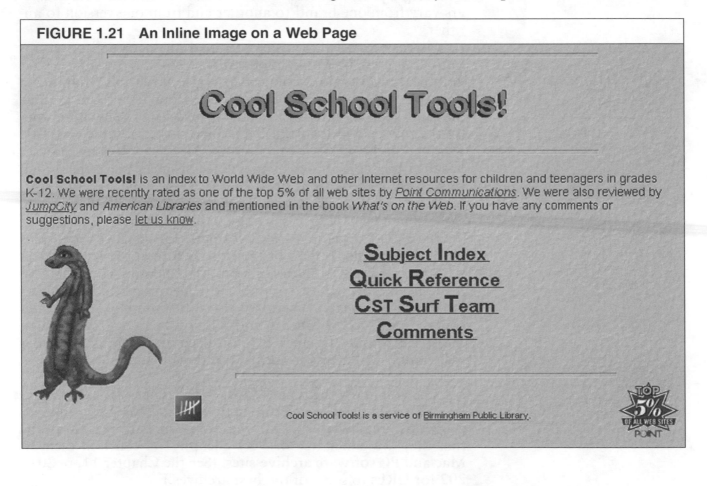

FIGURE 1.21   An Inline Image on a Web Page

When planning your library Web site, you can create your own images, find "clip art" archives on the Web, or purchase CD-ROMs that contain photographic and/or line images. Once you find the image you want to use on your Web page, you have to convert it to one of two graphic file formats. (To do this you need image editing software like Adobe Photoshop.) There are two reasons you have to do this. First, because Web browsers support only selected graphic formats and second, because graphic files are very large. Graphic format software reduces the size of files so they take up less storage space on Web servers and load and display more quickly.

FIGURE 1.22   An Image Used as a Link

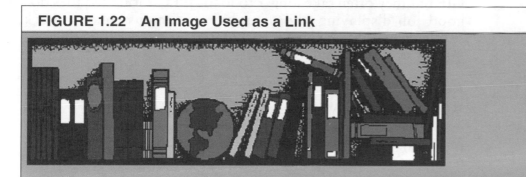

MULTNOMAH COUNTY LIBRARY
General Information

The Multnomah County Library serves Oregon's smallest county by size but the largest through population (estimated in mid-1995 at 620,000) and is centered in the Portland metropolitan area. We deliver our services through the Central Library in downtown Portland, 14 branch libraries and Library Outreach Services. Multnomah County Library also plays an important role in the coordination of regional library services through PORTALS and other interlibrary agreements.

- History and Description
- Mission and Philosophy
- Your Library Card
- The Library's Collection
- Governance
- This World Wide Web Site
- Library Publications

Return

Many graphic files are stored on Web servers such as GIF (Graphics Interchange Format) files (identified by the .gif file extension). GIF is a format developed by CompuServe. All graphical browsers can load and display GIF images, therefore most inline graphics on Web pages are in GIF format. GIF files load quickly because they are highly compressed. GIF formatted files do a good job displaying line drawings, cartoons, and graphic navigation buttons. They are less satisfactory for photographs and color pictures (as GIF files are limited to 256 colors).

Many other graphic files are stored on Web servers such as JPEG (Joint Photographic Experts Group) files (identified by the .jpg or .jpeg file extension). JPEG images are higher quality than GIF but they often take longer to load. JPEG formatted files do a good job displaying photographs, continuous tone artwork, scanned paintings, and complex colored images (as JPEG files can display up to 16.7 million colors).

AUDIO

When you visit a Web site you will mostly see links to external audio files. That is because few browsers, as yet, support automatically-loaded audio files. In order to hear audio files you need a computer than has a sound card, speakers, and audio "helper" software.

When planning your library Web site, you can create your own sounds or messages, download files from sound archives on the Web, or purchase CD-based "clip sounds." Just like graphic files, you have to convert sound files into common audio file formats. (To do this you need audio editing and conversion software, which is available on the Net as freeware or shareware.) The reason you have to convert sound files to specific formats is because often Macintosh and Windows computers support different audio formats. When setting up your Web site, consider converting sound files into different formats so that patrons using both Macintosh and Windows PCs can hear them.

AU (.au) and MPEG (.mpeg, .mpg) audio formats files can be played on both Macintosh and Windows PCs. AU and MPEG files produce high enough quality sound for spoken word files but not high enough quality sound for music files. MPEG is also commonly used as a video format file as discussed in the next section. AIFF (.aif) files for Macintosh and WAVE (.wav) files for Windows produce higher quality sound so they can be used for both spoken word and music files.

Another type of audio file just being developed is called "streamed" audio. Instead of waiting for the whole audio file to load, with streamed audio, pieces of the audio file are sent in sequence and play in real time as they arrive. So far the audio quality is a lot like AM radio, so voices sound better than music. Check out RealAudio's Web site http://www.realaudio.com/, for more information. RealAudio must be loaded onto your Web server to make it available to Web browsers.

VIDEO

When you visit a Web site you will mostly see links to external video files. That is because only a few browsers, as yet, support automatically-loaded video files. To view video files you need "helper" software. Video player software is included with new versions of operating systems (e.g., Windows 95). If your operating system doesn't include it, you will have to locate and download video player software from the Net.

When you are planning your library Web site, you can create your own video clips, locate and download clips from video archives on the Web, or purchase CD-based "clip videos." Like all media files, video files are large and take a lot of time to load. Just like graphic and audio files, you have to convert video files into common file formats. (To do this you need video editing and conversion software, which is available on the Net as freeware or shareware.) The reason you have to convert files to particular formats is because often Macintosh and Windows computers support different video formats. When setting up your Web site, consider converting video files into different formats, so that patrons using both Macintosh and Windows PCs can view them.

MPEG (.mpeg, .mpg) format audio files can be played on both Macintosh and Windows PCs. They are problematic, however, because they treat video images and accompanying audio as two separate files. QuickTime (.mov) video files for the Macintosh are becoming quite common also in the Windows environment. AVI (.avi) audio files as well are common in the Windows environment.

"Streamed" video is just being developed. Instead of waiting (often a long time) for an entire video file to load, with streamed video, pieces of the video file are sent in sequence and play in real time as they arrive. This makes it possible to view longer videos. Check out Xing Technologies Web site for more information http://www.xingtech.com/

TO LEARN MORE...

See Chapter 11 for complete bibliographic citations. Also refer to Chapter 11 for additional print and Web resources. For more information about Web media we recommend you connect to:

- *Setting Your Reader Properly* http://sunsite.unc.edu/wm/about/tech.html
- *Inline Image FAQ* http://www.uwtc.washington.edu/Computing/WWW/
- *Rob's Multimedia Lab* http://www.acm.uiuc.edu/rml/
- *Web Browser Test Page (Windows)* http://www.uky.edu/~macgree00/TestPage.html

2 THINK BIG—LOOK AT THE ISSUES FOR LIBRARIES

STARTING THE DISCUSSION

This section outlines how you can get staff discussing the Web and its impact on your library, your patrons, and your staff.

As you and your staff start planning for a Web connection or start planning your library's Web site, we recommend you take the time to discuss the many big and small issues the Web raises for libraries, librarians, and patrons. The earlier you discuss these issues the better. That way staff will be aware not only of "what" you are doing (acquiring the Web and setting up a Web site) but also know "why" you are doing it and "how" it will affect your patrons, your library, and their jobs.

We recommend you organize weekly "think big" discussions which focus on how the Web will affect your library. Plan to discuss the following topics (or some variation thereof):

- How is the Web different than other information tools?
- How will it affect your library building?
- How will it affect your services and organization?
- How will it affect patrons?
- How will it affect staff?
- How will it affect your community?
- What will the future be like?

The purpose of these meetings is four-fold; to familiarize staff with the issues, to encourage staff to discuss the issues among themselves, to provide you with their insights and opinions, and most importantly, to encourage staff to start thinking of themselves as a team, and your Web implementation as a team effort.

Full- and part-time staff, as well as student assistants, volunteers, board members, and trustees should be able to attend meetings and voice their opinions freely. Set up discussion rules so that those attending feel safe offering their ideas/opinions without fear of undue criticism or ridicule.

Prior to each meeting, provide staff with background readings and thought-provoking articles. You can find many relevant articles/readings in library and information technology journals as well as on library and information association Web sites. (See Chapter 11, p. 203–205 for selected articles and Web sites.)

Provide staff with "issues" outlines which contain statements and questions relating to each meeting topic. Staff can use them to start thinking (and start forming opinions) about each topic well before they attend each meeting.

SAMPLE "ISSUES" OUTLINES

This section provides you with outlines that will help focus staff discussions and get staff started thinking "big" about your Web connection and Web site.

You can use the following "issues" outlines as printed or modify them as needed. They do not, and cannot, cover all the issues you need to discuss. (If they did, they would comprise a book and not just a chapter.) Get creative with them, and use them as a vehicle to get your staff talking to you and to each other.

HOW IS THE WEB DIFFERENT THAN OTHER INFORMATION TOOLS?

The Web is a more global online information tool than you've ever had before.

- How is the Web different than other online tools?
- How is it better/worse?
- What new services and resources can you provide patrons?
- How will you staff training needs change?

The Web is a powerful and simple text and multimedia tool.

- Which current library tools or resources does the Web duplicate?
- Which materials should you consider cancelling once you have Web access?
- How do you decide what to cancel and what to duplicate?

The Web is famous and infamous for the wide range of opinions and viewpoints it contains.

- How do you educate patrons to be critical of where Web information comes from?

- How do you make patrons wary of misinformation?
- How do you train patrons to look for opinions on all sides of an issue?

The Web has no collection policy. You can't easily select or deselect Net or Web resources, therefore you have to deal with the types of materials to which you are not accustomed.

- How do you plan to deal with "adult" materials on the Web?
- Do you plan on using filtering/blocking software?
- Does your library support the Library Bill of Rights?
- What policies and procedures do you need to write?
- What kinds of discussions do you need to hold with community groups?

The Web makes both public domain and copyrighted text and images available.

- How do you plan to educate staff and patrons about copyright?
- What can you do to protect yourself legally?

HOW WILL IT AFFECT YOUR LIBRARY BUILDING?

The Web lets patrons access global and local information from home.

- Why will patrons still want or need to come to your library?
- What can you offer them that they can't get at home?

You will need to install clusters of computers all around your library.

- Where will you locate them?
- How will you balance patron privacy with service needs?
- How will you comply with ADA requirements?
- Will you put them in areas where there is no service desk or staff?
- Will you put them only in areas where staff are present?
- How will they affect your furniture arrangement, shelving, and service areas?
- How will they affect your heating/air conditioning system?
- Will you need to install air conditioning or upgrade your current system?

Computer clusters require lots of electrical outlets and should not be on the same circuits as other machinery (e.g., copy machines).

- How will your current wiring affect where you locate Web workstations?
- How will you budget for installing new electrical connections within your building?
- How will you manage until you can upgrade your wiring?
- How will local wiring regulations affect your installation?

If you have more computers in your library, you will need more ergonomic tables and chairs.

- How will you find the funds to purchase them?
- How can you "make do" until you can purchase them?

Many journals and government documents are now available only in electronic form via the Net and Web.

- How will this affect your collection areas?
- How will this affect your current shelving plan?

HOW WILL IT AFFECT YOUR SERVICES AND ORGANIZATION?

Your organizational structure will need to change.

- Will you need to set up new departments or units?
- Which staff members will run these units?
- How will you decide which staff gets reassigned?

You will have to purchase additional equipment, modify your library building, and maybe even pay staff more.

- Where will you find the funds to do all this?
- What will you stop purchasing?
- How can you save money on current services?
- Where can you go for financial support?
- How much money will you need?

Your library will become less of a physical place and more of a "a place to connect to other places."

- How will this shift affect what you collect and store in your building and what you access online via the Web?
- How will it affect your reference and other collections?
- What materials do you still need to provide in paper or CD-ROM format? Why?
- How will you use the Web to provide patrons with twenty-four hour-a-day access to information?

- How will you decide which materials to make available around the clock?

You probably will have to stop or cut back on selected services and materials in other areas.
- How will you find out what is available on the Net?
- How will you decide what to stop doing and purchasing?
- How will you decide what to cut back on?
- Who can you involve in making these decisions?
- How can you involve patrons in these decisions?

You will need to purchase more powerful computers and computer peripherals.
- How will you budget for upgrading library computers?
- Who can you ask for financial assistance and other forms of help?

HOW WILL IT AFFECT PATRONS?

Patrons can live miles away or just around the corner.
- What opportunities does the Web provide for distant patrons?
- What can you do to provide all patrons with access?
- What new forms of outreach will the Web make possible?
- What equipment and extra funds will you need?

Many patrons do not, and will not, have home computers.
- How will you ensure that they have access regardless of their connectivity at home?
- How will they know your library provides them with access to the Web?
- How can you get the word out to people in your community?
- What ways can you help these patrons get connected?

Patrons will need education and training to use the Web effectively.
- How much time can you afford to spend on training patrons?
- What kinds of training sessions will and can you provide for patrons?
- What other groups in your area offer computer or Internet training?
- Is there anyone in your community who can assist you?

Some patrons will immediately use Web workstations. Others will be hesitant to use them.

- How can you support enthusiastic patrons?
- How can you use their skills and enthusiasm to help you?
- How will you encourage reluctant patrons?
- How can you find out what will make them more comfortable?
- How might patrons be at a disadvantage when they don't want to use the Net or Web to locate information?

Patrons will often use the Net and Web without staff intervention or help.

- How will you know if patrons find what they need?
- How can you get feedback from patrons about their successes and failures on the Net?
- How can you use feedback to help patrons?

Patrons will start to expect real time availability of information. In some cases it is readily available, in other cases it isn't.

- How will you explain the disparity to patrons?
- How can you get them to have reasonable expectations?

Patrons will use the Web to visit informational and scholarly sites, but they will also visit recreational sites.

- How do you handle the intellectual freedom, privacy, and censorship issues?
- How will you deal with patrons who play online games, socialize in chat rooms, or view adult materials?

HOW WILL IT AFFECT STAFF?

Staff are used to working with paper-based and CD-ROM-based information which remains the same from month to month. The Web, on the other hand, changes daily. Keeping up with the Web will be almost impossible.

- How can you organize staff to keep up?
- How will you reward staff for making the effort?

Staff will no longer be information experts but will become information partners and explorers with patrons. This will be a new role that many librarians may have difficulty accepting.

- How will you encourage staff to accept their transition from "expert" to "fellow information explorer"?

- How can you get staff to view this change as an opportunity rather than a problem?
- How will you handle reluctant or resistant staff?

Staff job responsibilities will change.

- How will technical service jobs change?
- What new responsibilities will catalogers and collection development staff take on?
- How will public service jobs change?
- What new responsibilities will reference and circulation staff take on?
- How can you provide staff with time to get familiar with "virtual" tools and collections?

Staff job descriptions and staff pay classifications may change.

- How will you decide who gets assigned new responsibilities?
- How quickly will you need to update staff job descriptions?
- Where can you find the additional funds to pay staff more?

Newly hired staff need to have different skills.

- What skills will you want new staff members to have?
- How do these skills differ from those you valued in the past?

Some staff will have promotion and/or tenure requirements to meet.

- How will the Web change those requirements?
- What new categories of service and professional growth will you need to add to promotion and tenure documents?

Staff will be able to keep in touch with other professionals on a daily basis through e-mail and electronic discussion groups.

- How will you encourage staff to participate in discussion groups?
- How much time will you set aside during the day for staff to check and read their professional e-mail?
- How will you handle situations when a staff member spends too much time on this and ignores his/her other duties?

More staff will need to know how to answer basic computer questions and be able to troubleshoot equipment and connections.
- Will all staff have responsibility for computer trouble-shooting?
- How will they make the time while continuing their other duties?

HOW WILL IT AFFECT YOUR COMMUNITY?

Your community will be both local and global.
- How will you define your "community" of patrons?
- What services will you provide only to local patrons, but not offer to "virtual" patrons?
- How will you limit access to your community?
- What local community partners can you enlist to help your library?

Community members will often start thinking more positively about your library because of the Web.
- How will this help you pass your next library levy or bond issue?
- How will this help you get volunteers to assist staff?

Many local community groups will be interested in learning about the Web.
- How important is training community members?
- How will training impact the rest of your library services?
- How much time will you have to do this type of training?

Your Web site can and should include a lot of local community information.
- How will you decide what to make available through your Web site?
- How much time and money will you spend on such efforts?
- How can you get local assistance with these projects?
- What role can community members play in planning your Web site?
- What financial and staff support can they offer you?
- What formal agreements should you have with Web partners?

WHAT WILL THE FUTURE BE LIKE?

Information may not always be free.

- How will you handle subscription-based Net information?
- How will you handle pay-per-use charges?
- Will you pass the cost onto patrons or budget for it?
- How will you handle "hardship" patrons?

There will be a growing "information elite."

- What will your library do to counteract this trend?
- What new programs can you provide for the "information poor"?

There will continue to be enhancements to telecommunications and networking.

- How will high-speed ISDN connections help connect patrons and staff?
- How will cable modems affect your Web connection?
- How will ATM further enhance your connection?
- How will new versions of network software and hardware make setting up a Web server simple?

There will continue to be enhancements to existing Web tools (see Chapter 11 for definitions of the more technical terms below).

- How will real time audio and video enhance your Web site?
- How will virtual reality applications enhance your Web site?
- How will expanded HTML features and better HTML editing programs enhance your Web site?
- How will encryption and security programs make your Web site useful to patrons?
- How will CGI and JAVA applications enhance your Web site?
- How will SGML provide enhanced access to local text-based information?
- How will sophisticated statistical programs help you better analyze your Web site?

There will be different uses developed for the Web.

- How will you use the Web as a public relations tool?
- How will you use the Web as a publishing tool?
- How will you use the Web as a conferencing tool?

- How will you use the Web as a communication tool?
- What affect will the Web have on your local media (e.g., television, radio, newspapers)?

There will be too much information and a lot will be redundant.

- What will you do to help patrons sort through the mass of information?
- What sophisticated search tools will you need?
- What future classes will you need to teach?

TO LEARN MORE...

See Chapter 11 for full bibliographic citations. Also refer to Chapter 11 for additional print and Web resources.

For more information about the Web and libraries we recommend you read and connect to:

- "Untangling the Web" by P. Healy *RQ* (Summer 95)
- "The Wonderful World of the Web in the Library" by P. Ensor *Technicalities* (March 95)
- *American Library Association* http://www.ala.org/
- *Canadian Library Association* http://www.ncf.carleton. ca/freeport/prof.assoc/cla/menu
- *Coalition for Networked Information* http://www.cni. org/CNI.homepage.html
- *Coalition for Networked Information Discovery & Retrieval* http://cnidr.org/welcome.html
- *Consortium for School Networking* gopher://cosn.org

3 GOING ONLINE— GETTING AN INTERNET CONNECTION

THE DECISION PROCESS

This section describes who should decide what kind of Net/Web connection to get or who should review your current Net/Web connection. It also discusses important planning decisions.

WHO AND WHAT

The group of people you assign to either recommend the type of Net/Web connection your library should get or review your existing Web connection must be willing to wade through technical, and sometimes conflicting, details related to connection types. They must be familiar with existing library computers and their connections and be willing to take a look into the future and make some guesses about the way your library will use the Web in the next couple of years. Finally, they must be willing to tackle budget realities and recommend reallocating funds to get the best Internet connection.

Consider creating a group with the following overall skills:

- someone who is familiar with the Internet;
- someone who knows your computers and how they are connected together;
- someone who knows your library budget and where it can flex;
- someone who is good at knowing what staff want and need;
- someone who can cut through details, see the "big issues" and organize the group;
- someone from a local business or campus organization that has been through this process already;
- someone who understands telecommunications and can communicate using non-technical language; and
- someone in touch with patron needs.

The process of deciding on the right Internet connection or reviewing your current connection may take time. It involves getting technical specifications and prices from local Internet providers, trying to make sense of them, and comparing them to each other. It also may take time to come to some accurate conclusions about Web use now and in the future and to choose a connection type that will support staff and patron needs. Finally it may take time to find the funds so that you can sign a contract, or decide to upgrade your connection, and start the ball rolling.

How staff and patrons will use the Web (and other Internet tools) should be the most important factor used to determine what type of Internet connection you get. Before you start locating Internet providers, researching connection types and costs, or checking out local telephone options, you first need to find out from staff how they plan to use the Net/Web now and how they anticipate patrons using it in the future. (See Chapter 2 for issues to discuss and for some specific questions to ask.)

Once you know who will be using your library connection and what they will be doing with it, you need to investigate the various options for connecting to the Internet. You should spend time matching the type of Web access each type of connection makes possible, with the list of functions your library wants to make available to staff and patrons. (For instance, your group decides that graphical browser access is essential. You then eliminate a dialup shell connection from consideration because it only supports text-based Web access. Or you decide that multimedia applications like video and sound are essential. You then eliminate both dialup shell and dialup IP connections which are modem-based and basically too slow for transferring media.)

Cost is unavoidably a factor. Your group must choose the connection option that offers the best combination of functionality and price. If necessary, you must review your library budget to find the funds so that you can get the best, most appropriate Internet connection for your current and anticipated needs. You probably will find that prices vary wildly, from region to region and from state to state. A local Internet provider may or may not be the cheapest option. Many Internet providers offer deep educational discounts but are often not forthcoming about them. You need to press Internet providers for their best deal and be willing to "hold the line" on price and service options.

WHO CAN SUPPLY YOU WITH A CONNECTION?

This section discusses the different types of Internet connections offered by organizations.

Some organizations charge for connecting to the Net, others provide connections free of charge. Before you start paying for an Internet connection, check to see if there are free connection options available in your area. (However a free connection—if it does not meet your service needs—may not be your best alternative...just as "free" in other things in life doesn't always mean "best.")

PLACES TO GET A FREE CONNECTION...

- You may be able to get a free Net/Web connection from a local college. Many colleges that are connected to the Net provide guest accounts to local schools and libraries as part of their educational outreach program. These connections often can be limited to text-only Web access.
- Many local businesses with Internet connections provide guest accounts to local non-profit groups (including libraries and schools) as a community service (and get a tax write-off for a portion of their connection costs). These can be a good deal if they provide you with a connection which supports graphical Web browsers.
- Some states also provide free Internet connections for teachers and librarians through an educational network. Many of these connections are limited to text-only Web access.
- Local Free-Nets or bulletin board systems (BBSs) can provide you with free connections to selected Internet sites and tools such as e-mail. Most Free-Nets and BBSs, however, do not offer the type of Internet access that would support graphical browsers.

COMMERCIAL CONNECTION PROVIDERS

There are currently two major types of organizations that will sell you access to the Internet: Internet access providers and online services. Very soon you will also be able to get an Internet connection through your local telephone or cable company.

Internet Access Providers— Companies that provide or sell you an Internet connection.

Internet Access Providers

Internet access providers focus solely on providing you with a connection to the Internet. They provide various types of Internet connections from inexpensive dialup connections to more expensive dedicated connections. They often supply you with the software you need to navigate the Internet and the Web (along with the necessary telecommunication hardware). Soon your local telephone company may offer to be your Internet access provider.

Internet access providers can be local, regional, or national. Most provide you with local phone numbers for dialup connections. National providers offer dialup customers local phone numbers in larger metropolitan areas and 800 phone numbers in most other areas. Internet access providers charge you either by the minute, offer you a flat-fee for a specified number of hours per month, or offer you a flat-fee, unlimited use, per month. Be sure and comparison shop; prices vary greatly from provider to provider. You can easily find out which Internet access providers operate in your area. (See Chapter 11, p. 206–207 for these lists.)

Online Services— Commercial networks that offer subscribers both locally-loaded databases and a gateway to the Internet.

Online Services

Online services such as CompuServe, Prodigy, America Online, and Microsoft Network provide you with access to the commercial databases loaded on their computers as well as gateways to the Internet. This combination of commercial databases and the Internet can be a very attractive (but also a very expensive) option for school and public libraries. Most of these online services provide dialup, not dedicated, connections. Most online services have local or 800 phone numbers. Online services provide attractive, graphical displays of information resources. These displays make finding and using databases and the Internet simple.

It's easy to find out about online services. They advertise widely in computer and Internet magazines and many of you probably have received trial disks in the mail. Ask each online service for brochures that describe all their services and costs. Spend time comparing and contrasting all the services. There are differences in both cost and content. Which one you choose will depend on what information you want access to and how much you can afford to spend.

Before deciding to connect with either an Internet access provider or online service, spend time comparing costs for each type of company. Look at the differing types of services they provide. Many libraries find the convenience of having access to both online commercial databases and Internet access worth the cost of an online service. (Online services are not really cost effective for libraries planning to offer patron access to the Net.) Other libraries find that getting an Internet connection from an access provider suits their needs and saves them money at the same time.

Cable Companies

Your local cable company may soon be offering you an Internet connection. Reasonably priced cable modems are on the market and are being tested by the large cable providers. Cable modems can provide your library with a high-speed Net/Web connection similar to a dedicated connection. If your library or building already has cable installed, check with your local cable company about its plans for providing your community with Internet access.

CONNECTION OPTIONS AND EQUIPMENT

This section provides you with short descriptions of the types of Internet connections, their relationship to Web access, and the equipment your library will need to support such a connection.

Modem—A device for connecting a computer to a phone line and transmitting data.

There are two types of Internet connections: dialup and dedicated. Dialup connections use a <u>modem</u> or other similar device to connect your computer(s) to the Internet and also the Web. When you are using a dialup connection, you are connected to the Internet (and the Web) only when you make the connection via your modem. When you have a dedicated connection you are connected to the Net and Web twenty-four hours-a-day, seven days-a-week.

There are different types of dialup and dedicated connections available. Which option you choose will determine whether the Web will be instantly available or whether you will be required to dialup via modem every time you want to use it. The type of connection you choose determines whether staff and patrons will be limited to exploring the Web with a text-based browser, or will be able to take advantage of the Web's media capabilities by using a graphical browser. The type of connection you choose also determines what you can provide for patrons. Following are non-technical descriptions of the most common connection types, along with hardware and software requirements.

DIALUP CONNECTIONS

A dialup connection uses a modem or other device to connect your computer(s) to the Internet. There are three types of dialup connections—dialup shell connections, dialup IP connections (which come in two variations: SLIP and PPP), and dialup ISDN connections. Each connection type affects how you will both view and use the Web.

Dialup Shell Connections

Dialup Shell Connection—The most basic of Internet connections restricted to text-based access.

A <u>dialup shell connection</u> is the simplest of all Internet connections. You use a modem, telecommunication software (e.g., Procomm, Microphone), and a standard phone line to connect your computer to your Internet provider's computer, which is connected to the Internet. All the Internet software is loaded and ready to use on your Internet provider's computer.

When you choose this type of connection, your computer is not directly connected to the Internet. You are merely dialing into, and renting time on, a computer that is directly connected to the Net. This type of connection limits your computer to using text-based software to explore the Net. This means that you will be limited to using a text-based Web browser like Lynx.

Your computer doesn't have to be the fastest or the latest model. Because you are limited to a text-based connection, you can use older model computers that don't support Windows or Mac System 7.0+ (in other words, those old 286s and Apple machines). Having a fast modem (28.8kbps) is usually a necessity for accessing the Web, but this is not the case with a dialup shell connection and text-based browser like Lynx. Both work quite well with slower modems (9600 kbps).

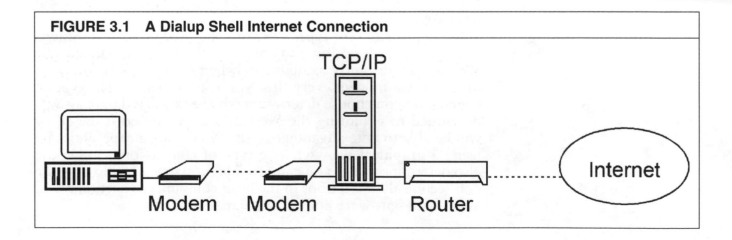

FIGURE 3.1   A Dialup Shell Internet Connection

Dialup IP Connection—A type of dialup connection in which you load TCP/IP, either SLIP or PPP software, and various types of client software onto your computer. Dialup IP connections allow you to be directly connected to the Internet and use graphical client software, such as Netscape, to browse the Web.

SLIP (Serial Line Internet Protocol)—The first popular type of direct Internet connection. With a SLIP connection your computer has TCP/IP loaded on it, has its own Internet address, and is directly connected to the Net. Having a SLIP connection means that you can use a graphical browser, like Netscape, to access media in addition to text.

Dialup IP Connections

With a dialup IP connection you connect via modem to your Internet provider's computer. With this type of connection, your library is directly connected to the Internet instead of indirectly connected like with a dialup shell connection. This means that you can load any Internet software onto your computer(s), including graphical Web browsers like Netscape and Mosaic. Finding and downloading Internet and Web software is simple. You can find it in software archives, on browser developer Web sites, or by doing a key word search in large Web indexes like Yahoo.

To set up an IP connection you need to first load TCP/IP and then load either SLIP or PPP software onto your computer to connect it to the Internet. (Often Internet providers will supply you with TCP/IP and SLIP or PPP software. If not, they usually will supply you with the URL of a software archive that makes them available for download.)

Using this type of connection, you are in charge of what software you load and what software you use. You can choose to load one or more graphical Web browser(s) and even a text-based browser if you want. To use a dialup IP connection, you need a computer capable of running Windows or MacOS7.0+ with a minimum 8 MB (16 MB is better) of RAM. You will also need a fast modem (28.8 kbps), and a regular phone line.

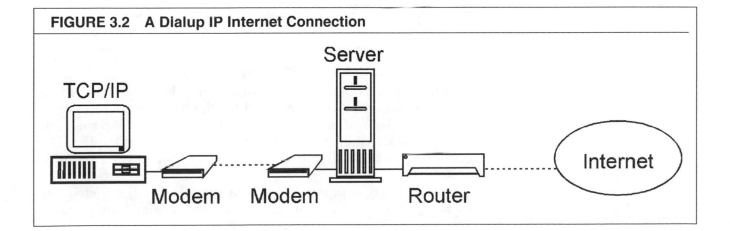

FIGURE 3.2   A Dialup IP Internet Connection

Terminal Adapter—A device, used with an ISDN connection, that acts like a modem and connects your computer to your Internet provider and the Net.

ISDN (Integrated Services Digital Network)—A type of phone line service. With an ISDN connection your regular phone line, that has been switched to ISDN service, can carry both digital (computer) and analog (voice) signals.

Dialup ISDN Connections

A dialup ISDN connection also provides you with a direct connection to the Internet. You load TCP/IP and PPP software onto your computer and any Web browser you choose. Instead of a modem you use a device called a <u>terminal adapter</u> to connect you to the Internet.

Dialup <u>ISDN</u> connections transmit information at much faster speeds than dialup connections that use a modem. (128 kbps or 64 kbps versus a 28.8 kbps connection for a modem.) A faster connection means that you can connect to, view, and download media resources that are too large to effectively access using a modem connection. ISDN connections are not available in all areas yet, so check with your local phone company to see if it's available in your area.

With a dialup ISDN connection you need to have a computer capable of running Windows or MacOS7.0+ with at least 8 MB (16 MB is better) of RAM, as fast a processor (e.g., Pentium) as you can afford, a terminal adapter, and a standard phone line that has been switched over to ISDN service. (You can use your ISDN connection to receive faxes and talk on the phone, sometimes at the same time you are using the Net.)

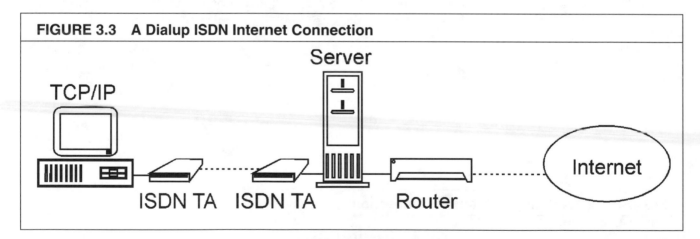

FIGURE 3.3   A Dialup ISDN Internet Connection

Costs (Including long-distance)

All three types of dialup connections are relatively inexpensive. Prices vary greatly, so shop around for the best service/price combination (and ask about educational discounts). Dialup shell and IP accounts are often billed on a per-minute basis. Dialup ISDN accounts and some dialup IP accounts are billed on a monthly basis.

If your library is in a rural area or outside a major metropolitan area, there are ways to avoid paying regular long distance phone charges to connect via dialup to an Internet provider. The easiest is to get a dedicated connection—you pay one flat fee per month for unlimited Internet access and don't have to worry about long-distance charges at all.

You can connect through an Internet provider that offers you a local phone number to dial. If there are no providers offering local phone numbers in your area, choose a provider that offers you an 800 phone number to dial for access. Or you can use a public data network, such as Tymnet or SprintNet, to connect at a lower rate than standard long distance to a provider that is out of your local dialing area.

DEDICATED CONNECTIONS

Dedicated Connection—A type of Internet connection that provides twenty-four hour-a-day, seven-day-a-week access to the Internet.

When you have a dedicated connection, your computer can be connected to the Net twenty-four hours-a-day, 7 days-a-week. A dedicated connection uses a special telecommunication line that is designed to carry computer data rather than voice messages. When you have a dedicated Internet connection you can create and store your library Web pages on the computer that acts as the server for your dedicated Internet connection.

If you have, or are planning to have, more than six computers in your library accessing the Net/Web, you will probably find that a dedicated line is less expensive and simpler to use and to maintain than six separate dialup connections. If your library already has a local area network (LAN), you should consider getting a dedicated connection rather than multiple dialup connections. A dedicated connection attached to your library's LAN server provides all computers that are part of the LAN with full-time Net/Web access.

LAN (Local Area Network)—A group of computers connected together and managed by a server computer. LAN-connected computers can share information, programming, e-mail and Internet connectivity.

There are different types of dedicated lines (56K, T1, and T3). The types are based on how fast data will travel over each connection. The faster data transfers, the more expensive the line. The faster the line, the more computers you can attach to it and the faster you can get information. If your library is small to medium sized, you will find that a 56K line is probably fast enough to handle your Net/Web connections. Larger public libraries, school districts, and most university libraries find that they need a T1 connection to handle both the types and number of connections. As more media-based information is available on the Web, you may need to get a faster dedicated connection to handle the increased amount of data that media files require.

When you get a dedicated connection you need a computer to act as your Internet/LAN server. It should be a Windows, Macintosh, or UNIX platform. You need TCP/IP and server software loaded on it (or LAN software that includes TCP/IP). You will not need a modem or terminal adaptor to connect you to the Internet, but instead you will need two different pieces of telecommunication equipment; a router and a <u>CSU/DSU</u>. This equipment translates your computer's signals into digital form and routes both incoming and outgoing messages and data to the correct computer. Your Internet provider will often supply you with

<u>CSU/DSU (Channel Service Unit/Data Service Unit)</u>—A device that allows your computer to talk to other computers over a digital phone line.

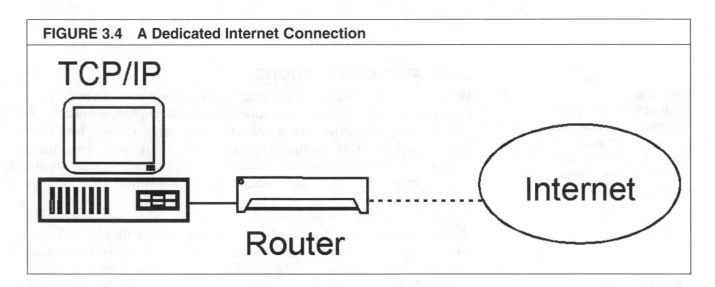

FIGURE 3.4   A Dedicated Internet Connection

TCP/IP

Router

Internet

<u>Router</u>—A telecommunication device that makes decisions about the path that incoming and outgoing Internet traffic will take.

both a <u>router</u> and CSU/DSU when you get a dedicated connection. Your decision to get a particular speed connection is not a permanent decision. Dedicated connections are relatively simple to upgrade, so you can get a faster connection as you need one.

Dedicated connections cost anywhere from $250 to $1,500 per month, depending on the speed of the line and the distance the line has to travel to reach your Internet provider. Costs can vary greatly and many providers offer deep discounts to schools and libraries. Finding Internet providers serving your area is relatively simple. (See Chapter 11 for a list of books and Web resources that can help you locate providers.)

To set up a dedicated connection locally you need to have someone on staff who has computer and Internet knowledge. This person needs to work closely with your Internet provider's staff to make sure all parts of the connection work correctly. That person probably will spend a few hours each week maintaining and troubleshooting your connection.

Computers That Support The Web and Graphical Browsers

Macintosh (Good)

Computer—Quadra
Hard drive—250 MB
Memory—8 MB RAM
Graphics card—1 MB VRAM
Operating system—MacOS7+
Modem—14.4 kbps

Macintosh (Best)

Computer—Power Mac
Hard drive—1 GB
Memory—16 MB RAM
Graphics card—2 MB VRAM
Operating system—MacOS7+
Modem—28.8 kbps

Windows PC (Good)

Computer—486 66MHz
Hard drive—500 MB
Memory—8 MB RAM
Graphics card—1 MB VRAM
Operating system—Windows 3.1
Modem—14.4 kbps

Windows PC (Best)

Computer—Pentium 150 MHz
Hard drive—2 GB
Memory—32 MB RAM
Graphics card—4 MB VRAM
Operating system—Windows 3.1
Windows 95
Windows NT
OS/2 Warp
Modem—28.8 kbps

TO LEARN MORE...

Chapter 11 gives complete bibliographic citations.

Also refer to Chapter 11 for additional print and Web resources.

For more information about Internet connections we recommend you read and connect to:

- *The SLIP/PPP Connection* by P. Gilster
- *The Internet Access Cookbook* by K. Schneider
- *Internet Connections: A Librarians Guide to Dialup access and use* by M. Engle et al.

- *Yahoo: Providers* http://www.yahoo.com/Business/ Corporations/Internet_Access_Providers

For more information about LANs, networking, and modems we recommend you read and connect to:

- *Networking Illustrated* by E. Lee
- *Networking for Dummies* by D. Lowe
- *Client/Server Computing for Dummies* by D. Lowe
- *Modems for Dummies* by T. Rathbone
- *ISDN FAQ* http://www.cis.ohio-state.edu/hypertext/ usenet/isdn-faq/faq.html
- *LAN/Ethernet FAQ* http://www.cis.ohio-state.edu/ hypertext/usenet/ethernet-faq.html

HOUSING YOUR WEB SITE

This section describes the decisions you need to make about where your Web documents will be stored.

Web Server—A computer that houses Web documents and that server and Internet software in order to communicate and share information with Web clients.

If you want to create a Web site you will either have to set up a local computer on which to store your Web documents, or you will have to find a computer that will store them for you. If you don't have an extra computer (or LAN computer), you may have to budget for and purchase a Web server. If you already have a decent-sized LAN server, it can often act as your Web server. (This depends on the computer you use as your LAN server and what other functions it performs besides running your LAN.)

The staff member in charge of your Internet connection should be in charge of your Web server because they often are housed on the same computer. (If not, the staff member in charge of your Net connection often knows more about the technical side of the Net than the rest of your staff.) If your library doesn't have such a person on staff, you may have to find someone in your community, on your campus, or in your school district to take responsibility for your Web server until you can train a staff member to do the job. Your "webmaster" can spend anywhere from 240 hours per week on tasks related to keeping your server functional and working with your staff to keep Web pages current, depending on how active and large your Web site is.

Webmaster/ Webweaver—The person in charge of the technical aspects of a Web site.

Setting up a Web server locally can be a complex task. This book does not go into detail on how to set one up, as there are books and articles that cover the topic in detail. (See p. 207–208 in Chapter 11 for suggested titles and URLs.) If you decide not to set up a local Web server there are lots of options for getting your Web pages housed and made available on a non-local computer.

- If you work in a university or large college library, check with your computing services or network staff. If they can't/won't host your Web documents, they probably know other computers/people on campus who might.
- If you work in a community college library, check to see if larger colleges or local businesses with a Web server might be willing to host your Web documents (perhaps in exchange for some training sessions or reference assistance).
- If you work in a public library, check with local businesses that already have a Web site to see if they would be willing to host your Web documents on their computer. (Companies often see this as good community PR.)
- If you are a member of a regional library (or educational) consortium, check to see if other libraries in the consortium know of a consortium member that might host your Web documents. You can also check with your local school district. It might have a Web server already, or be planning one, that might be able to help your library out.
- If you work in a school library, check with your local public library or a local college to see if either would be willing to host your Web documents. You can also check with local computer groups. Individual members might have a server or know of a non-profit group that would provide you with storage space.
- If all else fails, check with knowledgeable individuals to locate a company that will rent you space on their Web server. These companies are numerous and often provide non-profit groups (like libraries) relatively inexpensive storage for Web pages.

Qualities of a Good Webmaster/Webweaver

- Understands information services and librarianship
- Possesses a basic knowledge of computers, networking, telecommunications
- Is able to work with a wide variety of people and build consensus
- Is creative, interested in learning technical details
- Is able to understand and talk with "techies" and "non-techies"
- Possesses some graphic design sense
- Is willing to experiment, keep abreast of Web developments

TO LEARN MORE...

See Chapter 11 for complete bibliographic citations.

Also refer to Chapter 11 for additional print and Web resources.

For more information about Web servers we recommend you read and connect to:

- *How to Set Up and Maintain a World Wide Web Site* by L. Stein
- *The Web Server Book* by J. Magid
- *Web Weaving* by E. Tilton
- *The Complete Idiot's Guide to Protecting Yourself on the Internet* by A. Weiss
- *Web Server Primer* http://www.vuw.ac.nz/ Nathan.Torkington/ideas/www-servers.html
- *Internet Server Cookbook* http://web66.coled.umn.edu/ Cookbook/contents.html
- *Webmaster's Reference Library* http://www.webreference.com/
- *Security FAQ* http://www-genome.wi.mit.edu/WWW/ faqs/www-security-faq.html

4 ONCE YOU'RE CONNECTED—LEARNING AND TEACHING THE WEB

ORGANIZING LEARNING AND TRAINING

This section provides you with ways to organize staff and patron learning/training experiences.

WHO AND WHAT

Learning about the Internet and the Web in order to teach them may be daunting because of the technical nature of the topic, the new skills involved, and the pace at which the Net and Web change.

The Good News is...

- You don't have to learn everything about the Net/Web at the same time. You can start with basic skills and then learn other skills that build on the basics.
- You don't have to learn it all yourself. You can form a learning team consisting of interested staff members. Each team member can learn a specific Web skill and teach it to the whole team.
- You don't have to be a Web expert in order to teach. You can admit you don't know everything and then have fun exploring and learning right along with your patrons.
- Your library's "learning" team can become a "training" team. It can outline a training strategy/timeline, write individual session outlines, and teach courses for staff and patrons.

Planning and doing Net/Web training takes a basic knowledge of the Internet and the Web, an understanding of your library's vision for the Web, an appreciation of how they can enhance services to patrons, an understanding of patron needs and interests, a willingness to learn new things, and a desire to become an enthusiastic Web explorer. The group of people you choose for your learning/teaching team must:

- be willing to work closely together;
- be willing to share what they learn;

- have some experience teaching or a passion for teaching;
- be capable of explaining technical concepts simply;
- be capable of writing "user-friendly" handouts; and
- be open to constructive criticism.

The process of deciding who, what, and how to train staff and patrons is fairly straightforward. First you decide who you will teach, then you create an outline of what you want to teach, then you decide the best ways to teach. We assume that you will be forming a team that will train all library staff members as well as all interested patrons about the Web. We therefore discuss only the second and third steps (the "what" and "how"); creating a training outline and deciding the best ways to teach or provide information and assistance to staff and patrons.

START WITH A WEB TRAINING OUTLINE

A manageable way to tackle both learning about and teaching the Web to others is to break down what you need to know/need to teach into an outline. Each section of the outline builds on the previous one and provides you with a structure to build both a learning regimen and/or training program.

Background Knowledge

Learners need basic computer and modem skills in order to access the Internet and use the Web. Teach these skills or provide learners with other ways to get them (perhaps via videos) prior to teaching them about the Web. Skills include:

- basic MacOS or Windows structure;
- using icons and menu bars;
- opening windows/folders;
- creating, saving, and deleting files;
- printing, renaming, and moving files;
- Internet connection options;
- getting an Internet connection and the costs involved;
- purchasing and installing a modem;
- modem software basics; and
- using a modem to connect to the Net/Web.

Basic Internet/Web Concepts

Next, learners need to understand basic Internet and Web concepts. Use lots of analogies to make concepts clear. Avoid technical terms and provide learners with "plain and simple" definitions. Skills include:

- the Internet and how it works;
- the difference between the Internet and the Web;

- servers and clients;
- how Web servers and clients communicate;
- browsers and what they do;
- hypertext and how it works;
- home pages; and
- URLs demystified.

First Steps That Get Results

After understanding basic concepts, learners want pragmatic skills yielding quick, positive results. Teach these skills in a hands-on environment whenever possible, or follow up demonstration sessions, with practice time and trainers present, on your Web workstations. Skills include:

- browser basics; moving around, buttons, and menus;
- working on your library Web site;
- connecting to the Web by selecting a hyperlink;
- typing in a URL;
- printing information you find on the Web;
- saving information from the Web to disk;
- e-mailing information using the Web;
- using bookmarks; and
- using Web indexes or search engines to find information.

Web Indexes—Web sites that categorize Web resources into groups or disciplines, so you can locate them easily. Yahoo and Galaxy are well-known Web indexes.

Web Skills and Strategies

After learning basic skills that get results, learners want to know how to search more effectively and how to find quickly the information they want. Teach these skills in either a hands-on or demonstration environment. Spend time working with individual learners, either during sessions or in follow-up one-on-one sessions. Skills include:

- Boolean searching basics;
- how and where to do general searches;
- understanding search results;
- how to tell where Web information comes from;
- how and where to find information on specific topics;
- how and where to do technical or scholarly searches;
- how and where to find software to download;
- what is virus check software and how to use it;
- where to find graphics, sound bites, and videos; and
- finding and using helper applications.

Using the Web as a Toolbox

Finally, learners want to know how to access Internet tools such as Gopher, Usenet newsgroups, and FTP sites using the Web and your Web browser. Teach these as short, separate sessions with hands-on time available. Skills include:

- URLs for Gophers, FTP, and Usenet;
- Gopher structure and keyword help tools;
- FTP sites and Archie on the Web; and
- accessing and reading Usenet newsgroups through the Web.

Trainer Tips

- Don't count on having a live Net connection.
- Provide your students with important information and/or skills that they can immediately put to use.
- Provide your students with an interesting and interactive learning experience.
- Avoid "techie speak." Use analogies to clarify technical concepts. Supply students with user-friendly glossaries during each session.
- Remember that your goal is to help your students learn, not to make yourself look good.
- Invite students to ask questions or to stop you for a clarification whenever the need arises.
- Encourage knowledgeable students to contribute to the session, and acknowledge them when they do.
- Be willing to change your presentation style or take a short stretch break if students become restless.
- Save the most interactive or fun part of your presentation for right after lunch to keep people aware after their meal.
- Check out your equipment the day before and again just prior to each training session. Be sure there are spare projector bulbs, that your Internet connection works, and that your Web browser is set up for the session.
- Always have backup computer-based demos or transparencies ready in case your Net/Web connection decides to stop working.
- Use transparencies for summarizing points, when time is short, or when response time is slow.
- Regularly review and update your handouts. Create customized handouts whenever possible

---

CONSIDER YOUR LEARNING/TRAINING OPTIONS

Training can be conducted through a variety of methods: Web-based training, trainer-based training, and video-based training.

Web-based training

Prior to the Web, libraries provided little in the way of computer-based real time training or assistance. The Web makes it relatively simple for you to provide online in-context help and training. Web-based training and assistance is based on either hypertext/hypermedia links or browser toolbar options.

Text information links. You can include "For More Information" or "Basic Training" hypertext links on individual Web pages which will provide staff and patrons with a basic skills course, questions and answers about the resource, tips for using it, technical support information, and where and when to get further assistance.

Video/audio clip information links. You can also create audio and/or video versions of text-based skill and resource information and include them as a hypermedia link. Imagine providing patrons with short video or sound clips about how to conduct a Web search, how to download a file, etc. instead of describing these processes in words. You can create individualized video/audio clips for different types of patrons and place them on patron-focused Web pages (e.g., graphically interesting instructions for computer-savvy kids, "executive summaries" for busy adults, basics for computer-novice seniors).

Toolbar information/assistance. The other way you can provide information or assistance for staff and patrons is to build in-context help file options into your browser's toolbar. Building help/training into each computer's toolbar ensures that users will have a consistent place to look for help. No matter where a user is in your Web site they know that the toolbar is where they will find local customized assistance. The key to such assistance, as any software developer will tell you, is to ensure that you have the most useful information at each location. No matter how much information you provide, always include who to contact for more information or assistance.

Trainer-based training

One-to-one training sessions. This is the best type of session for learners who need occasional individualized attention (e.g., busy faculty members, reluctant teachers, kids, seniors). You can customize sessions to individual interests and needs. One-on-one sessions encourage learners to ask questions that they might not normally ask in a group session. (Note: Good for closet technophobes.) You should set up sessions at the learner's convenience and limit them to one hour. Use one-on-one sessions as follow-ups to group sessions. One-on-one sessions take a lot of preparation time. Many learners prefer this type of training because it doesn't require them to take risks in public. Don't use this training method unless it's for a limited time.

Half-day training sessions. Half-day sessions are long enough to go into depth on a single topic or subject, but short enough not to totally overwhelm learners with too much detail. They are ideal for following up on short introductory sessions. Such sessions are long enough for lab-based hands-on teaching. They are also long enough to answer most questions. Many busy staff and patrons find it hard to break free time to attend a half-day session, so you need to schedule them whenever is most convenient (often evenings or weekends).

Full-day training sessions. Full-day sessions provide learners with time to investigate a Web topic or subject in-depth. Many learners enjoy full-day sessions because they can get all their questions answered and have plenty of time to practice what they have learned. Other learners find them totally overwhelming and therefore frustrating. Full-day sessions should provide learners with a mix of lectures and lots of hands-on practice using focused exercises. Full-day sessions should include no more than six hours of instruction and practice time, and at least an hour-and-a-half lunch, so learners can relax. Scheduling staff and patrons to attend a full-day session can be difficult. Many times you have to schedule these sessions on holidays or weekends to ensure attendance.

Subject-focused training sessions. Instead of teaching learners skills only, this type of session teaches them both skills and information resources relevant to a single subject or area of interest (e.g., genealogy, science resources, resources for Latinos). Learners find these sessions appealing because they can easily see the benefits to them. Subject-focused sessions can be one-on-one sessions, "brownbags" or longer sessions, depending on learner interests and time constraints. These sessions take time to plan and research. You must customize handouts for each session. Surveying patrons is one good way to find out the subject-focused sessions you should schedule. Providing "on location" Web subject training sessions for your patron community can be an excellent form of outreach for your library.

"Brownbag" training sessions. "Brownbags" are more fun and less threatening than formal training sessions because they are both informal combined social events and learning sessions. They are great for teaching big concepts or skill overviews and should always include time for questions and answers. Since they are no more than one hour in length and concentrate on only one or two concepts per session, learners who need a little extra time to think about and assimilate information find these sessions exceptionally useful. You can schedule one or a series of "brownbag" sessions at breakfast or lunch so busy staff and adults can attend. You can also schedule "brownbags" for kids, young adults, and parents after school and on weekends. Some learners find "brownbags" too general. There is often not enough time to answer detailed questions. You should schedule longer, more focused training sessions as follow-ups to "brownbags" based on learner feedback.

Bibliographic instruction sessions. Folding Web training into existing library BI sessions has its advantages and disadvantages. The advantage is that staff teaching these courses merely have to add teaching Web skills into their existing course structure. Another advantage is that BI sessions reach a wide audience in most libraries. One disadvantage is that Web training tends to get "lost" amid the myriad of subjects normally covered by BI sessions. Many staff feel that BI courses already cover too much in too little time, and that adding Web skills further reduces the entire course's effectiveness.

Video-based training

Sometimes learners don't feel computer-savvy enough to use Web-based training or assistance options. Sometimes learners don't have the time to come to trainer-based sessions, or are reluctant to attend because they fear they will not understand what is being taught or look stupid if they attend and ask questions in front of others. Video-based training offers learners flexibility as to when and where they learn, the ability to rewind the tape and review what they just learned, and the ability to learn in private. Most of all, people like to learn from videos because there are visually stimulating and present information in an entertaining manner.

Commercial computer videos. Videos about computers provide learners with a conceptual framework that will help them better understand your trainer-based Web sessions and any Web-based assistance your library provides. There are a number of good general computer, Windows, Macintosh, and modem videos on the market. These videos can help learners who first have to figure out how their computer, modem, or operating system works before they can understand your library Internet or Web training sessions. Providing these basic videos cuts down the need for library staff to teach a lot of basic computer, modem, and Windows/Macintosh skills during Internet/Web training sessions.

You can also purchase and use general Internet videos during introductory training sessions to explain basic concepts. The same videos can be used by learners to review what you have covered in an introductory training session (or help someone unable to attend your session catch up).

Local library videos. You can create locally produced, low-budget, videos of trainer-based Web sessions. You can provide these videos to individuals who cannot attend the actual sessions or to local groups that will play them at their meetings. These videos are another kind of outreach that may encourage individuals to attend future library-based Web training sessions or may encourage groups to sponsor trainer-based Web sessions "on location."

You can also create short instructional videos on very specific skills (e.g., how to open a connection using a URL, how to navigate your Web site) which play continuously on TV monitors or on cable TV channels where there are a large concentration of Web workstations, thereby eliminating the need for staff to continuously answer basic questions. You can also use these short instructional videos as hypermedia links on Web pages.

Given how fast the Internet and Web changes you will probably want to create new or revised library-produced videos every three to four months. Advertise them widely and make multiple copies so patrons can get them when they want them.

ENCOURAGING STAFF TO BECOME WEB EXPLORERS

This section provides you with some ideas for encouraging staff to learn the Web and become "Web savvy."

In addition to providing staff with formal Web training sessions, you can encourage your staff to become independent and motivated Web explorers. There are lots of ways you can do this, listed below are our favorites.

- Provide staff with uninterrupted time away from their regular duties to practice the Web skills taught in training sessions.
- Create interesting exercises that encourage staff to have fun and learn at the same time.
- Provide staff with weekly, uninterrupted time to explore the Web and learn about resources relevant to their job or patron interests. Most staff feel they have little time, given their regular duties and schedule, for such exploration. In order to encourage staff to explore the Web, you need to work with each of them to decide what gets put on hold so they can spend time exploring the Web.
- Provide staff with lists of "cool" Web search engines and indexes, links to the best virtual reference desks and subject-based Web sites, as well as fun links to explore. (See Chapter 11 for a bunch of interesting URLs to start sharing with staff.)
- Create Web learning partnerships. These partnerships are especially effective when staff work in the same area (e.g., reference). Let staff choose their own partners when possible and supply them with short, subject-related exercises on an ongoing basis.
- Get staff to ask questions informally and learn something new about the Web when they are ready by creating Web

Web Search Engines—Programs that search the Web using key words which you supply. Webcrawler, Lycos, and Excite are well-known search engines.

mentors. Mentors can provide casual, ongoing training as well as non-threatening answers to questions. Staff who wouldn't consider doing formal training often are willing to be mentors and share their knowledge on a one-on-one basis.

- Set up a regular "I found it on the Web" column in your library newsletter, so that staff and patrons can share interesting Web sites and information they have found.
- Create an "I found it" library Listserv for staff.
- Make staff responsible for writing subject-related "Netographies."
- Make staff responsible for keeping a section of your library Web up-to-date. You will need to structure their work week so that they have time to find new resources, check new links suggested by patrons, review existing links, and do the HTML work to update their assigned section of your Web.
- Make staff responsible for teaching subject-based or skill-based workshops to patrons.

TAKING THE NEXT STEP—TEACHING PATRONS

This section discusses how to organize and start educating patrons about the Web and its resources.

WHO AND WHAT

Your training team and the library staff you assign to do subject- or skill-based workshops should organize workshops for patrons. In addition, you can enlist others to help in both planning and teaching sessions.

- In a college, university, or school library, you can ask computing teachers and technical staff to teach basic computer skills courses as background sessions to your Web sessions. You can also identify interested and knowledgeable students who can assist you during sessions and help you do one-to-one follow-up with learners. You can enlist volunteer staff and students to become Web mentors and provide interested patrons with informal instruction and assistance. Often you can have knowledgeable students co-teach a skill or topic with you (e.g., Homework help on the Web, Research help on the Web).

- In a public library, you can ask for volunteers from local computer clubs or computer stores to teach basic computer skills courses. You can also identify knowledgeable patrons, both young and old, to help you during sessions, and become Web mentors for other patrons. You can also ask knowledgeable patrons to teach sessions on a particular skill (e.g., kids know a lot about Usenet newsgroups and BBSs) or on a topic (e.g., seniors are often willing to teach other seniors about what's on the Net/Web for the over-60 crowd).

TRAINING OPTIONS

You can offer in-library training sessions, either demo-based or hands-on (if you have a computer cluster or wired classroom where you can gather patrons together). See the section on staff training options on page 66 for the types of sessions you can offer. You also have the opportunity to take your Net/Web training sessions "on the road."

- In a K-12 school library, you can offer after-school, weekend, or evening training sessions for parents, interested community members (e.g., pre-school or day-care staffs) or "learn more" sessions for interested students. Often you can partner with public librarians to co-teach or host these sessions at the public library. You can also offer to do short presentations about the Net/Web at PTA meetings, school board meetings, and relevant community group meetings (e.g., scouts, YMCA/YWCA, boys/girls clubs). You can do short presentations for interested parents during parent/teacher conference periods or during school open houses and educate them about censorship and intellectual freedom issues related to the Web.
- In a college or university library, you can offer to teach continuing education or non-credit Net/Web courses through your college or university CE program. You can take subject-specific Web training sessions to academic departments in order to teach faculty and graduate students about the Web resources unique to their research and study. You can volunteer to teach "outreach" Web courses to local businesses and establish an ongoing Net/Web mentor relationship with them.
- In a public library, you can offer customized Net/Web training sessions to a wide variety of community groups (e.g., small business groups, civic clubs, senior groups, professional fraternal organizations, unions, investment clubs). These sessions can take place in your library or at

their location. (Be sure and have a laptop computer with modem, overhead projector, and LCD panel available for staff to use during "road" training sessions.) You can partner with your local schools, community college, or university to jointly hold hands-on training sessions for interested patrons.

WHO TO TRAIN

When you first get your Net/Web workstations installed and functioning you need to decide who you will train first. We suggest that you get input from all staff to help you decide your training strategy and timeline.

- In a K-12 school library environment you will want to discuss which students to train first based on input from teachers, school and district administrators, and school board members. You will want to take a look at their computer skills and decide which students or grades to select (e.g., honors classes, TAG students, college track high school students). You will want to check to see what training (if any) is being done by either your local public library or colleges. You will also need to decide what you will train the first wave of students to do, and if you want them to then become Net/Web mentors for other students or assistant instructors in your training sessions.

- In a college or university environment you will want to discuss which departments or student groups to train first based on input from faculty, administrators, and even the students themselves. A short survey of student library users can provide you with valuable input. Often the first students who are anxious for training are those in the sciences, math, social sciences, and engineering. On some campuses, medical-related majors will be most anxious to learn how to use the Web. You will want to check to see if other campus groups (e.g., computing staff) have been providing Net/Web training to students and work with them to coordinate your training efforts (or better yet to set up a joint series of courses taught by both computing and library staffs). It is likely that many students already use the Web, so you may want focus training sessions on refining Web search skills or subject-related sessions.

- In a public library environment you will want to discuss which skills to teach first, which patron groups to teach (e.g., kids, teens, seniors, businesses), and in which subjects they would be most interested (e.g, reference resources, business resources, schoolwork resources). You will want to involve library staff, administrators, library board members, "friends" members, and interested patrons and library volunteers in deciding on who gets trained first and what subject areas will be highlighted first. You will want to coordinate your efforts with the schools and colleges or universities in your area to decide what and who to teach (or better yet to jointly teach a series of workshops for your community).

TRAINING RESOURCES

Probably the hardest part of getting ready to train patrons is creating instructional handouts, exercises, and "Netographies" of Net/Web resources. This is where staff bog down quickly. You can prevent this by having your learning/training team put together a core packet of user-friendly handouts and exercises (including glossaries of terms, simply explained) to be used by all library staff. The team needs to constantly update and revise this packet of handouts since new tools and resources become available daily and older resources often disappear without warning. We recommend that handouts be reviewed, and URLs checked, at least every thirty days.

Subject-based training sessions require that staff create unique lists of Web resources for each session. One of the ways that you can make this task more manageable is to make various staff members responsible for creating and maintaining subject specific lists of Web resources that can be used both in training sessions and as subject hyperlinks on your library Web. Staff who are responsible for locating subject-based Web resources end up becoming "mini experts." They, in turn, can either teach subject-related Web sessions or work as Web mentors specializing in a particular subject (e.g., math, business, law, literature). (See the list of selected patron/subject resources in Chapter 11.)

TO LEARN MORE...

See Chapter 11 for complete bibliographic citations.

Also refer to Chapter 11 for additional print and Web resources. For more information about learning and teaching the Web we recommend you read and connect to:

- *Learning the Internet* by J. Burke
- *The Internet Training Guide* by D. Kovacs
- *Crossing the Internet Threshold* 2nd ed. by R. Tennant
- *Net Etiquette Guide* by A. Rinaldi ftp://ftp.lib.berkeley.edu/pub/net.training/FAQ/

- *Nettrain (e-mail discussion group)*
  listserv@ubvm.cc.buffalo.edu

For more information about doing research on the Web we recommend you read:

- *The Official Internet World Guide to Electronic Styles* by X. Li
- *Finding Government Information on the Internet* by J. Maxymuk
- *Web Search Strategies* by B. Pfaffenberger
- *Internet World WWW Yellow Pages*
- *New Rider's Official WWW Yellow Pages*

We recommend you connect to the following Web search engines and indexes:

- *Excite* http://www.excite.com/
- *DejaNews* http://www.dejanews.com/forms/dnquery.html
- *Galaxy* http://galaxy.tradewave.com/galaxy.html
- *Lycos* http://lycos.cs.cmu.edu/
- *Savvy Search* http://guaraldi.cs.colorado.edu:2000/form
- *WebCrawler* http://webcrawler.com/
- *WWW Search Engines* http://ugweb.cs.ualberta.ca/%7Ementor02/search/search-all.html
- *Yahoo* http://www.yahoo.com/

We recommend you connect to the following reference resources:

- *Citylink* http://www.neosoft.com/citylink/
- *Free-Nets Home page* http://herald.usask.ca/~scottp/free.html
- *Michigan Clearinghouse Guides* http://www.lib.umich.edu/chhome.html
- *Reference Resources via the WWW* http://vm.cfsan.fda.gov/reference.html
- *Federal Web Locator* http://www.law.vill.edu/fed-agency/fedwebloc.html
- *Legal Information Institute* http://www.law.cornell.edu/lii.table.html
- *Library Resources on the Internet* http://www.library.nwu.edu/resources/library
- *Master Listserv List* http://www.tile.net/tile/listserv/index.html
- *Yahoo: Reference* http://www.yahoo.com/Reference/

We recommend you connect to the following diversity resources:

- *Galaxy: Cultures* http://galaxy.tradewave.com/Community/Culture.html
- *Yahoo: Society and Culture* http://www.yahoo.com/Society_and_Culture/Cultures
- *African American Haven* http://www.acu.edu/~tpearson/haven.html
- *Berit's Kids Sites* http://www.cochran.com/theosite/Ksites.html
- *El Mundo Latino* http://www.bart.nl/~dtheb/
- *Gay, Lesbian, Bisexual Links* http://txdirect.net/~slakjr/glb/
- *Judaica Web World* http://www.nauticom.net/users/rafie/judaica-world.html
- *Native American Resources* http://www.ota.gov/nativea.html
- *Uncle Bob's Kids Page* http://gagme.wwa.com/~boba/kids.html

SAMPLE INTERNET/WEB BROWNBAG SERIES

We provide you with these sample training sessions to illustrate one type of session you can create for patrons. School libraries can use these sessions to train both teachers and students. Public libraries can use them to train both staff and the public. College/ university libraries can use them to encourage faculty, staff, and graduate students to learn about the Web in an informal environment or as separate bibliographic instruction sessions for undergraduate college students.

DESCRIPTION

Six weekly one-hour BYO breakfast, lunch, or dinner seminars introducing the Internet and the Web. Seating is informal and social time is built into each session. Each session combines an informal lecture with a live Internet/Web demonstration. Participants get handouts, primarily summaries of Internet/Web skills, bibliographies, and terms covered in each session. There is time set aside at the end of each session for answering questions.

Session 1
What is the Internet? What Can It Do For You?

Objective

To provide you with an overview of the Internet including basic Internet functions and tools, its history, and where it is going.

Topic Outline

What is the Internet?

Who developed it and why?

How does it work?

What can you find using the Internet?

How do you get an account and what will it cost?

Basic Internet functions and tools.

Session 2
The Internet's Power Tool—The Web

Objective

To provide you with an introduction to the World-Wide Web.

Topic Outline

What is the Web?

How is the Web different from other Internet tools?

Why should you be excited about the Web?

Hypertext—Where it all begins.

HTTP—How information is shared.

Web servers—Where information is stored.

Web browsers—How you see information.

Home pages—Where information is organized.

URLs—How you connect to a specific site.

Session 3
Web Browsers—Your View of the Web

Objective

To provide you with an introduction to Web browsers and provide you with some basic skills for using the Netscape browser.

Topic Outline

Text and graphical browsers—what's the difference?

How to choose a browser for your computer.

Browser basics.

Moving around the Web.

Using a URL to connect with a Web site.

Printing, saving, and e-mailing information.

Bookmarks (optional).

Web shortcuts and timesavers.

Session 4
Finding It on the Web

Objective

To provide you with an introduction to Web indexes and search engines so you can easily locate and access information.

Topic Outline

What are Web indexes and where can you find them?

What are Web search engines, where can you find them, and how do they work?

What is Boolean searching and how can it help you find information?

Which is the best index or search engine for different types of searches?

Session 5
Using the Web to Search Gophers

Objective

To provide you with the basics of another Internet tool named Gopher. To acquaint you with Gopher-based tools such as Jughead, Veronica, and Hytelnet.

Topic Outline

What is a Gopher and why is it still an important tool?

How do you access Gopher through the Web?

How is Gopher different than the Web?

Moving around Gopherspace.

What are Veronica and Jughead?

What are some good Gophers to search?

Session 6
Using the Web to Get Software, Graphics, etc. and Read Usenet newsgroups

Objective

To provide you with ways to get software, graphics, audio, and video from the Net. To acquaint you with reading Usenet newsgroups using the Netscape browser.

Topic Outline

How can you find software, graphics, etc.?

What tools can help you?

Isn't retrieving software/graphics hard to do?

What about computer viruses?

What is Usenet?

How can you read Usenet newsgroups using Netscape?

5 TAKE TIME TO THINK IT THROUGH—PLANNING YOUR WEB SITE

WHO AND WHAT

This section provides a framework for making decisions about the planning needed before work can begin on your web site.

It's important that you take time to think through and plan out each step in the process of creating your library Web site. There are lots of decisions to make, lots of technical details to consider, lots of people who you need to talk to and get input from, and lots of talent on your staff and in your community that you need to draw upon as you proceed. Your whole staff should be involved along the way. One of the reasons you will want to spend time planning is to make sure that all library staff and relevant community members who need to be involved are indeed involved, and giving you feedback, support, and most importantly their resources and expertise to help you build a great Web site.

One way to begin the planning process is to hold brainstorming sessions with staff and interested patrons. To help you structure your planning, you can also hold focused discussions with teachers, faculty, and community leaders. You should spend at least a couple of weeks structuring your planning, discussing important issues to be resolved, assigning staff to various tasks and committees, and getting feedback. It is important that you constantly inform staff of changes to the planning process. It is even more important, though, that you work with all staff to put as many routine tasks as possible on temporary "hold" so that planning will not be viewed as "one more thing we have to do."

Planning a Web site is different than planning any other type of library service because:

- your Web will constantly be revised and enhanced;
- your "patrons" can reside anywhere on the globe; and,
- it requires that library staff learn new information search skills and become familiar with "virtual" reference collections and other electronic resources.

Taking a positive approach to the decisions and challenges that the Web presents, through positive planning and team building, can make the process of integrating the Web into your library an enriching, rather than unpleasant, experience for both staff and patrons.

PLANNING STEPS

This section provides you with suggested planning steps and issues that you should discuss/decide along the way.

BEFORE YOU START

Your Web site will represent your library to your patrons, your community and the world. As such, you should create a Web site that reflects positively on libraries in general and on your staff's professionalism.

- In a K-12 school library, your Web will represent your library, your school, your district, and your community.
- In a college or university library, your Web will represent your library, your particular department or school, your institution, and your community.
- In a public library, your Web will represent your library, your community, its citizens, community groups, and businesses.

Next, remember that you should build your Web site to serve the informational needs of your patrons. As such, you should plan to build in mechanisms for getting feedback from patrons, whether they are located around the block or around the globe, so that you make your Web site "their" Web site.

Finally, remember that planning a Web site is a continual process in which you are constantly updating your Web's content to serve your patron's ever-changing needs. As such, you should both encourage and support staff to become enthusiastic Web explorers, teachers, Web authors, and guides for patrons.

IDENTIFY YOUR PATRONS

Deciding who your patrons are (so you can later decide how you will serve them) must be the first step in the planning process. In a Net/Web environment your traditional definition of "patron" must be rethought, as your patrons can now be part of your local community or part of the global community.

This issue should be discussed widely by all library staff. It should be also discussed with your library board, faculty advisory committee, or trustees, depending on your type of library. We suggest you appoint a small working group consisting of one library administrator, one institution representative, one board/ trustee member, and one community representative to come up with a statement of who your primary library patrons are in a virtual environment. It should only take the group a week or two to come up with a draft which then should be discussed by all staff and your library board. The group needs to recommend who your primary patrons are. It also needs to recommend who your library's secondary patrons are.

- In a K-12 school library, your primary patrons will be students who attend your school as well as students in your local school district. However, you will want to discuss if students who attend private schools in your area, student parents, and school staff will be considered primary or secondary patrons.
- In a college or university library, your primary patrons will be tuition-paying students who attend classes and faculty. However, you will want to discuss if staff at your institution, continuing education and non-credit students, and related community program participants and staff will be considered primary or secondary patrons.
- In a public library, your primary patrons will be individuals in your local community or region. However, you will want to discuss if businesses, colleges, and schools in your local area, as well as your state, will be considered primary or secondary patrons.

Next, you need to identify different primary patron groups so you can create Web pages that respond directly to their needs and interests.

- In a K-12 school library, you can group patrons by age, grade level, or ability (e.g., primary, elementary, middle, high school, special education). If you also include staff as primary patrons, you can group them by grade level or subject taught (e.g., math teachers, librarians, school guidance counsellors).
- In a college or university library, you can group patrons, faculty, and staff by college or school they attend (e.g., college of engineering, school of nursing) or by major (e.g., physical therapy, psychology). You can also group patrons into undergraduate, graduate, and faculty categories, so you can be sensitive to each group's unique research needs.

- In a public library, you can group patrons by age, educational level, interests, and their knowledge of computer technology.

DECIDE WHO WILL BE INVOLVED

Once you decide who your primary patrons are, you need to take a step back and look at the planning process in relationship to them. You need to set up a general planning group to oversee the creation of your library Web. Depending on who your primary patrons are, you will want to include representatives from various patron groups in your general planning group. You should also decide if you want to hire an outside consultant to help with overall planning or specific aspects such as telecommunications or graphic design.

- In a K-12 school library, you will want your planning group to include at least one: teacher, librarian, administrator, district representative, parent group representative, and student representative.
- In a college or university library, you will want your planning group to include at least one: faculty member, librarian, administrator, computing staff member, and student representative.
- In a public library, you will want your planning group to include at least one: librarian, administrator, community official, and one community member/patron.

The first decision your planning group needs to make is whether your Web site will focus solely on your library or whether it will have a wider focus (e.g., school/district site, community site). If your Web site will have a wider focus, you need to get representatives from appropriate groups involved from the very start. The planning group for a wider focus Web must agree on the amount of time and resources each group will contribute to the effort. They must identify who will be responsible for what and must set up formal agreements among all Web site partners.

- In a K-12 school library, you will want to decide on the relationship between your library Web site and school/district, local college, and public library Web site.
- In a college or university library, you will want to decide on the relationship between your library Web site and other campus Web site, as well the relationship between you and other college, library, and library-focused Web sites.

- In a public library, you will want to decide on the relationship between your library Web site and other community, library, business, and government Web sites.

UNDERSTAND YOUR WEB CONNECTION/PATRON CONNECTIONS

After deciding who your patrons are and who will be involved in planning your Web site, you need to review your Internet connection to make sure it supports the type of Web access you want to provide patrons. You also need to take a look at your library computers to see if they are capable of running the Web client software you select. Finally you need to understand how patrons from your school, campus, or community will be accessing your Web site.

The group of people who agree to tackle this job should be familiar with telecommunications, computers, and Web client software (or be willing to learn about them). They should hire a consultant or find community experts to help if necessary. They should be willing to work with computer-savvy patrons to get input on how patrons will be connecting to your library Web site.

The group needs to understand the nature of your library's Net connection and how it limits or enhances patron access to your Web. They also need to understand the computer equipment you have in your library and how it will limit/enhance the patron's use of the Web. The group should recommend purchasing new computing equipment, creating a library LAN, or upgrading your Internet connection as needed. They also should recommend whether your library will set up its own Web server or find another computer to house it. Finally they should recommend whether your library will provide patrons with remote dialup access and library-based e-mail accounts.

WRITE A VISION STATEMENT FOR YOUR WEB SITE

Creating a vision statement for your Web site will help you focus broadly on the needs of patrons and how your library will meet them, as well as help you create specific objectives and outcomes for each primary patron group. Your Web vision statement must be complimentary to your regular library vision statement. You must regularly review and revise it as the Net/Web changes.

Your Web vision statement should be based on who your primary patrons are, the focus of your Web site and how your patrons access it, your Web site connection and library hardware and software, and finally how you plan to fulfill patrons' informational needs through your Web site.

Since your Web vision needs to be regularly revised, the group you assign to write your vision statement should consider writing more than one statement. The first vision statement (what your first Web site will look like and provide for patrons) will have a limited life span. The second vision statement (how you envision enhancing your Web site once staff and patrons are trained and using it on a regular basis) should be reviewed and updated on an ongoing basis. A third vision statement (a long-term vision of what you would like to include eventually as staff expertise increases and Web enhancements become a reality) will keep your staff thinking creatively about your Web site.

The group can also write different vision statements for the various primary patron groups (e.g., kids, adults, seniors, businesses, campus groups, faculty, teachers) in order to start focussing on outcomes for each group.

GATHER TOGETHER RELEVANT INFORMATION AND DOCUMENTS

Taking the time to gather together information and documents will help you decide what to include/not include on your library Web site. It will also help you begin to organize individual Web pages. The group you assign to this task must gather together library policies, procedures, newsletters, point-of-use guides, bibliographies, and forms. If your library is partnering with community or campus groups to create a wider focused Web site, the group also needs to gather together related materials from community, campus, and institutional partners.

- K-12 school libraries need to gather school policies, district guidelines, lists of staff, information on school clubs and sports teams, school lunch menus, calendars of activities, parent-related information, and URLs to other school and district Web sites.
- College or university libraries need to gather university policies, procedures, catalogs, class schedules, staff listings, information on financial aid, scholarships, and student employment, student housing information, social clubs, sports schedules, campus maps, and URLs to campus and other library/college Web sites.
- Public libraries need to gather local government information, business information, community organization information, other local library information, local maps, school information, information related to community happenings, parks, local and regional attractions, festivals, museums, concerts, social groups, and URLs to state

and local business, community, university, school, and other public library Web sites.

Once it has relevant documents and information in hand, the group needs to start deciding which information is most important. It also needs to begin arranging and editing the information. It's tempting just to take written procedures, policies, and library handouts, scan them and put them up on library Web pages. However, people don't read Web pages like they read paper documents. Hypertext linking makes it possible for patrons to move easily from one bit of text to another. The group should read through all existing documentation, select the most important text, edit it, and divide it into text and graphic bits that can be turned into hypertext links and arranged meaningfully on Web pages.

WRITE SPECIFIC OBJECTIVES AND OUTCOMES FOR YOUR WEB SITE

At the same time as some staff are gathering information and documents together, the rest of the staff should be involved in writing specific Web objectives and outcomes for patrons. Getting staff to think about and write detailed objectives and outcomes for your Web site will help staff better understand their role in helping patrons adjust to this totally new information environment. Staff should write objectives for primary patrons and specific patron groups (e.g., kids, seniors, staff). They should also write objectives for non-primary patrons. All objectives should be outcome-based, have a time frame, and assign responsibility to a group of staff or individual staff members. Your staff should review and revise Web objectives every six months, in order to celebrate their accomplishments and add new objectives to the list.

Sample Objectives and Outcomes for a Library Web Site

Objective: Create a homework help Web page so K-12 students (and parents) can get answers to reference questions and find information for school projects while visiting the library anytime day or night, from home.

1. Locate Web and Gopher resources related to homework; decide on the best for different grade levels and interests.
2. Locate other good homework help Web pages to help decide on the content and arrangement of our page.
3. Create an outline of a homework help page with links to Internet resources.
4. Include links to in-house documents explaining the library's homework help tutor program.
5. Compose a Web-based form so parents and students can sign up for the local program.
6. Offer informational programs on how to use the homework help page to students, parents, local teachers, and interested community groups.
7. Ask the local newspaper to write a story on it, when it is finished.

Timeline: January - March
Responsibility: Childrens' and YA librarians

GET FEEDBACK FROM STAFF ON WHAT HAS BEEN DECIDED SO FAR

Once staff finish writing specific Web objectives (a huge and tiring task) they should take a breather, look at what they have accomplished, discuss it all, change what they feel doesn't or won't work, and add things that were inadvertantly missed. Staff should have a chance to spend time thinking about and reacting individually, have a chance to discuss planning steps and decisions in both small and large group settings, and have a chance to volunteer to be responsible for accomplishing individual objectives.

WRITE POLICIES AND PROCEDURES RELATED TO YOUR WEB SITE

Next, you should start to create policies related to the Web. Following are some of the policies, procedures, and statements you should consider writing.

- A general philosophical statement on why you provide patrons with Net/Web access.
- A statement that Net/Web access is a privilege, not a right.
- A series of statements that make it clear that your library is not responsible for 1) the content of the Net or Web; 2) the accuracy of information found on the Net or Web; 3) non-library server or network outages.
- A policy related to patron access to Net-based resources. For school and public libraries, this policy should include a statement on a parent's responsibility for deciding on his or her child's access to certain information or images. It should include procedures for getting parental permission should library policy require this.
- A policy related to connectivity and Web access. This policy should define Net/Web privileges according to patron groups. It should define how patrons will be able to access your Web site either from the library or through dialup access from home or office. It should also define the level of support that your library will provide for patrons connecting to your Web site internally and remotely.
- A policy on the types of assistance and training your staff will provide to patrons. This policy should outline the various computer ethics, netiquette, and skill courses you will be offering. It should define to whom these courses will/will not be offered. It should address the types of assistance your library will not offer (e.g., configuring patron computer software, debugging patrons' programs, recommending specific Internet access providers).

- A policy on system security. This policy should cover patron log-ins and passwords and the importance of not sharing them with others. It should also cover cracking library computers and software, and breaching the security of other systems using library computers.
- A policy related to Web use. This policy should describe when and how long patrons may use library computers, delineate any costs involved for printing or disks, and describe specifically the Internet tools your library will provide for patrons and staff. It should include statements related to each tool and procedures that need to be followed (e.g., downloading files to library computers, virus checking, and use of patron supplied diskettes). It should also include statements related to for-profit and non-educational use of your library computers.
- A policy related to Net/Web behavior. This policy should let staff and patrons know how you expect them to behave in your library while using the Web and how you expect them to treat others on the Net. It should include specific statements on posting obscene/sexist or harassing messages via e-mail, Listservs, or Usenet newsgroups. It should address accessing "adult" Web site in public areas, and include rules of "netiquette" for all patrons.
- A policy related to remedies and recourses. This policy should let staff and patrons know what will happen if they don't adhere to your Net/Web policies. Steps to remedy the situation and recourse to sanctions should both be specific and incremental based on the seriousness of the misbehavior and how often it occurs. It should coincide closely with your general policy related to patron misbehavior.
- A policy related to using library Net/Web computers for illegal activities. This policy should address violating copyright, downloading illegal software, and using library computers to run illegal businesses and scams. It also should address plagiarism.
- A policy related to staff use of Net/Web computers during work hours and from home. It should provide staff members with formal time during work hours for exploring the Web. It should also clarify for staff if they can use staff Web accounts for non-library business.

TO LEARN MORE ABOUT POLICIES AND PROCEDURES...

See Chapter 11 for complete bibliographic citations.

Also refer to Chapter 11 for additional URLs. We recommend you connect to the following sites to locate individual library policies

- *ERIC Policies Archive* gopher://ericir.syr.edu:70/11/ Guides/Agreements
- *Rice University Policies Archive* gopher:// riceinfo.rice.edu:1170/00/More/Acceptable
- *The Freedom Pages* http://www.bluehighways.com/ freedom/

DECIDE THE ORGANIZATION AND CONTENT OF YOUR WEB SITE

Having defined your primary patrons and patron groups, having gathered information and documentation together, and having created specific written objectives and policies, your staff will be able to quickly decide how your Web will be organized. The group of people you assign to this task should take all input and turn it into a conceptual map of your Web site. They need to decide what is most important, what information gets included and what does not, and how it all gets organized. They need to decide on the overall organizational structure (or combination of structures) for your Web and actually draw it on paper for your Web design team.

Once you have your basic Web organization mapped out, it is important to share it broadly with staff and Web partners and get feedback on what works and what doesn't. Taking the time, if necessary, to "go back to the drawing board" now will save you lots of time once you get to the design and authoring stages. This is also a good time to select a staff member, or someone local to be your "Webmaster" (if you are setting up your own Web server).

DESIGN YOUR WEB PAGES AND OVERALL LOOK

Taking time to design your Web site is important for two reasons. The first is that your Web site represents your library and/ or institution and as such should well represent your professionalism and skills in organizing information. The second is that a well designed Web site makes it simple for patrons to locate and get to information.

Designing a Web is a lot like designing a brochure, newsletter, or other publication. It involves deciding on graphics and graphic placement, text placement and arrangement, white space, etc. The group of people involved in this task should have a variety of talents, from text editing, to graphics creation, to HTML knowledge. Hiring a graphic/Web designer to help you at this stage might be a good idea.

Your design team's job is to create an overall plan for your Web site and how individual pages fit together. They need to decide on the basic look of pages for different patron groups, and the three most important pieces of information on each Web page. They need to create page templates showing where graphics, text, navigation buttons, etc. will be placed. They also need to create a "storyboard" version of your Web that they will pass onto your HTML authors. After your design team has finished its initial design they should present it to staff and Web partners, get lots of feedback, and make changes to the design as appropriate.

WRITE YOUR WEB PAGES AND ADD HYPERTEXT LINKS

Writing HTML documents for individual Web pages based on your organizational map, design team templates, and "storyboard" documents is often a quick and simple process. Often though, what designers imagined creating cannot be always be done, given the limitations of HTML. It is important, then, that designers and HTML authors work together to create a Web site as close as possible to the original design concept.

Your HTML authoring team needs to decide on a common HTML style that all authors will follow and set up a common directory for all HTML and graphics files to be saved into. They need to create HTML documents that will be friendly to both text-based and graphical Web browsers, and contain hypertext links that are organized well and worded succinctly.

TEST YOUR WEB SITE AND GET LOTS OF FEEDBACK

Before you "go public" with your Web site it is important to test it thoroughly. Staff, patrons, and Web partners, should:

- make sure that important information is prominent;
- make sure that information is organized so that patrons can easily find it;
- make sure than hypertext links work the way they should;
- check for spelling and grammar errors;
- check for graphic and textual consistency between pages;
- monitor load times for pages; and
- check how your Web looks using different browsers.

Let testers tell you the three most important pieces of information on each page and compare their answers to your "storyboard" design. Ask them what they like most/least about your Web, and what information they had a hard time finding. Give testers a couple of weeks to explore your Web site so they can give you meaningful feedback. If necessary, rearrange, redesign, and reorganize.

SET UP PROCEDURES FOR KEEPING YOUR WEB SITE UP-TO-DATE

Thousands of new Net/Web resources are being made available daily. In order to keep your Web site up-to-date and "fresh" for patrons you need to make staff responsible for regularly reviewing and adding new information and links to your Web site. You can create e-mail links and Web-based forms to help staff and patrons give you suggestions for adding new resources and links. You also need to set up an ongoing staff/patron group responsible for reviewing suggestions. Finally, you should assign at least one person the responsibility for maintaining the site (and give them time each week specifically to carry out this essential task).

TRAIN STAFF ON HOW TO USE AND UPDATE YOUR WEB SITE

Training staff on how to use the Web site can be easy and fun. Structure both classes and follow-up hands-on time for staff to practice what they have learned. Teach concepts and then skills that build on one another and provide staff with interesting exercises. Provide staff with time to cruise the Web on library time (putting job assignments on temporary hold) so that staff can feel comfortable using Web tools and "virtual" information resources. Once staff can use the Web, teach them HTML (or how to use HTML editor programs) so they can keep the Web site up-to-date.

PUBLICIZE YOUR WEB SITE, GET IT INDEXED

Once your Web site "goes public" you will want to get creative about letting patrons, community members, and "the world" know about your library Web site. Set up open houses, get the local press to write an article on your Web site, and offer to do presentations and demonstrations of your Web site to local and regional groups.

- In a K-12 school library, hold a ribbon cutting ceremony and party for students and teachers. Set up an open house for parents during a parent/teacher conference period, give presentations at your PTA, at your local public library, and at preschools and kids clubs in your area. Encourage colleges and other local libraries to add your Web site as a link on their home page.
- In a college or university library, have an open house/dedication ceremony for your Web site, invite administrators

to speak, and extend an invitation to all faculty and graduate students. Offer "get to know it" brownbag sessions for faculty at which you highlight your Web site's resources for research and instruction. Encourage department and college-based Web sites to include a link back to your Web site.

- In a public library, hold an open house for the public. If your Web is also community-focused, have your partners publicize your Web site through their regular communication channels. Give presentations on your Web site to local civic and social groups, as well as invite local colleges and universities to create a link to your Web from their home page.

After you decide how you will let local patrons, citizens, and groups know about your Web site, you should let Net citizens know that you are online. There are lots of ways to get the word out on the Net. Post announcements to Usenet newsgroups set up for that purpose, use Web announcement services, and add your Web site's URL to large Web indexes and library-related indexes.

EDUCATE PATRONS ABOUT YOUR WEB SITE

You can set up both formal and informal in-library training sessions. For patrons unable to attend, you can video tape sessions and circulate them widely. You can also set up "on the road" training sessions for all types of patrons. These sessions can be skill- or subject-based. You can also build Web-based training/assistance right into your Web site.

SET UP AN ONGOING PLANNING PROCESS FOR YOUR WEB SITE

The last step is planning for the future. Review your vision statement and objectives often. Use link check software to help your keep links current. Add something new to your Web site each week so that people will want to visit it often. Send out press releases to the local press (community, campus, or school) when you make a major change to your Web site. Encourage patrons to help you enhance your Web site by making it easy for them to suggest new resources and services while online.

Finally, keep abreast of Web developments that may affect how you present information to patrons in the future. Form a committee and assign members to learn about trends and future enhancements, so that when they become reality, you already know about, have planned for, and are ready to add them to your Web site.

6 LOOKS ARE IMPORTANT— DESIGNING YOUR WEB SITE

THE DESIGN PROCESS

This section outlines some of the steps for designing your library's Web site.

In the last chapter you decided the purpose for your Web site, clarified who your audience was, and wrote some specific objectives for your Web. The next step is designing your Web in order that its purpose is instantly apparent, it is appealing to your patrons, and is visually organized so that your objectives come across loud and clear.

WHO AND WHAT

Designing your Web site takes a good eye, knowledge of basic graphic design principles, an understanding of your Web's purpose, audience, and objectives, some knowledge of HTML, and a willingness to try out ideas, trash them, and start all over again. The group of people you assign to come up with draft designs of your Web must be willing to support each other creatively, critique each other fairly, and be able to incorporate existing graphic elements (e.g., your logo or colors) into your Web site. They must be willing to continually ask themselves how their design supports the content and focus of each page. They must be willing to actively listen to feedback on their draft designs from staff and patrons, and if necessary "go back to the drawing board" if the design doesn't work. Finally they must be able to communicate what they want to your HTML authors.

We recommend you consider the following people when forming such a group:

- someone who designs your library's posters and flyers (or a graphic designer);
- one of your HTML authors;
- someone who is a good writer and text editor;
- someone who is a natural organizer; and
- a patron who is visually sophisticated and vocal about patron needs.

We recommend you keep the group small in order to foster creativity and create a safe environment for critiquing ideas.

THE DECISION PROCESS

The process of designing your Web site should take much more time that authoring the pages using HTML. When you author pages using HTML you create documents, which when loaded to a Web server, make it possible for staff, patrons, and the world to see the information you provide. When you design your Web site you organize that information in a logical and visually appealing way that makes it come to life for patrons. Organizing information is what libraries are all about, so be sure and take the time to do a good job for you and your patrons.

Depending on the complexity of your Web site, you can spend anywhere from two–four weeks on design, feedback, and redesign. Depending on whether you have good graphics already, or need some new ones, you can spend anywhere from zero to hundreds of dollars on graphics and/or hiring a designer to create the graphics for you. Following are some steps your design group needs to take:

Gather and review information

Get together existing library graphics and documents (logos, samples of brochures, point-of-use guides). If part of a larger organization (e.g., school, school district, college) or planning a community Web site, gather together existing publications, logos, and samples of their Web pages. Search the Web for, and print out, Web sites you like (both library and non-library).

Decide what's important

Use your Web's purpose and objectives to decide what are the three most important pieces of information on each page you will be designing. Decide how important graphics are to each page. Decide how your Web pages will relate to each other and begin to "storyboard" your Web structure.

Take into account your limitations

Make decisions about the wording and arrangement of text based on patron interests, and how much time they have to look at your Web site. Make decisions about the size and number of graphics you will use on each page based on the type of Internet connection your library has, the types of connections dial-in patrons have, how relevant the graphics are, and how important they are to the structure of the page. Finally make decisions about the design of your Web site based on how it looks when viewed through different browsers, each running customized viewer "preferences."

Develop an overall look

Decide on what elements are common to each page (e.g., logos, lines, title, arrangement of text, menu bars, navigation buttons, author information). Create templates for each page, taking into account how your Web is structured (e.g., home page, major sub-pages and their related sub-pages). Create templates showing where common design elements are to be placed, outline page structure, and suggest to HTML authors header sizes and list types.

Take a stab at designing

Start designing each page in relation to every other page. (This can be done by individual group members trying their hand at it and then having the group discuss each member's ideas, or by the group collectively creating a first draft Web design. Either way, group members need to be open to all ideas and to critique each other supportively.) Design pages so that you can see each page's relationship to other pages and the structure of the whole Web. Looking at the whole Web, see if it works in terms of graphic design and if the three most important pieces of information on each page pop out at you.

Get feedback

Get staff to look at your design and arrangement of information. Ask them what are the first three things they see when they look at each page (it should be the most important piece of information.) Ask them if any important information is hard to find. Ask them what the most interesting thing on each page is. Ask them what they find least interesting/most distracting. Ask them for their opinions on color, size, placement, and relevance of pictures and other graphic elements (e.g., buttons, lines).

Go back to the drawing board

Use feedback from staff to make your draft Web even better, or use the feedback to start redesigning your Web from scratch. Either way, think of any changes you make as positively affecting access to your library and the Net, rather than seeing them as a failure to get your Web pages perfect on the first try. Consider your Web site as a dynamic entity, always changing and improving.

Work with HTML authors

When you have revised versions of your Web pages ready to be converted into HTML documents, work with your HTML authoring group so that they understand the rationale and design principles behind your page structures and how the whole Web site is organized. Pass around the final "storyboard" version of your Web site to your authoring group. It will provide them with a visual representation of what you want them to create and help them divide up the various authoring tasks.

Ways to Design Your Web

If you know how you want it organized....
- Create templates for your home page and main pages.
- Design your home page and include links to all main pages.
- Then write the pages that link to your home page.
- After that, write sub-pages that link to the main pages, etc.
- Add navigation links from page to page.

If you're not sure where to start....
- Create a template for an individual page.
- Write individual pages.
- Organize individual pages.
- Create templates and a design for your home page and main pages.
- Add navigation links from page to page.

TO LEARN MORE...

See Chapter 11 for complete bibliographic citations.

Also refer to Chapter 11 for more print and Web resources. For more information on designing a Web site we recommend you read and connect to:

- *Designing and Writing Online Documentation* by W. Horton
- *The Web Page Design Cookbook* by W. Horton
- *World Wide Web Design Guide* by S. Wilson
- *Web Style Manual* by P. Lynch http://info.med.yale.edu/caim/StyleManual_Top.HTML

BASIC DESIGN PRINCIPLES

This section outlines some basic design principles that you need to keep in mind when designing a Web site.

Graphic design is defined as the application of type, color, and images to a document—artistically and skillfully—to create a clear and effective whole.

DESIGN	TEXT
<ul><li>Graphic design is a means of enhancing communication, not just decoration.</li><li>Design doesn't call attention to itself; it leaves you aware only of the communication, not the mechanism.</li><li>Design leads your eye through a document and highlights the most important information.</li><li>Each design element should be relevant to your page's purpose.</li><li>Each design element should help people understand the message you want to convey.</li><li>Clarity, organization, and simplicity are as important to page design as they are to writing.</li><li>Design elements create visual consistency between documents.</li><li>Good design creates interesting documents that invite people to interact with them.</li></ul>	<ul><li>Choose words appropriate for readers.</li><li>Keep sentences simple and to the point.</li><li>Keep sentences thirty–forty characters long for best reading comprehension.</li><li>Use the active voice.</li><li>Seven times more people read headlines than blocks of text.</li><li>Outlines interest people more than paragraphs of text.</li><li>Subheads draw your interest down a page; they act as a transition between headlines and body text and let you find information quickly.</li><li>Numbers stand out more than letters. If a number is important, use the numeral.</li><li>Text set in all capital letters is difficult to read. Use bold or italics to set off a word or phrase.</li><li>Use centered text sparingly and only for short phrases or headlines.</li></ul>
READING PATTERNS	**TONE AND CONTRAST**
<ul><li>You start reading at the top left of a page, work your way across and down, moving left to right, until you get to the bottom right corner.</li><li>Any design that works in opposition to the way you read interrupts your reading flow. You often stop reading at this point.</li><li>Each page has a focal point that is 1/3 of the way down the page and slightly to the right of center. This focal point is the best place to locate the most important information.</li><li>You often quit reading a page about two-thirds of the way down a page and go on to the next page, so put your least important information towards the bottom of a page.</li></ul>	<ul><li>Contrast (dark and light) creates visual excitement and encourages you to read/look further.</li><li>Dark areas draw your eye like a magnet.</li><li>Use tone and contrast sparingly for the greatest impact.</li></ul>

BORDERS AND LINES

- Text within a border gets read before text outside a border.
- Use only one border/line style per page.
- Use lines to separate text with one purpose from text with another purpose.
- Use borders and lines very sparingly and consistently throughout your series of documents.

BACKGROUNDS

- Medium to dark backgrounds obscure dark text and make reading difficult.
- Avoid dark backgrounds with light text. Research shows that there is a 70 percent good comprehension rate for black or dark text on a light background and 0 percent good comprehension for light text on a black or dark background.
- Light colored (10-20 percent tint) backgrounds make documents more attractive and don't negatively impact reading comprehension. Choose non-standard colors whenever possible.

PICTURES

- Pictures must be completely relevant to the text around them.
- When in doubt about the quality of a picture, don't use it.
- Pictures invite you to look at a page, but at the same time they are barriers to reading. Each time you stop reading to look at a picture you have to find where you left off reading and many times you decide not to continue reading.
- Use pictures sparingly and consistently throughout your series of documents.
- Color pictures get more attention than black and white pictures.
- Large pictures get more attention than small ones.
- A sequence of pictures that tells a story gets more attention than single pictures scattered throughout.
- People and action pictures get more attention than "thing" pictures.
- Pictures of children and close-ups of faces get the most attention.

Patron-Centered Design Tips

- Get input from patrons before you start, after you have a first draft of your design, and before you "go public" with your Web.
- Design your Web site so new and experienced users can easily see how information is arranged.
- Make it simple for patrons to move around your Web site. Use navigation buttons and links. Place them in consistent places on each page.
- Start each Web page with a short, descriptive title. Include a short description of what the page contains immediately after the title.
- Create customized pages for different patron groups (e.g., kids, seniors, businesses). Be sensitive to the words and content you select.
- Design Web pages that load quickly so patrons don't have to wait, or provide them with a link to a text-based Web page.
- Be sensitive to patrons with older equipment and slow modems. Include customized descriptions of graphics for patrons with text-based browsers.
- Supply patrons with plenty of help files. Place them in a consistent place on each page so patrons can easily find them.
- Get patrons involved in updating your Web design. Consider forming a patron feedback group to give you ongoing advice on how well your pages are designed.

HOW DESIGNING A WEB SITE IS DIFFERENT THAN DESIGNING A PAPER DOCUMENT

This section explains how designing a Web Site is different than designing a paper document.

YOU CAN'T CONTROL A LOT OF THE GRAPHIC DESIGN ELEMENTS.

With a desktop publishing or word-processing program, you are in complete control of the font and size of text, the amount of white space, and placement of text and graphics. This is not the case with the Web.

Each page you design can have a different look depending on the browser you use to view it and the browser options you choose. HTML makes it difficult to put a set amount of white space into a document. Each browser seems to interpret white space included around the header and paragraph tags slightly differently. Whether someone sees/or does not see your graphics is totally up to them. They can turn on and off graphics at will.

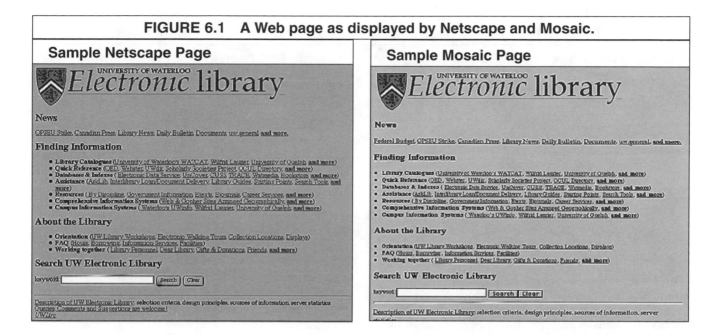

FIGURE 6.1 A Web page as displayed by Netscape and Mosaic.

Designing a Web in this kind of environment can be frustrating for staff used to having total control of how things look (especially those used to doing desktop publishing). Designing a Web Site is mostly a case of doing the best you can to make sure text elements are well-worded and logically arranged and that graphic elements enhance, rather than distract from, text content.

Testing to see how your design fares using different browsers is the only way to see if your design does or does not work. The best design is one that works well for all types of browsers and not just one browser, even if that means that it isn't as "pure" a design as you would like.

YOU WON'T ALWAYS SEE THE WHOLE WEB PAGE ON YOUR COMPUTER SCREEN.

When you design a paper document you assume that patrons will see the whole page at once. Web page design is different because unless each document is very brief, it is rarely all seen at once. Not seeing your whole document can change the effect of your design and basic page organization.

How much of a page you see depends on the size of your computer screen, your browser's navigation displays (e.g., URL window, navigation buttons), and the size of font you choose your browser to display. (Ten point text, for example, will display more of your page on a computer screen than will eighteen point text.) Creating short pages, with simple, obvious structure will help to offset this problem as much as possible.

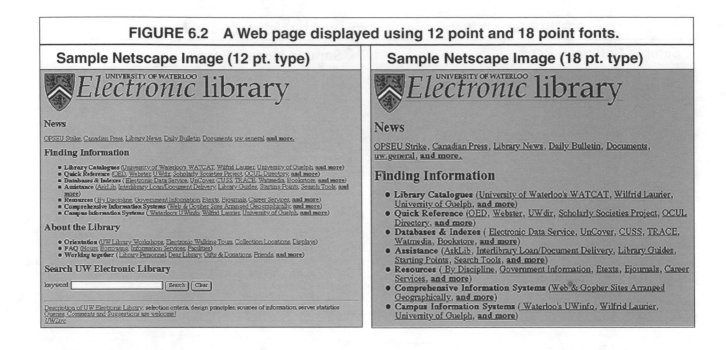

FIGURE 6.2 A Web page displayed using 12 point and 18 point fonts.

YOU HAVE TO DESIGN FOR DIFFERENT CONNECTION SPEEDS.

When you design a paper document you don't have to concern yourself with how long it will take people to view it. With the Web you need to design Web pages for all types of connections, both slow and fast, and take this into consideration in your Web page design. For instance, you should consider creating two versions of your Web, a text-based version for people with slow connections, and a graphic version for people who have fast connections and can use graphical browsers. Even on graphic versions of your Web, you should include text link alternatives to slow loading graphic links. You should also consider designing a single Web version that loads quickly using a wide range of browsers at differing telecommunication speeds. This may mean simplifying your Web design and stifling the impulse to include lots of graphic embellishments just because you can do them or just because "everyone has them."

FIGURE 6.3   A Web Page Displaying Both Graphic and Text Links

| Help/Search | Your Comments | About the Libraries | Collections & Resources | Library Catalogs |
| Map of the Libraries | UC Berkeley | Digital Library SunSITE |

YOU SHOULD DESIGN FOR BOTH GRAPHICAL AND TEXT ENVIRONMENTS.

You have to assume that not everyone has a computer capable of running a graphical Web browser. This is also essential since you will want to serve all users—including those with disabilities—for both maximum service and in order to comply with ADA regulations. Most screen readers for visually-impaired people only work with character-based (nongraphical) text. Therefore, you should design your Web to look good in a text environment as well as a graphic one. Testing your Web is the only way to find out what works/doesn't work in both environments. You may find that you have to make some tradeoffs in the graphical environment in order for your Web to look good in a text environment and vice versa.

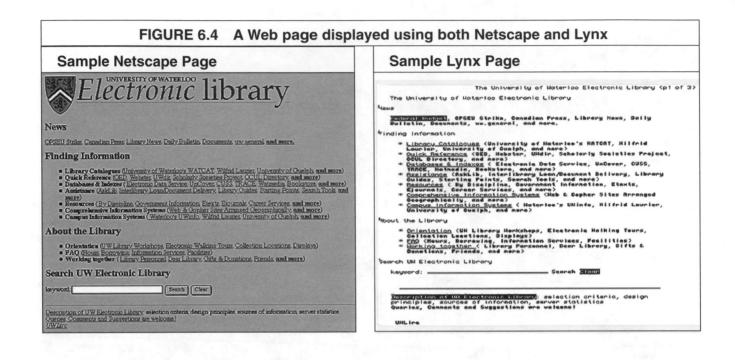

FIGURE 6.4 A Web page displayed using both Netscape and Lynx

THERE ARE LIMITS TO WHAT YOU CAN DO WITH HTML.

When designing a document in a paper environment you can do almost anything with text style, white space, and text placement. HTML is far from being as flexible as desktop publishing programs like PageMaker or Ventura. Additional HTML tags will soon make HTML authoring similar to creating a document using a desktop publishing program. In fact, within a couple of years, most desktop publishing programs will include HTML editing features. For the time being, though, you can't do everything with text and white space using HTML.

YOUR WEB IS A PERPETUAL DRAFT.

When you design a paper document, once it is out of draft stage, printed, and distributed, it is considered in final form (until you go back, review, and update it). This is not the case with a Web site which is in a perpetual draft state. New Web developments, continued improvements in HTML capabilities, and faster Web connections mean that your Web can and should be constantly updated in terms of content, graphic capabilities, and features only possible with high-speed connections (e.g., sound, video). Lots of people include "under construction" signs on their Web pages. These are not really necessary since all Webs are constantly under construction *and* reconstruction.

WEB ORGANIZATION

This section describes the various ways you can arrange individual Web pages in relationship to each other. It also provides you with advantages and disadvantages to each type of organization.

There are three basic organization schemes you can use to structure your library Web site—hierarchical, linear, and interconnected.

HIERARCHICAL ORGANIZATION

This type of organization is built on a pyramid model, with one starting place (or home page) that contains links to other major sections, each of which has subsequent sub-sections. This is the most common form of Web organization. It is often used by libraries because it mirrors the way libraries organize themselves administratively (director on top, department heads immediately below, and staff in units under each department head). The hierarchical arrangement also mirrors the way library resources are organized. (Catalogs/indexes as the starting place, major subject disciplines arranged together by floor, and specific subjects arranged together on shelves.)

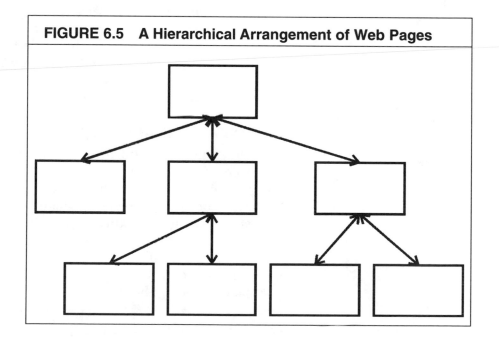

FIGURE 6.5   A Hierarchical Arrangement of Web Pages

Advantages
- Hierarchical organization presents patrons with a logical starting place that makes their search for Internet-based information as logical as using your online catalog to locate a book in your stacks.
- Hierarchical organization places important information that the majority of patrons want and need high up in the hierarchy, so that they can find it quickly.
- It is the easiest to create and maintain because it reflects the way libraries already arrange information.

Disadvantages
- It assumes that all patrons search from the same starting point. (This isn't true in your library now. Lots of people use your online catalog to start their search, while others choose CD indexes and others just cruise the shelves.)
- It assumes that patrons always start their search from your home page. (Not necessarily the case, given that patrons can bookmark any of your Web pages and return directly to them and not your home page.)
- It arranges information in a hierarchy of importance for the majority of patrons. For the patron whose information needs match your Web organization, important information is easy to find and probably only one level down in the Web hierarchy. For the patron with specific information needs that don't match your Web organization, information may be buried three or four levels down in your Web hierarchy, or may not be there at all.
- It doesn't allow you to easily customize approaches to finding information, a major Web benefit.

LINEAR ORGANIZATION

This type of organization assumes that patrons start from your home page and then proceed from one page to another in a set progression. This is an easy Web structure to organize in the abstract because it moves logically from page to page. It is not so easy to create in reality because it has to be designed to take into account all your patron needs and then structure those needs in a set order. This is not a common type of organization for a whole Web site as it leaves patrons little or no freedom to skip over a page or move about as they like.

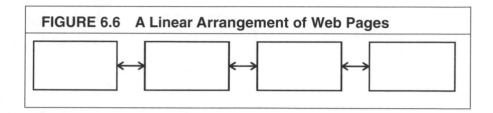

FIGURE 6.6   A Linear Arrangement of Web Pages

Advantage

- It can be used effectively within either a hierarchical or inter-connected Web structure, or to lead patrons through a series of instructions or steps in a process (e.g., how to use the self-checkout, how to fill out an inter-library loan request, or visit an exhibit).

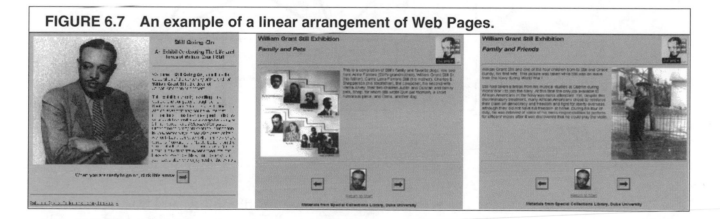

FIGURE 6.7   An example of a linear arrangement of Web Pages.

Disadvantage

- It mandates what people look at rather than giving them a choice. Patrons generally want the freedom to explore information freely and react badly to excessive use of linear organization, except when explaining steps in a process. Use linear organization sparingly to get across information you don't want patrons to miss.

INTERCONNECTED ORGANIZATION

This type of organization assumes that there are multiple starting points for exploring your Web site. This type of organization interconnects every page with every other page so that patrons can move freely through pages and find information based on their own needs. It also assumes that patrons can and will access your Web presence from different starting points, so every page is a potential "home page" for someone.

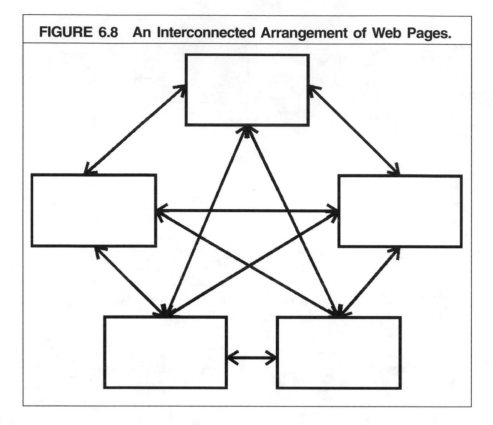

FIGURE 6.8 An Interconnected Arrangement of Web Pages.

Advantages

- It allows for maximum flexibility and customization of information. Since all pages are equal and referenced to each other, users are in control of what they see, and are not forced into any sort of imposed hierarchy.
- It doesn't assume that libraries know what information patrons need.
- It is relatively simple to create, since every page is linked to every other page. So there is less of a need to decide which information is more important than other information—you let your patrons decide for themselves.
- It is the most forward-looking type of Web structure. It gives patrons the "feel" of how the Net and Web are structured, or more properly, not structured.
- It can be used within a hierarchical Web organization to give patrons a choice of subjects to explore, or to give patrons a choice of what library policies and procedures they wish to view or not view.

Disadvantage

- It forces patrons to explore on their own. They must be willing to make decisions about what they want to see. Those with little time or inclination for exploration may view it as frustrating or inefficient.

WHICH TYPE OF ORGANIZATION IS BEST?

Most libraries start out choosing the organization style closest to their current structure—namely hierarchical. Many good Web sites have been built solely using the hierarchical model. The best Web sites also have linear and interconnected organizational elements incorporated into them.

When starting to design your Web presence you might want to stick with a hierarchical structure, focusing on arranging information for the majority of patrons. As you continue to develop your Web you might want to next incorporate linear direction/procedure pages as well as clusters of interconnected subject or resource pages. The end result will be a Web site that works better for all your users, not just the majority. Such a Web presence will provide structure for those who like structure and freedom for those who like to explore on their own.

WEB DESIGN ELEMENTS

This section discusses individual design elements and the issues you need to address when considering using them.

Web Design Hints

- Design each Web page so it is easy to read.
- Think of each Web page as an outline. Use headings and lists to organize information.
- Make each page complete in itself.
- Design each page so that people see the three most essential pieces of information first.
- Keep text simple, in active voice, and to-the-point.
- Be brief; people don't like to read long paragraphs of prose on computer screens.
- Add a graphic only if it is meaningful and relevant, otherwise leave it out.
- Be sensitive to the amount and size of graphics and the time it will take to load the page.
- Make sure all links add significantly to the page's usefulness.
- Make it simple for people to move between pages; put in navigation links or use graphical buttons on each page.
- Spell-check and proofread each page.
- Sign and date each document.

GRAPHIC ELEMENTS

Headline Graphics

This is the graphic that can include your logo, picture of your library, your library's name, etc. It acts as the headline to your home page and/or subsequent pages and is the first thing that people look at. Make sure that the information and images you include are relevant, professional looking, and quick loading. Make sure it gives people the information they need to see immediately and encourages them to read or look at the rest of the page. The size of the graphic and the number of colors you use should be relative to the speed of your Internet connection and your patron's ability to load it quickly from home using modem connections.

FIGURE 6.9   A Web Page Headline Graphic. (Westerville Public Library)

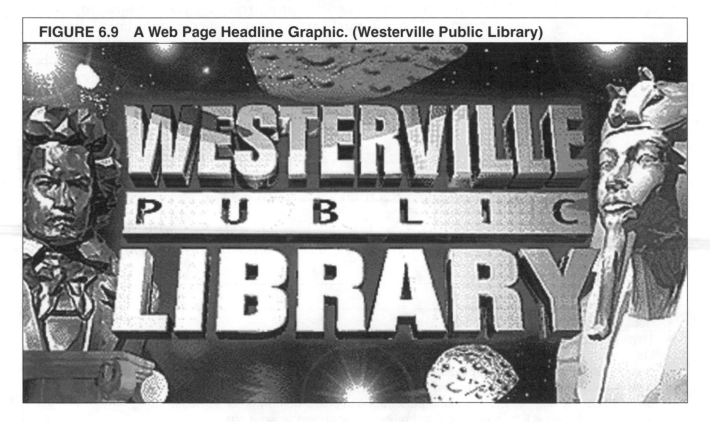

Logos

Most libraries want their logo on their home page and subsequent pages. This is an important graphic element because it visually identifies your library. Keep your logo small, unless you have an especially well-designed, well-liked logo. Lots of Web page designs incorporate library logos into the headline graphic that is displayed at the top of each page. This is a conservative, and very standard, place to put them.

Consider using a tiny version of your logo as a navigation button to other resources. Consider putting it at the bottom of the page along with your library address, phone, and fax information instead of the top of the page. (Especially if you have a more interesting picture to start off each page.)

FIGURE 6.10   Web Page Graphics With Logos.

Pictures

Most libraries also want pictures on their Web pages. Make sure every picture is both relevant and interesting. (Refer to the section on basic design principle for ideas on the subject matter and the positives and negatives of including pictures for readers.) Take into account the speed of your library Web connection when deciding to include/not include pictures. Take into account your connection speed when deciding how big a picture will be and how many colors to use. (The smaller a picture it is, and the fewer colors it has, the faster it loads.) Also take into account how fast your page (with pictures) will load for patrons who dial-in from home or office using different speed modems.

FIGURE 6.11   A Web Page Picture. (Rochester Hills Public Library)

Navigation Buttons

These small thumbnail graphics, used as hypertext links, navigate people around your Web site easily (e.g., back to your home page). You can use navigation buttons with simple pictures on them to connect patrons to your online catalog, or let them know where to find science information or resources for kids. There are an number of "button" archives on the Web where you can locate and download non-copyrighted images to use on your library Web page (See Chapter 11, p. 221 for URLs) or you can use CD-ROM images and reduce them to thumbnail size.

FIGURE 6.12 Web Page Navigation Buttons. (Multnomah County Library)

Graphic Lines

HTML has the horizontal rule tag <hr> that creates a simple line on your Web page. If you want to use a colored line or a line with a texture that matches your other graphics, you can use graphic lines. These can be found in "line" archives on the Web. Use them sparingly for best graphic effect and to reduce the load on your Web server. (See Chapter 11, p. 221 for URLs) or you can use programs like Corel Draw! or Adobe Illustrator to create your own lines. Because these can bog down a page, use them only when they significantly increase user comprehension of your page.

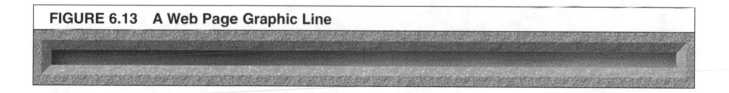

FIGURE 6.13 A Web Page Graphic Line

Backgrounds

These are graphics that load behind the text on your pages and give your pages both texture and color. Most graphical browsers support loading backgrounds, but exactly how they look depends on which browser you use to view them. Be careful when using dark backgrounds. They obscure text and discourage people from reading them. Dark backgrounds with light text also negatively affect a patron's ability and willingness to read the text of your Web page. It's best to choose light and simply textured backgrounds for the most readable and professional look. There are "background" archives on the Web (See Chapter 11, p. 221 for URLs) or create your own background using programs like Corel Draw! and Adobe Illustrator. You can use different backgrounds for different pages. (We recommend the same texture for all pages, but differing colors.) Bright colors, like yellow, work well on children's pages, cooler and more neutral colors are more appropriate for adult pages.

FIGURE 6.14   A Web Page Background (With Logo). (Case Western Reserve University Library)

Image Maps

These are pictures that also contain hypertext links. Some libraries use <u>image maps</u> instead of words to highlight library services. For instance, clicking on the circulation desk in a picture of your library service desks will bring up information on circulation policies, hours, fines, and procedures. Campus and public libraries with branches often use campus or city maps to show the location of branches and at the same time provide patrons with links to information about branch collections, hours, etc. Like any graphic, images maps should be used sparingly for best effect and to reduce the load on your Web server.

Image Maps—Graphics that have hypertext/media links imbedded in them. By clicking on a spot on an image map you select a link, and you ask your browser to make the connection for you and display the information you request.

FIGURE 6.15   A Web Page Image Map

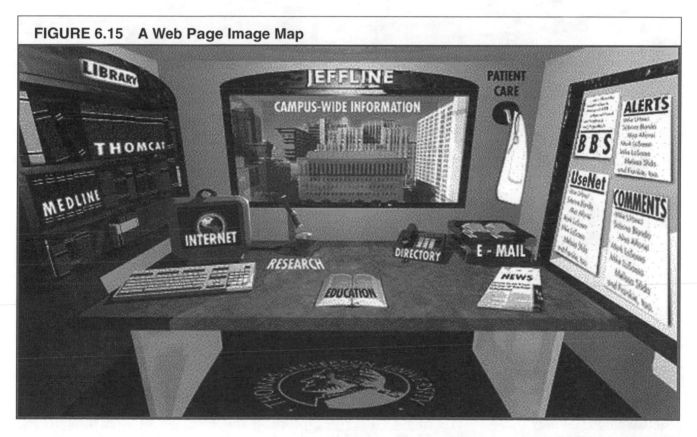

Image maps are load intensive transactions for your Web server. Be sure when deciding to use one that you have the connection speed to support one (at least a 56K connection). Be aware that dialup patrons will have to wait for some time to see the whole graphic, so provide them with a text-only Web page alternative or text links that they can click on instead of waiting for your image map to load.

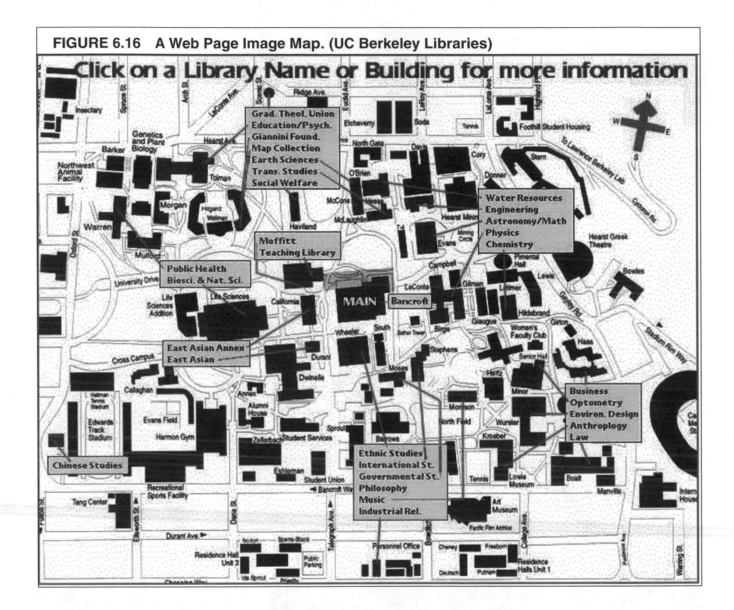

FIGURE 6.16   A Web Page Image Map. (UC Berkeley Libraries)

CGI (Common Gateway Interface)—A program that links an external program and a Web server. CGI scripts are often written in C, Perl, or Applescript languages. They are commonly used to process Web-based image maps and forms.

Creating an image map today is a complex process that involves creating CGI scripts, plotting the location of each link in the graphic, and building that location into each link. If you have a fairly knowledgeable bunch of HTML authors, creating an image map should not be a problem. If you have a bunch of fairly new HTML authors, you might want to wait until they have done the first public version of your complete Web before they learn to do mapping. Canned image map scripts available on the Net can help get them started. Image maps are in the "bells and whistles" category of graphics for most library Web pages. You can create a great Web without using them at all.

Forms—Information, created as HTML documents and processed by CGI scripts, that looks like a form you can fill out. Forms are used for such things as key word searching, suggesting book purchases, or providing patron feedback.

Forms

Forms are supported by a wide variety of graphical browsers. They are a powerful addition to any library Web site. You can create fill-in forms for people to suggest library material purchases, to get patrons' input on services and staff, to put a hold on a book, to request a book from interlibrary loan, or to interact with your library in countless other creative ways.

Creating forms involves using CGI scripts. It is a more complex process than writing simple HTML documents. If you have fairly knowledgeable HTML authors, try creating some forms for your first public Web site. If your HTML authors are fairly new at it, it's best to wait till your first Web site is complete and add forms as an enhancement. There are also "canned" forms scripts available on the Net to help you get started. (Until you get forms up, you can use "mailto" links at various spots around your Web, to get patron suggestions.) (See Chapter 11, p. 222 for URLs to help you learn more about creating forms.)

FIGURE 6.17   A Web Page Form

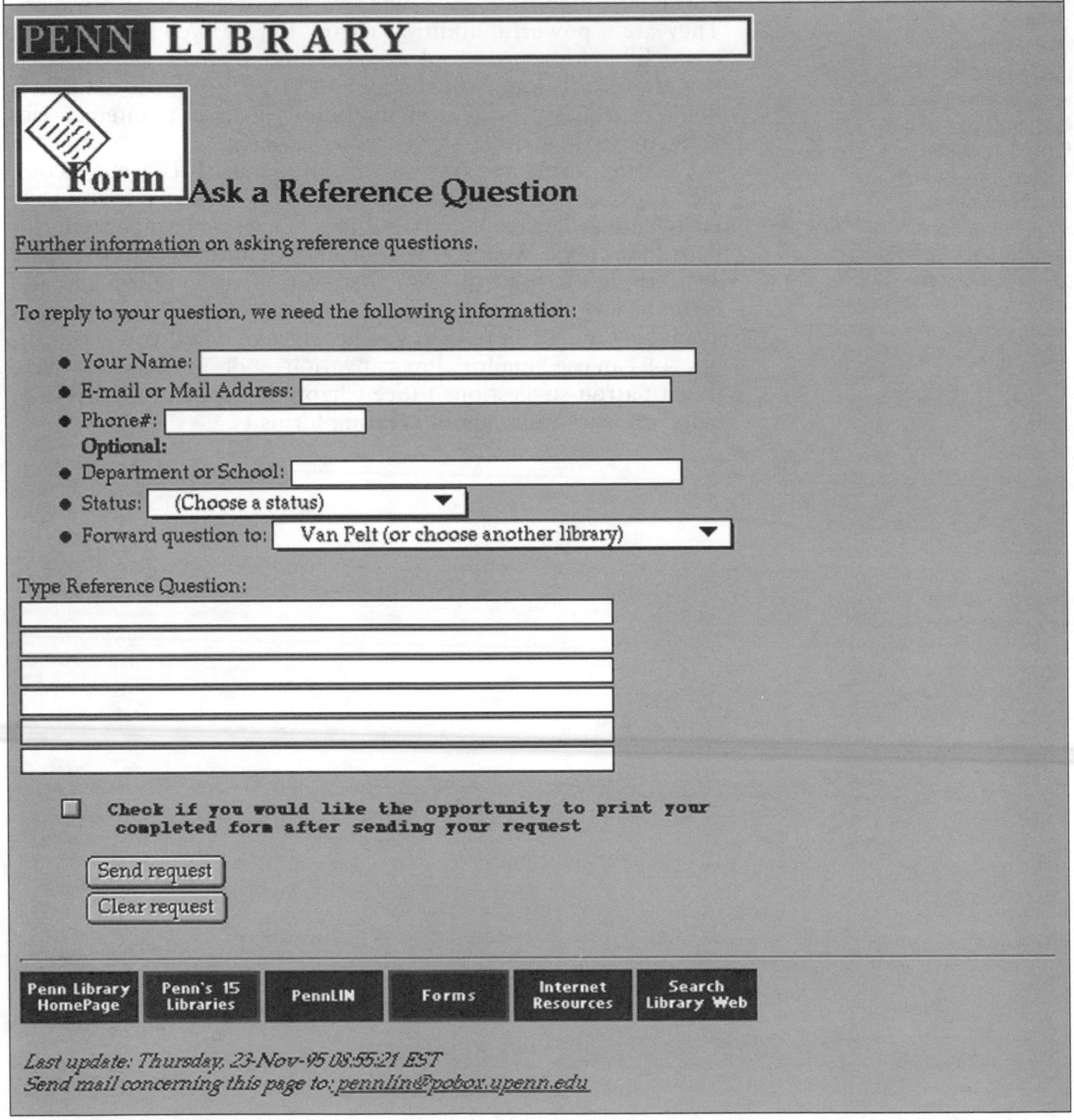

PENN **LIBRARY**

Form **Ask a Reference Question**

Further information on asking reference questions.

To reply to your question, we need the following information:

- Your Name: [   ]
- E-mail or Mail Address: [   ]
- Phone#: [   ]
  Optional:
- Department or School: [   ]
- Status: [(Choose a status)   ▼]
- Forward question to: [Van Pelt (or choose another library)   ▼]

Type Reference Question:

[   ]
[   ]
[   ]
[   ]
[   ]
[   ]

☐   Check if you would like the opportunity to print your
    completed form after sending your request

[Send request]
[Clear request]

| Penn Library HomePage | Penn's 15 Libraries | PennLIN | Forms | Internet Resources | Search Library Web |

Last update: Thursday, 23-Nov-95 08:55:21 EST
Send mail concerning this page to: pennlin@pobox.upenn.edu

FIGURE 6.18   A Web Page "Mailto" Form

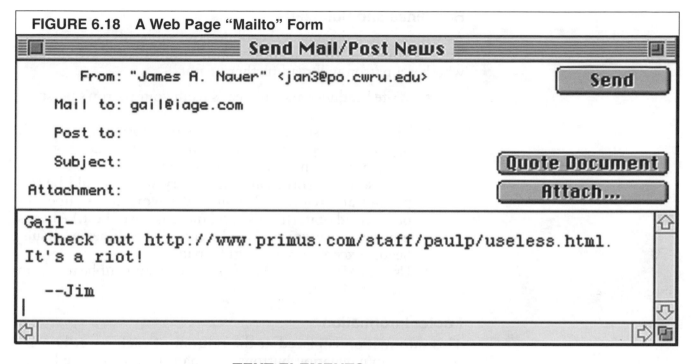

TEXT ELEMENTS

Text Style

Pictures may be more visually appealing to readers, but the content and style of text you provide readers will make or break your Web. Here are some specific text tips for Web pages:

- Keep sentences simple and short. Consider using phrases as long as they are understandable.
- Arrange text on pages in a logical manner, highlight words with italics, and bold sparingly for maximum effect. Use an outline form or lists if possible.
- Choose words carefully based on who will be reading the page. Wording for kids' pages, teen pages, business pages, and senior pages should all be different to be the most effective.
- Don't just scan your policy and procedure manual. Pick and choose the most important information, carefully edit the text, and create links to the important bits. If you include the whole document, make it an option to read or not read.
- Keep "techie" terms and library jargon to a minimum. If you use a term that you think someone might not know, consider creating a definition link, so that a patron can click on the word to see its definition.

Headlines and Subheads

As with any text document, headlines and subheads get read first. The wording of your headlines and subheads greatly affects whether a patron will read further or not.

- Write headlines and subheads from your patron's perspective.
- The three most important pieces of information on each page should be found in a headline or subhead (not buried in a list or in a paragraph of text).
- Choose your words carefully; every word should be important and relevant, If you find a word to be superfluous, get rid of it. (In this case, more is never best.) Always use the active voice. Avoid "cutsie" headlines and subheads (except maybe on kids' pages).
- Use HTML tags to set off headlines and subheads from the rest of text.

Footer Information

This information is placed at the bottom of each page. Footers often contain navigation buttons or "mailto" links for feedback. They also contain text information such as the document's URL, the name of the person responsible for the Web page's content, the date the page was last revised, a copyright statement, and sometimes your library logo, address, phone, and fax number. Keep words to a minimum and only include essential information.

WEB PAGE TEMPLATES

This section provides sample templates you can use to create a consistent look for your Web site.

When you create page templates, plan to include the following elements:

- a short, descriptive title near the top of the page;
- an optional graphic that relates to the content of the page;
- a brief statement of the purpose of the page (somewhere near the title);
- an outline structure, showing how text and links will be arranged;
- lines that separate the title from the body and the body from the footer information;

- navigation buttons or text links for moving around your Web;
- information about who wrote the page, when they wrote or revised it, and how to contact them; and
- an optional logo graphic identifying your library.

Creating templates for a hierarchical Web (e.g., home page, major pages, and their subsequent pages) makes it possible to have a consistent look that helps patrons to visually understand how your Web is organized. Below are examples of some hierarchical templates you might consider using, or modifying, when designing your Web site.

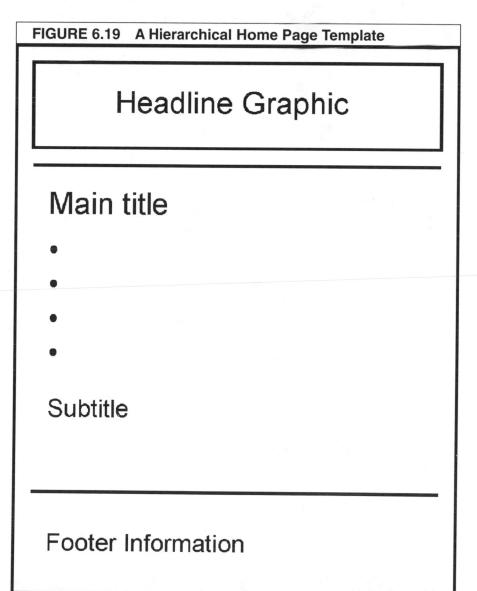

FIGURE 6.19   A Hierarchical Home Page Template

FIGURE 6.20   A Hierarchical Major Page Template

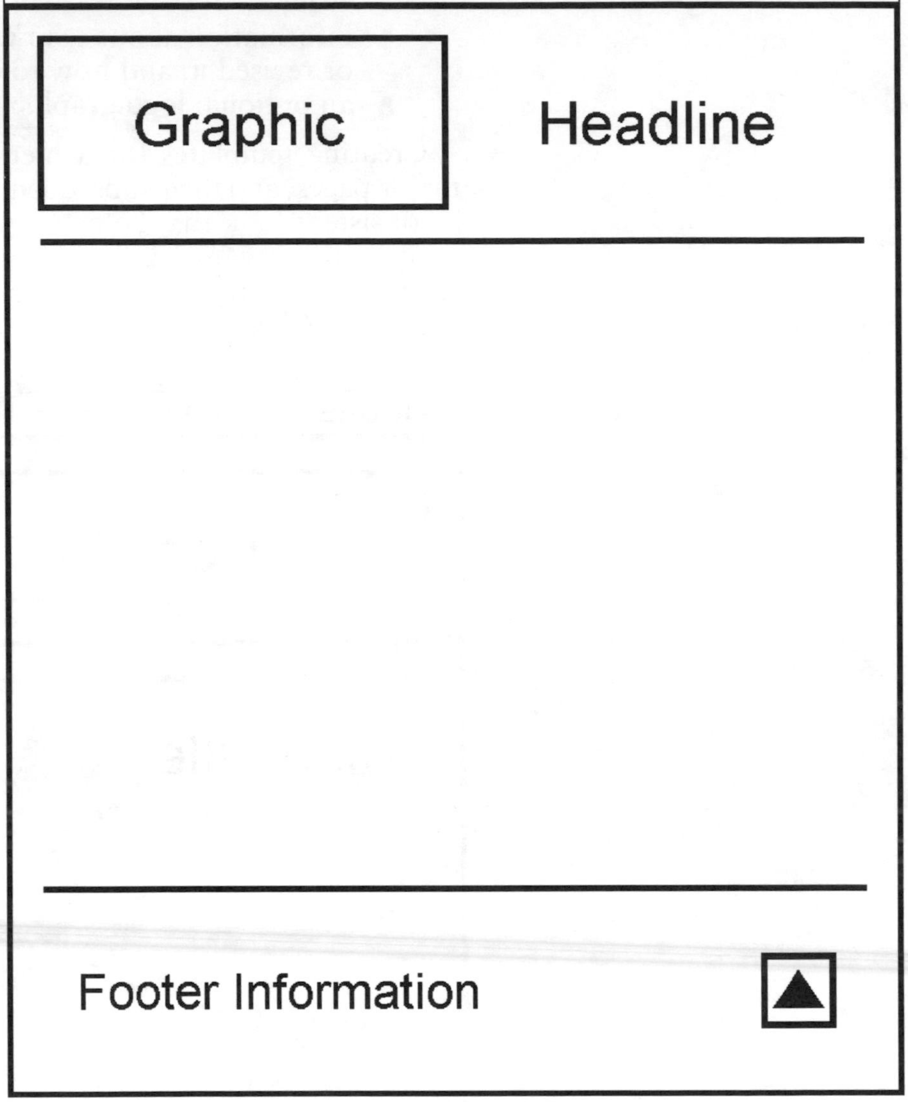

Graphic   Headline

Footer Information ▲

FIGURE 6.21   An Interconnected Page Template

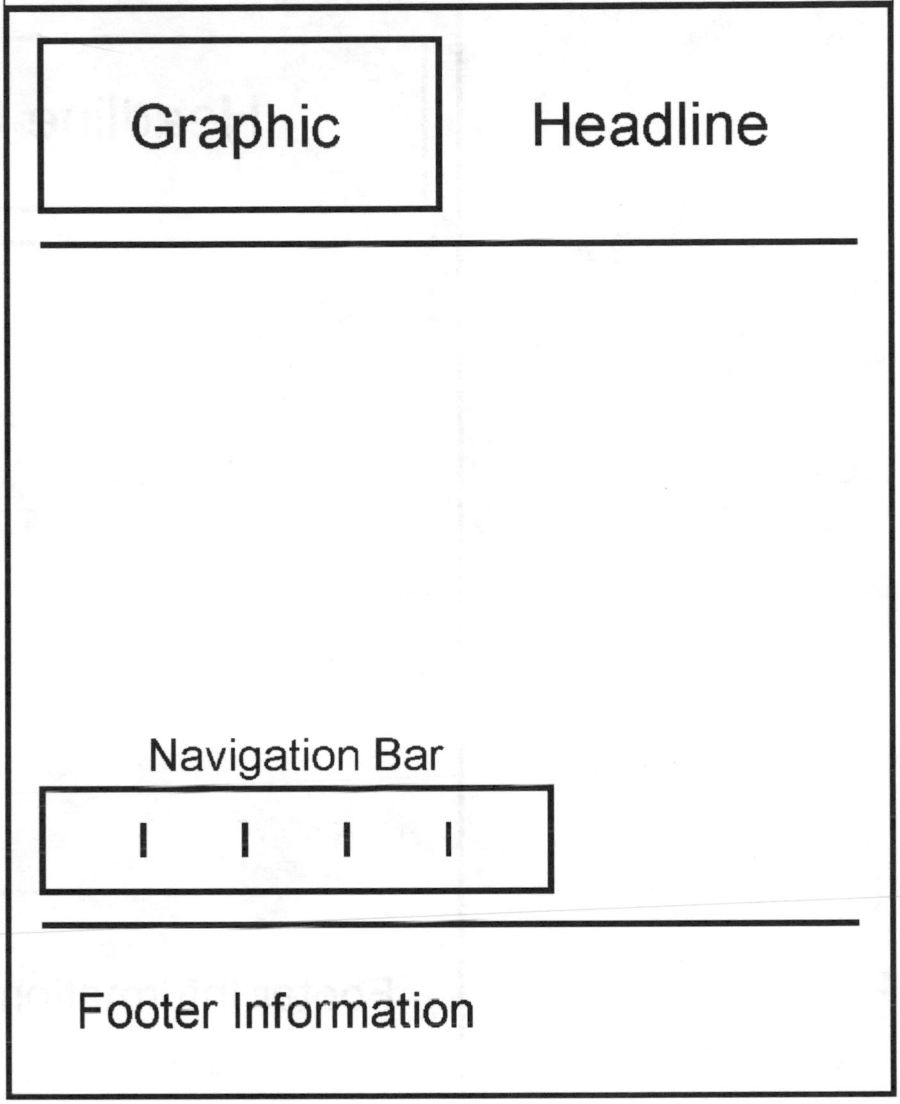

Graphic   Headline

Navigation Bar

Footer Information

Creating a template for all the pages of an interconnected Web helps patrons understand how pages relate to each other, and how they are all interlinked.

FIGURE 6.22   A Linear Page Template

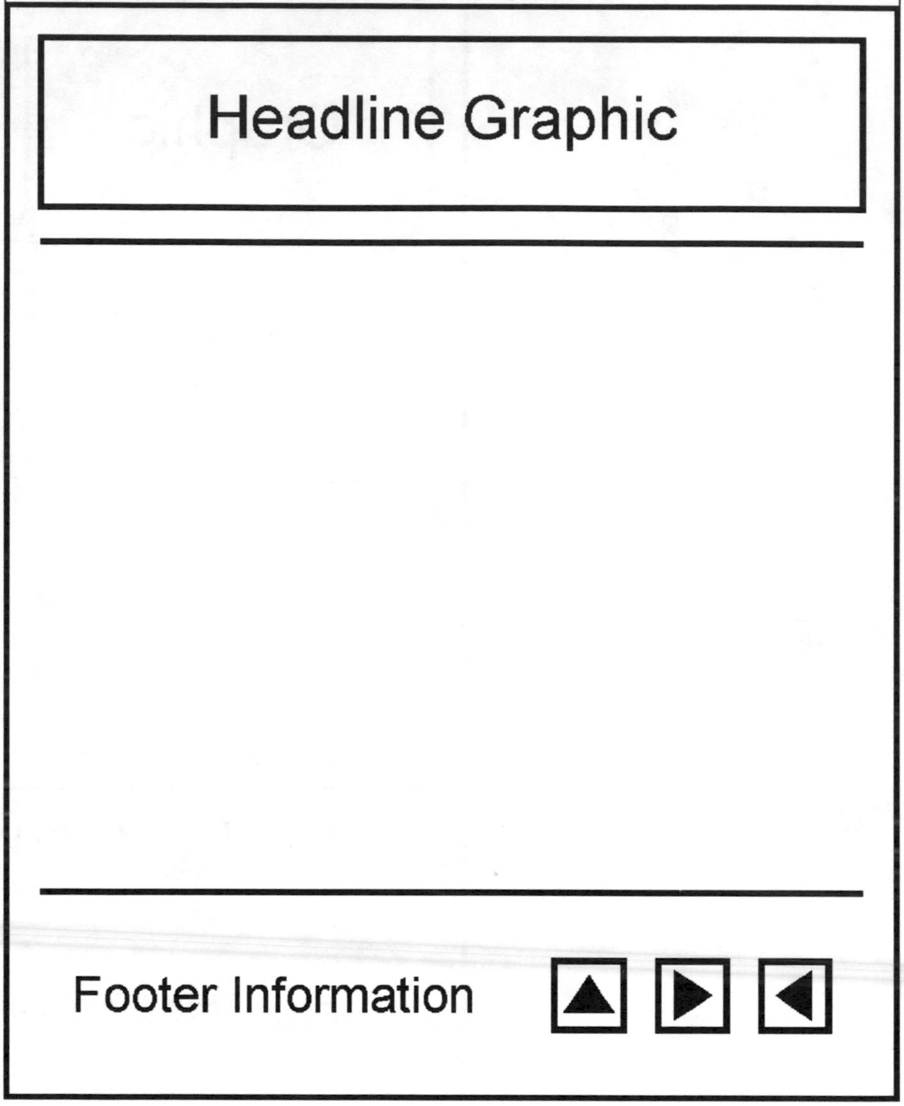

Headline Graphic

Footer Information ▲ ▶ ◀

Creating templates for a sequence of linear Web pages helps patrons understand better the process or steps they are learning, and helps them see the relationship between the pages before and after.

7 GETTING DOWN TO IT—AUTHORING YOUR WEB SITE

THE AUTHORING PROCESS

This section outlines some of the basic steps you need to take to start getting your library Web site written.

WHO AND WHAT

Basic HTML is quite simple. It can be mastered by any of your library staff, including student assistants. There are, however, natural HTML authors already on your library staff. HTML tagging is similar conceptually to MARC tagging of cataloging records, in that unseen tags govern the display of data. Staff who do bibliographic searching or cataloging usually understand the relationship between HTML tags and text very quickly. To start creating your library Web site, we recommend you create a team of HTML authors. This team might consist of a cataloger (copy cataloger, bibliographic searcher), a reference librarian, your graphic designer, an administrator, and a "techie." Once you have your Web site created, tested, and implemented, we recommend that you teach more staff HTML so that they can be involved in keeping your Web site current.

LIMITATIONS OF HTML

HTML is conceptually similar to desktop publishing programs like Ventura and PageMaker in that it provides for text variations that makes information visually appealing, and therefore more readable. Desktop publishing programs let you control what a document will look like (e.g, font type and size, white space, illustration location, and size). HTML lets you control some, but not all of the ways that your Web site information will display. HTML will undoubtedly become more robust in the future and allow for more flexibility in presenting information.

The first limitation of HTML is that not all the formatting tricks of desktop publishing programs are as yet available in HTML. The second limitation is that HTML documents cannot mandate how browsers will display the information you provide. HTML

129

describes the content of the document, not how the content is to be displayed. Because you do not have total control of how your Web site will display, you must write your Web pages keeping in mind that patrons will be using different browsers and will choose different browser display options for viewing your Web site.

STARTING OUT

Assuming that you have done the requisite planning and design work for your Web site, the actual authoring can be done in relatively short order. This will depend on how many hours you have to spend and how complex your initial Web site will be. A lot of HTML authoring involves typing the same <u>tags</u> again and again as well as proofreading tags and text for typographical errors. Having your HTML team proof each other's HTML documents can relieve the tediousness of proofreading while eliminating most typographical errors.

Before you start tagging documents, spend some time trying out different tagging styles to see which works best. Decide on one style that all teams members will use. (One style you might consider uses tabs and indents in your HTML text to make clear the structure of the document. Since tabs and indents are ignored by browsers when displaying the document, a pseudo-outline style can make it easy to review and update each document.) Be consistent in your tagging from document to document. Lastly, decide on a naming scheme for all HTML documents the team will create and agree on folder or directory names where they will store draft and final versions of HTML documents. As more members of your staff learn HTML, provide them with an HTML "style sheet" so that all documents retain a consistent look.

There are a number of ways you can create HTML documents. You can start by creating the text first, using any word-processing program that allows you to save text in ASCII format (e.g., ClarisWorks, Word, WordPerfect). After you finish writing the text, add the HTML tags to it with the same word-processing program.

You can also add HTML tags to an existing document. This is a quick way of getting documents converted to HTML and made available on your Web. There is one problem with simply adding HTML tags to an existing document. People read Web sites differently than they do paper documents. When tagging an existing document you can easily fall into the trap of solely adding tags and forget abut doing the necessary text editing. Use this option with care. Web pages should, as a rule, contain concise information arranged for ease of use.

Tags—Instructions placed around regular text to indicate how Web browsers should display the text (e.g., Oh Boy!).

HTML Editing Program—A program that simplifies the creation of HTML documents. HTML editors provide you with menu item or button choices for inserting HTML tags into text. They eliminate the need for you to type in HTML tags manually.

You can also use an <u>HTML editing program</u> to add HTML tags to either a pre-existing document or to one you create from scratch. Using an editing program, you can get documents quickly tagged and available on your Web site. Editing programs such as PageMill, HotDog, HoTMetaL or HTML Assistant provide you with menu choices or templates for creating HTML documents. (See p. 157–159 for a further explanation of the different types of HTML editing programs you can use. See also Chapter 11, p. 220–221 for URLs of specific editing programs.)

HTML editing programs can be more effective when you already know the basics of HTML tagging. They are great tools for keeping Web sites up to date. HTML editing programs can be less useful for beginning HTML authors who may not know enough about HTML to choose wisely from the many options available. If you are simultaneously learning HTML and writing Web pages, we recommend you manually key HTML tags into your text documents rather than using an HTML editing program. This keeps your task focused on the two most important things: HTML tags and the content of your Web site. Once you have the basics of tagging down and know how they display on different browsers, then start using an HTML editing program to make writing and updating HTML documents more efficient.

CREATING AN HTML DOCUMENT

Creating Web pages from scratch consists of three steps. First you write Web document text using your favorite word-processing program. After you have finished writing the text you go back through the document, adding HTML tags and hypertext links as appropriate. You then save the document, being sure to include either .htm or .html as the extension to the document file name (e.g., homepage.html). While experienced Webweavers tag as they go, we recommend you use this three-step process until writing in HTML becomes a natural process for you.

Using an HTML tag editing program is quite similar. You first write Web document text using your favorite word-processing program. If your word-processing program also includes an HTML editing subprogram, you can start it and add HTML tags by choosing from the menu or button options. If your word-processing program does not include an HTML editing sub-program, save your text document, open up your HTML editing program, retrieve the document, and add HTML tags to it using the program's menu options. When you are done, save the document and include either .htm or .html as an extension to the document's file name.

CHECKING YOUR WORK

It is simple to see how your draft HTML documents will look using a Web browser. You can view the document you just created using the Web browser(s) loaded on your computer. To do this, start your Web browser. Then choose the menu option to "view a file". Select the directory/folder where your document is stored, locate your draft HTML document, and take a look at it using your browser. If you like what you see, fine. If not, exit your browser and restart your word-processing or HTML editing program. Try some different tags or arrangements of text, checking with your browser until it looks the way you want it to.

TO LEARN MORE...

See Chapter 11 for complete bibliographic citations.

Also refer to Chapter 11 for more print and Web resources.

For more information on HTML we recommend you read and connect to:

- *HTML and CGI Unleashed* by J. December & M. Ginsburg
- *HTML Sourcebook* by I. Graham
- *Teach Yourself Web Publishing with HTML in 14 Days* by L. Lemay
- *Teach Yourself Web Publishing with HTML 3.0* by L. Lemay
- *HTML Bad Style Guide* http://www.halsoft.com/html-val-svc/index.html
- *HTML Quick Ref.* http://www.ncsa.uiuc.edu/General/Internet/WWW/HTMLQuickRef.html
- *Yahoo: HTML Editors* http://www.yahoo.com/Computers/World_Wide_Web/HTML_Editors

HTML CONCEPTS

This section provides you with basic HTML concepts and how HTML and browsers work together to display your Web site.

HTML is short for Hypertext markup language. HTML describes the contents of Web pages so that your browser can display them. HTML also makes it possible for you to create hypertext links from your Web site to resources on the Internet or from one Web site to another. HTML is a subset of Standard Generalized Markup Language (SGML).

There are several versions of HTML. The basic version is called HTML 2.0. There are additional HTML tags, which are included in a version called HTML 3.0. Before your authoring team starts writing HTML documents, it must decide which version of HTML they will use.

There are essentially two parts to an HTML document, text and tags. HTML documents start as text documents. You then add HTML tags to the document to give it both structure and hypertext capabilities when saved and displayed as a Web page. Most tags come in pairs that surround text. All tags are surrounded by angle brackets <>. This means that the text inside of tag pairs will display the attributes of the tag when viewed with a Web browser. The beginning tag turns the tag "on" and the ending tag (along with the slash mark) turns the tag "off".

<tag>text</tag>

Tags can be written in either upper, lower or mixed case.

<html> <HTML> <HtMl>

HTML ignores all document formatting like returns, tabs, and spaces as well as character attributes you produce by holding down the CTRL or ALT keys in combination with keyboard keys (e.g., bold, underline).

There is no one standard way of tagging documents. Some people prefer to write HTML documents so that there is only one tag or tag group per line; others write HTML documents as long continuous paragraphs of text and tags. Most people fall in between these two extremes.

FIGURE 7.1   Different HTML Document Styles

```
<HMTL>
<HEAD>
<TITLE>Sampler</TITLE>
</HEAD>
<BODY>
<H1>Sample HTML Files</H1>
This shows you what an HTML document with
<B>tags</B> looks like.
<P>
This sentence contains a <a
HREF="hlink.html">hypertext link</a> to another
document.
</BODY>
</HTML>
```

```
<HMTL>
<HEAD>
<TITLE> ERO STAFF</TITLE>
</HEAD>
<BODY>
<A HREF="emrls.htm"><IMG SRC="emrls.gif"></A>
<H3><I> EMRLS STAFF </I></H3>
<P><H3><A HREF="lbmail.htm">Linda W. Braun,</
A></H3><H4>Youth Services Consultant</H4></P>
<HR>
<H3>Back to EMRLS <A HREF="emrls.htm"> Main
Menu</A></H3>
</BODY>
</HTML>
```

HTML AND BROWSERS

When a Web browser requests your home page, your Web server sends it an HTML document full of tags. The browser's job is to take your HTML document and display it in a user-friendly way for the requestor. HTML tags describe the content of the document so that the browser software can format, arrange, and display the information. The options that you set up locally on your Web browser (e.g., font type and size, page background color) also affect how your document will display. The resulting document will display as text and graphics with different looks, placement and formats.

BASIC HTML TAGS

This section provides short descriptions and examples of the most common HTML 2.0 tags (and a few Netscape extensions). It includes the tags you need to know to start creating a basic Web site (or will provide you with a basic knowledge of HTML tags so you know what your HTML authors are doing).

HTML tags can be broken down into five basic categories:

- starting and ending tags
- structure tags
- list tags
- appearance tags
- linking tags

STARTING AND ENDING TAGS

Starting and ending tags help browsers display your Web pages correctly. These tags do not affect the line-by-line appearance of your documents, but give browsers instructions about the nature and length of each document and how different pages are labeled.

HTML Tag

The first and last tag of every HTML document is the <html> </html> tag pair. These tags indicate to browsers when an HTML document starts and when it stops.

```
<html>
your document
</html>
```

Head Tag

The <head> </head> tag pair is usually the second tag of every document. It contains the <title> tag and nothing else.

```
<html>
<head>
<title>Racine HS Library</title>
</head>
your document
</html>
```

Title Tag

Title—The title of a single Web page, as named by the HTML author. The words you use in a title become the phrase that is bookmarked by your browser.

The <title></title> tag pair is found inside the <head> tags. It identifies the <u>title</u> of the document (which, depending on the browser, will be displayed in the window bar or indented at the start of the home page text). The text you put in the title tag also describes the document when you save it as a bookmark. You can have only one title per HTML document and it can only contain text (no links). Many browsers limit the number of letters/numbers that display for the title, so it is best to keep titles short (thirty–forty characters).

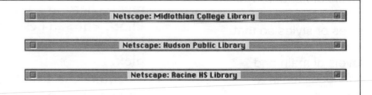

```
<title>Midlothian College Library</title>
<title>Hudson Public Library</title>
<title>Racine HS Library</title>
```

Body Tag

The <body> </body> tag pair tells browsers that all the text and tags inside these two tags contain the information you want people to view.

```
<html>
<head>
<title>Racine HS Library</title>
</head>
<body>
your home page
</body>
</html>
```

Structure Tags

Structure tags help create the basic look of a Web page. You use them to create headlines and to break up information into meaningful pieces. List tags are also structure tags, but because there are so many ways to create lists, we describe them in a separate section.

Header Tags

Header tag pairs (e.g., <h1><h1>) are used to structure your document like an outline. It is best to use <u>header</u> tags in descending numerical order starting with <h1> and ending with <h6>.

```
<h1>Hudson Public Library</h1>
<h2>Virtual Reference Desk</h2>
<h3>Business Resources</h3>
```

Hudson Public Library
Virtual Reference Desk
Business Resources

Header—A type of HTML tag that makes text larger or bolder in order to set selected text apart from regular text. There are different levels of headers which display in different sizes or styles so that you can create various levels of main and subheadlines in a document.

First level <u>header</u> tags <h1> are like the major section heads in an outline. (<h1> tags are often used as the main "headlines" for individual Web pages.) Second level header tags <h2> are like the second level of headings in an outline. (They often are used to subdivide major parts of Web pages.) Third level header tags <h3> often indicate important subcategories under major text groupings. There are fourth, fifth, and sixth level header tags <h4>, <h5>, <h6>. These are normally not used in a basic Web site unless the Web page structure is solely in outline form or very complex.

Unlike the title tag, there is no limit to the number of words, you can use inside header tags. Like newspaper headlines or outline head text, use common sense and keep text short and to the point. Each header tag displays differently (e.g., bold and indented, bold not indented). You can include either plain text and/or hypertext links in headers. Each browser displays the various levels of headers slightly differently, so it's important to check how each type of header displays (especially when using a text browser like Lynx).

Paragraph Tag

The single paragraph tag <p> puts space between lines or blocks of text. Paragraph tags should not be used to separate text so that it is more readable. If you use more than one <p> tag to create multiple lines of space, you may find that some browsers will ignore all but the first <p> tag and only create one space for you.

```
<p>
This is text
<p>
This is more text
```

This is text
This is more text

Horizontal Rule Tag

This single tag <hr> does not contain any text. It simply creates a line that can be used to separate headlines from body text at the top of a page, to separate major sections within the body text, and to separate body text from navigation buttons and Web page information at the bottom of a page. Like any graphical element, use it sparingly and consistently for the greatest impact.

Text Break Tag

This single tag <br> is used to stop text and restart again on the next line (similar to a hard return in a word-processing environment). It is placed at the end of each line of text you want to break.

```
Roses are red<br>
Violets are blue<br>
I think HTML is easy<br>
And so will you<br>
```

Roses are red
Violets are blue
I think HTML is easy
And so will you

Address Tag

The <address> </address> tag pair is often found at the bottom of each page. It contains information about the Web page author or library and often a copyright statement, e-mail address of the Webmaster, and a date when the page was last revised. Address information displays differently on various browsers. One browser may italicize it, another indent it, and still another may right justify it.

```
<address>
Hudson Public Library<br>
copyright 1996<br>
revised 2/21/96<br>
</address>
```

Hudson Public Library
copyright 1996
revised 2/21/96

Center Tag

The   tag pair will center the text on your computer screen. Not all browsers currently handle this tag, so check to see how it looks with a variety of browsers before you use it.

```
<center>
2418 Main Street<br>
Racine, WI 53403<br>
414-555-1234<br>
</center>
```

2418 Main Street
Racine, WI 53403
414-555-1234

HTML Document—A document that displays on your browser as a Web page. An HTML document is one that contains tags that advise your browser software how you want the document to display.

Comments Tag

This odd looking single tag <!-- --> is important because browsers don't display the text included inside it. The comments tag displays in your HTML document and contains internal comments that you want your staff to see. You can use this tag to ask fellow HTML team members to check your tagging or to include information about who added/revised a link or to indicate the source of information. You can also add key words in comments tags so that Web search engines can find them when they index your Web site. You can compose comments using upper and lower case letters, or just upper case letters, so they stand out more in your HTML document. (This is one case where using all capitals doesn't translate into "screaming" your message, like it does in Usenet newsgroups.) There is no limit to the length or content of comment tags, so be creative when using them.

```
<!--Sam, is this the tag you wanted me to use?-->
<!--Link suggested by patron 3/1/96-->
<!--URL REVISED BY R.S.T. ON 4/15/96-->
```

LIST TAGS

Directory and Menu Lists

These two list types are the simplest kind. Both are designed for lists of briefly described items. <dir> lists are designed for items that can be described in twenty characters or less and <menu> lists are designed for items that can be described in a short sentence. Both <dir> and <menu> come in tag pairs. The single <li> tag comes before each item in the list. Browsers display both of these lists with some form of bullet or an asterisk. Often the items on the list are indented.

```
Library Personnel Manual
<dir>
<li>Orientation
<li>Policies
<li>Procedures
<li>Job titles
</dir>
```

Library Personnel Manual
- n   Orientation
- n   Policies
- n   Procedures
- n   Job titles

```
Summit Library Archives
<menu>
<li>Hours and services offered
<li>Circulation to community members
<li>Interlibrary loan policy
<li>Summary of collections
<li>Special exhibits for 1996
</menu>
```

Summit Library Archives
- n   Hours and services offered
- n   Circulation to community members
- n   Interlibrary loan policy
- n   Summary of collections
- n   Special exhibits for 1996

Numbered List—A list of items on a Web page, arranged hierarchically by number.

Numbered (Ordered) List

The <ol> </ol> tag pair and the single <li> tag combine to form what is called an ordered, or <u>numbered list</u>. When you use these tags together, your browser will display all the text following each <li> tag in numerical order (some browsers also will indent this kind of list). If you edit and remove an item from the list your browser will automatically renumber the items. Use ordered lists to display information in a specific sequence. If the order of items in a list is not important, use one of the unordered list types.

```
Putting a Book on Reserve
<ol>
<li>Make a list of books for reserve
<li>Fill out a form for each book
<li>Give the list and forms to staff early
<li>Check with staff the first week of class
</ol>
```

Putting a Book on Reserve
1. Make a list of books for reserve
2. Fill out a form for each book
3. Give the list and forms to staff early
4. Check with staff the first week of class

Bulleted (Unordered) List

Bulleted List—A non-numerical list of options on a Web page, each of which is preceded by a graphical dot or asterisk.

The <ul> </ul> tag pair and the single <li> tag combine to form what is called an unordered, or a bulleted list. When you use these tags together, your browser will display an asterisk or some form of bullet graphic in front of all the text following each <li> tag. Some browsers will also indent the listed items. Use an unordered list when the sequence of items is not important.

```
Virtual Reference Desk
<ul>
<li>General reference
<li>Business
<li>Education
<li>Law
<li>Federal government
<li>State/local government
<li>Campus/city
<li>Just for kids
</ul>
```

Virtual Reference Desk
n General Reference
n Business
n Education
n Law
n Federal government
n State/local government
n Campus/city
n Just for kids

Definition (Glossary) List

The <dl> <dt> tag pairs and the single <dd> tag combine to form what is called a definition or glossary list. The <dl> tag stands for "definition list." The <dt> tag stands for "defined term" and the <dd> tag stands for "defined definition." This list type can be used in many more ways than its name implies. When you set up a glossary list, your browser will display "term" <dt> information justified to the left and "definition" <dd> information as indented with a bullet or asterisk. You can use glossary list tags anytime you want to easily indent text.

```
Midlothian Library
   <dl>
   <dt>Services
       <dd>Circulation
       <dd>Reference
       <dd>Interlibrary Loan
   <dt>Collections
       <dd>Monographs
       <dd>Periodicals and microforms
       <dd>Special collections
   </dl>
```

```
Midlothian Library
Services
    Circulation
    Reference
    Interlibrary Loan
Collections
    Monographs
    Periodicals and microforms
    Special collections
```

** Note that the indentions make it easier to see the structure of this type of list (and are ignored by browsers).

Combining Lists

It is possible to combine one type of list with another to create a variety of visual effects. Browsers display each type of list differently. When combining different list types, check to see that they create the visual effect you want.

```
Putting a Book on Reserve
<ol>
<li>Make a list of reserve books
<li>Fill out a form for each book
    <ul>
    <li>Include your course number
    <li>Include your phone extension
    <li>Tell us if the book is on order
    </ul>
<li>Give the list and forms to staff early
<li>Check with staff the first week of class
</ol>
```

```
Putting a Book on Reserve
1. Make a list of books for reserve
2. Fill out a form for each book
    n Include your course number
    n Include your phone extension
    n Tell us if the book is on order
3. Give the list and forms to staff early
4. Check with staff the first week of class
```

** The indentions in the HTML document above help make the structure of the list clearer. Since Web browsers ignore tabs and indents, you may also want to use this style of tagging on your Web pages; it makes reviewing and revising pages much simpler.

APPEARANCE TAGS

Appearance tags affect the graphical look of the text itself. There are two main types of appearance tags: logical tags and physical tags. Logical tags indicate how the text is used but do not dictate how browsers must display them. Physical tags, on the other hand, tell browsers precisely how you want the text displayed (e.g., italics). Of the two types, logical tags are more flexible because they let browsers decide how to display the text in the manner appropriate for that browser. As a result, HTML documents with logical tags have a better chance of displaying well with a variety of browser software. A few kinds of appearance tags fall outside these two main categories and are discussed at the end of this section.

Logical Tags

Emphasized Text Tag. The <em> </em> tag pair indicates that the text should be treated as emphasized text. Most graphical browsers display <em> tagged text as italics. (Be cautious in your use of italicized text. On many workstations with low-resolution display, italicized text appears fuzzy and difficult to read.)

<em>How</em> did you do that?	*How* did you do that?

Strongly Emphasized Text Tag. The <strong> </strong> tag pair indicates that the text should be treated as strongly emphasized text. Most graphical browsers display <strong> tagged text as bold.

This is <strong>very</strong>important	This is **very** important

Keyboarded Text Tag. The <kbd> </kbd> tag pair can be used to show what a patron would either see on a computer screen or type using a computer keyboard. Most graphical browsers display <kbd> tagged text as a fixed-width, mono-spaced font such as Courier.

<kbd>telnet</kbd>	`telnet`

Variable Text Tag. This tag pair <var> and </var> shows variable information that a patron would type using a computer in order to make something happen. Most graphical browsers treat <var> tagged text as either italics or underlined.

<kbd>telnet</kbd><var>Internet address of remote computer </var>	telnet*Internet address of remote computer*

Defined Text Tag. This tag pair <dfn> and </dfn> is used to emphasize a word that is being defined. Most graphical browsers display <dfn> tagged text as bold.

<dfn>ILL</dfn> is short for Interlibrary Loan	**ILL** is short for Interlibrary Loan

Cited Text Tag. This tag is used to make a citation stand out from regular text. Most graphical browsers display <cite> tagged text as italics.

<cite>M. Cronin, 1994.</cite>	*M.Cronin, 1994.*

Physical Tags

Bold Text Tag. The <b> </b> tag pair tells browsers to display the text as bold.

This is <b>very</b> important	This is **very** important

Italicized Text Tag. The <i> </i> tag pair tells browsers to display the text as italics.

<i>How< /i> did you do that?	*How* did you do that?

Typed Text Tag. The <tt> </tt> tag pair tells browsers to display the text a fixed-width, mono-spaced font such as Courier.

To exit, type <tt>logout</tt>	To exit, type `logout`

Other Appearance Tags and Features

Nesting Tags. You can combine (or nest tags) inside other tags for a combined graphic effect. Check various browsers to make sure nested tags produce the visual effect you expect to see.

`<b><i>Fun Internet Resources for Kids</i></b>`   ***Fun Internet Resources for Kids***

Preformatted Text Tag. Using the `<pre> </pre>` tag pair you can take pre-existing text and tag it quickly for inclusion on your Web site. You can use the `<pre>` tag to create columns of information (keep columns to eighty characters or less), put in white space around text without having to master more complicated HTML tags or tag aspects, or add temporary (or rapidly changing) information to your Web pages. Preformatted text has one less-than-optimal feature: it displays text in a mono-spaced font such as Courier. If you use too much pre-formatted text on your Web pages, it will look quite amateurish and dull, so use it sparingly and only when necessary.

`<pre> 1,200 books 2,327 periodicals 1,544 books 945 periodicals</pre>`

```
1,200 books    2,327 periodicals
1,544 books      945 periodicals
```

`<pre>March 9th is the last day to return your books</pre>`

```
March 9th is the last day to return your
books.
```

Character Equivalents. Since you can't use the SHIFT, ALT, or CTRL keys to create special characters in HTML documents, there are character-based and numerical equivalents for these characters that you can code into your documents to get the characters to display. In addition, special characters used in HTML documents, namely angled brackets (<>), quotation marks ("), and ampersands (&) don't normally display. If you need to display one of these characters you will need to use equivalent characters, otherwise your browser will not be able to tell a bracketed word in the text from an HTML tag in brackets, or a hypertext link address (URL) in quotation marks from a quoted piece of text.

There are many character equivalents; we list only the most commonly used here. All HTML texts have complete lists of character equivalents that include foreign diacritical equivalents as well as symbols and subscript/superscript numerals.

Character	Named	Numbered
<	& lt;	& #60;
>	>	& #62;
"	& quot; & #34;	
&	& amp;	& #38;
(	——	& #40;
)	——	& #41;
!	——	& #33;
#	——	& #35;
$	——	& #36;
%	——	& #37;
?	——	& #63;
@	——	& #64;
+	——	& #43;
=	——	& #61;
^	——	& #94;
*	——	& #42;
/	——	& #47;
\	——	& #92;

This is & quot;very & quot; interesting	This is "very" interesting
This is & #34;very & #34; interesting	This is "very" interesting
Smith $amp; Smith	Smith & Smith
& #40;M. Cronin, 1994. & #41	(M. Cronin, 1994.)

LINKING TAGS AND CREATING HYPERLINKS

Hypertext/ hypermedia Link— Text containing HTML commands to connect you to text, graphic, or audio information.

Creating <u>hypertext/hypermedia links</u> in Web documents so that patrons can access different parts of your Web site or information that is located on computers around the world is just as important as tagging document text so that it displays in a way that it is easy to read and interpret. This section discusses link concepts and provides you with step-by-step directions for creating different kinds of basic hyperlinks for your Web site. This section does not include directions for creating imagemap links because they require more than a basic knowledge of HTML.

Links consist of three elements:

- HTML tags and attributes;
- information you want to link to, expressed as file names or URLs; and
- words or graphics which act as links to URLs or file names.

Anchor Tags—An anchor in an HTML document indicates where a link is located. Anchor tags show both the start and end of a hypertext link.

Anchor tags <a></a> identify links for browsers. Information inside of anchor tags identifies the location of the information and how the link will be displayed on your Web page.

You can create different types of links. Links to information on your Web server (called internal links) and links to information out there on the Internet (called external links). Links can be represented by words or pictures (or both). In order to make creating links to HTML documents and URLs to Internet tools as simple as possible, we provide you with step-by-step directions for creating basic kinds of internal and external links, as well as examples of basic links to media sources.

Creating an Internal Link (with text)

You will be creating many internal links within your Web. These links refer you to and from HTML documents stored on your Web server, from one part of your Web site to another, and from general to more detailed information. To do this, create a text phrase that describes where you will find yourself if you choose that link. Follow the steps below to create an internal text link.

1. Decide on a short text phrase that will represent the link.

   Virtual Reference Desk

2. Put <a> tags around the text.

   <a>Virtual Reference Desk</a>

3. Inside the first <a> tag, add the file name of the locally stored HTML document (in quotation marks).

   <a "vrdesk.html">Virtual Reference Desk</a>

   If the file "vrdesk.html" resides in a different directory than the file containing this link, you must include the complete path to that file.

   <a"desks/vrdesk.html">Virtual Reference Desk</a>

4. Finally, inside the first <a> tag, insert HREF= before the HTML document name. (HREF= indicates that what follows it is a hypertext link.)

   <a HREF="vrdesk.html">Virtual Reference desk</a>

5. The phrase will appear as an underlined, highlighted, or colored hypertext link on your Web page. When you select it, you will be connected to and view the HTML document stored on your Web server.

   Virtual Reference Desk

Creating an External Link (with text)

You will also want to add external links to your Web pages. These links can point to Internet tools and HTML documents stored on computers anywhere in the world. When you select these links you will be leaving your Web site and connecting somewhere else. To do this, you can create a text phrase that describes where (outside of your Web site) you will find yourself if you choose that link. The process of creating an external link is very similar to, but not identical to, creating an internal link. Follow the steps below to create an external text link.

1. Decide on a short phrase that will represent the link.

    Library of Congress MARVEL Gopher

2. Put <a> tags around the text.

    <a>Library of Congress MARVEL Gopher</a>

3. Inside the first <a> tag, add the URL (surrounded by quotation marks).

    <a "gopher://marvel.loc.gov">Library of Congress MARVEL Gopher</a>

4. Finally, inside the first <a> tag, insert HREF= before the document name.

    <a HREF="gopher://marvel.loc.gov">Library of Congress MARVEL Gopher</a>

5. The phrase will appear as an underlined, highlighted, or colored hypertext link on your Web page. When you select it, you will be connected to and view the information stored on the Library of Congress's computer which is located in Washington, DC.

    Library of Congress MARVEL Gopher

Choosing the Best Wordings for Links

There are two ways you can use words as links.
- You can write a paragraph of text and choose selected words to act as links.
- You can write short phrases that act as links and arrange them into lists.

Links in Paragraphs

- Paragraphs work best when you want to provide a short description of each link.
- Write what you want to say first, then go back and identify single words or short phrases as links.
- Be sensitive to reading flow. Links tend to slow or stop people from reading further, so make sure that the words you choose as links don't disrupt the flow of the paragraph too much.
- Avoid links that start with "Click here for..." Instead describe what information people will find and why they might want to select the link.

Link lists

- Use link lists when you want to provide lots of links or links can adequately be described in short phrases.
- Add a short paragraph of plain text at the beginning of a link list to explain the hidden benefits of connecting to the links you list.
- Write the link text first. Avoid wordiness, but make the link phrase long enough to be understandable.
- Make wording, voice, and tense consistent throughout the list.
  Connecting to Internet resources
  Using Eudora e-mail
  Subscribing to electronic discussion groups
- Consider using only a word or two of the text as the link.
  Oakland University <u>software archive</u>
- Avoid library jargon as much as possible.
  ILL Policy
  LC Marvel
- Avoid "click here" links.

Creating a Link (with a graphic)

Instead of using words to represent a link, you can also choose to let a copyright-free picture do the job instead. Graphics can make your Web pages more appealing. Many Web sites use graphics to help you quickly select particular tools or information (e.g., your online catalog, specific collections) or go back to the site's home page. Instead of patrons selecting a link by reading and clicking on a text phrase, this type of link provides you with a picture to click on. The process of creating a graphic link bears some similarity to creating a text link, but is slightly more complex. You first need to prepare and load an image onto your Web server. You can either scan and size your own pictures or use CD-ROM and Web-based graphic libraries. (Try browsing Yahoo and other Web indexes under terms like "art" and "graphics" to find Web clip art collections.)

This book does not discuss how to scan, size, or load graphics onto your Web server. How you do this depends on the type of computer and scanning equipment you have and the type of machine that acts as your Web server. The details of how to scan and size pictures and graphics can be found in books about setting up a Web server. (See Chapter 11, p. 221 for a list of titles.) Once you have your graphic scanned and sized, follow the steps below to create graphic links.

1. Decide on the graphic that will represent the link.

2. Download it from the Web or from a CD-ROM graphic collection, scan it, then convert it to a graphic file format (e.g., JPEG, TIFF, GIF), size it, name it, and store it on your Web server.

3. Type the graphic's name and surround it with quotation marks

    "libref.jpg"

4. Next, add IMG SRC= (which indicates that the link is a graphic file) and surround the whole thing with a set of angle brackets. (IMG is the HTML tag and SRC= is an <u>attribute</u>. Both parts let browsers know that the link is to an image and not text.)

    <IMG SRC="libref.jpg">

5. Put <a> tags around the whole thing.

    <a><IMG SRC="libref.jpg"></a>

6. Inside the first <a> tag, add the name of document or URL you want retrieved, surround it with quotation marks, then add HREF=.

    <a HREF="vrdesk.html"><IMG SRC="libref.jpg"></a>

7. The picture, surrounded by a colored line, will appear as a hypermedia link on your Web page. When you select it, you will be connected to an HTML document (in this case the Virtual Reference Desk).

Attribute—A unique quality than an HTML tag can take on. Attributes are added to HTML tags and specify the special conditions for that tag.

Creating a Graphic Link that is Friendly to Text-Only Browsers

When you use a graphic link, those people using text-based browsers like Lynx (or people with slow modems who have to turn off graphics to get the page to load within a reasonable time) are at a disadvantage because they can't see your graphics. Instead of a picture, they see the generic message [IMAGE]. This doesn't give them any idea what they are missing.

There is a way to provide them with a text description of the graphic they can't see. (e.g., [LIBRARY LOGO], [REFERENCE DESK]). Adding customized graphic descriptions for text-based patrons is quite simple. The process is almost identical to creating a graphic link with one extra step added to create the customized message in brackets. Follow the steps below to create text-friendly graphic links.

1. Decide on the graphic that will represent the link. Scan, name, save, and store it on your Web server.

2. Place the graphic name in quotation marks, add IMG SRC= and surround the whole thing with angle brackets.

    <IMG SRC="libref.jpg">

3. Add ALT= and the customized text description of the graphic in square brackets, surrounded by quotation marks. (ALT= is an optional attribute of the IMG tag which indicates that there is an "alternative" description of the graphic.)

    <IMG SRC="libref.jpg" ALT="[REFERENCE DESK]">

4. Put <a> tags around the whole thing.

    <a><IMG SRC="libref.jpg" ALT="[REFERENCE DESK]"></a>

5. Inside the first <a> tag add the HTML document name or URL you want retrieved, surround it with quotation marks, and then add HREF=.

    <a HREF="vrdesk.html"><IMG SRC="libref.jpg" ALT="[REFERENCE DESK]"></a>

6. Those visiting your Web with a graphical browser, with the graphics turned on, will see the picture link. Those using a graphical browser that delays loading graphics until after

the text has all loaded can take advantage of the ALT description to decide if it is worth waiting for the graphics to load before they select the first hypertext link. (This is especially useful over slower modem connections.) Those using text-based browsers will see the customized description of the graphic.

[REFERENCE DESK]

Creating a Link (with a graphic and text)

Often it is wise to give the people who visit your Web site choices. Some people prefer pictures and others prefer words. You can satisfy them both by creating a link that comes in both picture and text form. This process is a combination of the text and graphic steps described previously. Follow the steps below to create both picture and text links to the same HTML document.

1. Decide on the text phrase that will represent the link.

    Virtual Reference Desk

2. Decide on a graphic that will also represent the link. Scan, name, save, and store it on your Web server.

3. Place the graphic name in quotation marks, add IMG SRC= and surround the whole thing in angle brackets.

    <IMG SRC="libref.jpg">

4. Add the short text phrase.

    <IMG SRC="libref.jpg">Virtual Reference Desk

5. Put <a> tags around the whole thing.

    <a><IMG SRC="libref.jpg">Virtual Reference Desk </a>

6. Inside the first <a> tag add the HTML document name or URL you want retrieved, surround it with quotation marks and then add HREF=.

    <a HREF="vrdesk.html"><IMG SRC="libref.jpg">Virtual Reference Desk</a>

7. You will see a picture (libref.jpg) surrounded by a colored line as well as underlined, highlighted, or colored text (Virtual Reference Desk). When you choose either one, you will be connected to an HTML document (in this case the Virtual Reference Desk).

Virtual Reference Desk

Creating Links to Media

You can create links to media resources stored on your Web server or located on Web servers anywhere in the world. When you create media links, patrons selecting them will view graphics (e.g., pictures, maps, diagrams), hear speeches and music, or view short video clips (e.g., cartoons, news shorts). The structure of a media link is identical to a text link, with one minor exception. With media links you need to include the media format and the size of file in the link description. So that people know how big the media file is and what "helper application" software they may need to view or hear it.

<a HREF="libpic.jpeg">Library photo. 120K JPEG</a>
<a HREF="circ.mpeg">Check-out video.</a>650K MPEG
<a HREF="speech.au">Welcome from the Director.</a>AU format, 392K.
<u>Library photo. 120K JPEG</u>
<u>Check-out video. 650K MPEG</u>
<u>Welcome from the Director.</u> AU format, 394K.

You can also create small versions of graphic images (called thumbnail images) and use them as links to full size images. To do this you create two versions of the image using a conversion/sizing program, one full size and one small (less than 5K). There are a number of advantages to using thumbnail images. Being small in size, thumbnail images load quickly. They also allow you to view the image before deciding whether or not to load or download the larger image.

<a HREF="bigcom.gif"><IMG SRC="smalcom.gif"></a>

FIGURE 7.2 Thumbnail and small picture

Creating a Link That Opens Up an E-mail Form

This kind of link is called a "mailto" link. When you create this kind of link, you instruct browsers capable of handling them to open up a form so that patrons can send suggestions or comments via e-mail. Use them wherever you want patrons to provide you with information. "Mailto" links make it possible for patrons to easily comment on library services, suggest materials that the library purchase, or send messages to library staff members. These links are also often found at the bottom of pages along with information found in the <address> tag.

```
<address>
Hudson Public Library<br>
Copyright 1996<br>
<a HREF="mailto:webmaster@
hudson.lib.oh.us">webmaster@hudson.lib.oh.us</a><br>
revised 2/21/96<br>
</ADDRESS>
```

Hudson Public Library
Copyright 1996
webmaster@hudson.lib.oh.us
revised 2/21/96

** In the example above, selecting the link webmaster@ hudson.lib.oh.us opens up an e-mail window on browsers. In order to take advantage of your "mail-to" links, your patrons will need to know how to tell their browser software the name and address of your library's mail server so it can send the e-mail messages to the right place.

GRAPHICS IN HTML DOCUMENTS

This section provides you with some simple ways you can begin to include graphics on your Web site. It does not discuss forms and image maps because they require more than a basic knowledge of HTML.

INLINE GRAPHICS

Inline graphics are not the same as external graphic links. You select and click on a graphic hyperlink to get external graphics to display. Inline graphics are part of HTML documents and load automatically when a Web page loads. Common inline graphics include logos, bullets, directional buttons, fancy graphic lines, and thumbnail images.

<IMG SRC="music.gif">

Inline Images—
Graphics that are part of a Web document and its HTML tagging. When you ask your browser to display a Web page that contains an inline image, it loads right along with the Web page text.

You should discuss the use of <u>inline images</u> during your Web site's design phase. Questions to ask when deciding on the size and number of inline graphics are:

- How important are graphics to the "look" of the page?
- How important are graphics to the content of the page?
- How fast can library-connected computers load pages?
- How fast will most patron computers with modems load pages?
- How many patrons have graphical browsers and how many have text-based browsers?
- How long will patrons wait for pages to load before they give up and go away?

Inline images can come from Web or CD-ROM "clip art" archives. Be sure that images are not copyrighted. (Check for copyright statements on the Web site's home page. When in doubt, ask, don't assume the image is not copyrighted.) You can also scan and size images that you already have on hand (e.g., logos, photographs, maps). This book does not go into detail on how to scan or size images, as this depends on your equipment, expertise, and type of computer you have.

You can insert images into any line of text in an HTML document. Images can either substitute for a word or illustrate a word. Use them sparingly for the greatest effect.

Please <IMG SRC="stop.jpg"> at the Circulation Desk

Please at the Circulation Desk.

You can also control to some degree how text and pictures relate to each other. Text can be aligned with the top, middle, or bottom of a picture by using the ALIGN= attribute.

<IMG SRC="home.gif" ALIGN="top">Our new home
<IMG SRC="home.gif" ALIGN="middle">Our new home
<IMG SRC="home.gif" ALIGN="bottom">Our new home

Our new home

Our new home

Our new home

BACKGROUND TEXTURES AND COLORS

Adding a colored or textured background to each of your Web pages is simple.

1. First locate a texture or color graphic file. Yahoo has a large number of sources for these files. (See Chapter 11, p. 221 for the URLs). Simple, light-colored, subtle backgrounds work best. (You can also create your own colored or textured background graphic file using a program like Corel Draw!)

2. Next, download the background graphic file into the same folder/directory that houses your Web page HTML files.

3. Then, go into each HTML document and add the background attribute and graphic file name, in quotes, to the opening <body> tag

    <body background="white-mi.jpg">

4. Your Web pages now have a textured or colored background that will load whenever anyone accesses them.

5. Check to see how your colored or textured background looks using various graphical browsers. (Results can be fine on one browser and pretty bad on another...)

Image Tips

- Limit the number and size of images as well as the number of colors so that your Web pages load quickly.
- Keep images relevant to your page. When in doubt, don't use an image.
- Be sensitive to copyright laws. Just because you find an image on the Web doesn't mean that is not protected under copyright.
- Get written permission to use images prior to adding them to your Web pages.
- View all images in both black-and-white and color using different browsers.

TO LEARN MORE...

See Chapter 11 for complete bibliographic citations. Also refer to Chapter 11 for additional Web resources.

For information on Web graphics, forms and imagemaps connect to:

- *HTML Goodies Page* http://www.cs.bgsu.edu/~jburns/gifs.html
- *Terry Gould's Graphics* http://www.netaccess.on.ca/~kestrel/list.html
- *Carlos' Forms Tutorial* http://robot0.ge.uiuc.edu/~carlosp/cs317/cft.html
- *Info. Map Tutorial* http://wintermute.ncsa.uiuc.edu:8080/map-tutorial/image-maps.html
- *Imagemap Help Page* http://www.hway.net/ihip/
- *Introduction to CGI and HTML Forms* http://kuhttp/cc.ukans.edu/info/forms/forms-into.html

HTML EDITING PROGRAMS

This section provides you with a brief overview of the different types of HTML editing programs and the features of each.

There are three types of HTML editing programs:

- HTML tagging programs;
- "View as you create" programs; and
- HTML conversion programs.

When you first learn HTML we recommend you manually key in both document text and HTML tags in order to experience first hand how HTML tags are structured. As you become more familiar with HTML you should start using an HTML tagging program to more quickly create error-free tagged documents. If you have a staff member who is familiar with word-processing software, but doesn't have time to learn HTML, or if you will be relying on students to input Web page text, you might consider using an HTML conversion program to convert their word-processed documents to HTML format. Word-processing software combined with "View as you create" programs and HTML conversion programs (such as Internet Assistant) will soon be the norm. The HTML aspects of these programs will be transparent to users and just another feature of standard word-processing software.

HTML TAGGING PROGRAMS

HTML tagging programs help you create documents by inserting HTML tags into a text document for you. (In other words, you don't need to type tags into your document.) Tagging programs come as either stand-alone programs and as "add-ons" to popular word-processing programs. Tag editors provide you with window menu options or tag-specific buttons that place HTML tags around the text you select.

Tagging programs can help you create Web documents faster once you have learned how the different tags work, because they remember all the details about each tag and insert them correctly (a boon for non-expert typists and bad spellers). When you start using a tagging program, it is best to compose your text document first, then use the "tagger" to add HTML tags to it. After a while, you might try writing text and tagging it simultaneously. Some people like this one-step method, others prefer the two-step method because it focuses on one task at a time.

There are lots of both freeware and commercial tagging programs available on the Net and for sale in your local computer store. This is an area of the Net/Web development that is changing almost daily. As we write this book, the most popular Windows tagging programs are: HTML Assistant, HotDog, HTML Easy, and WebEdit. The most popular Macintosh tagging program is HTML.Edit. Check Web indexes like Yahoo to find additional HTML tagging programs. (See also Chapter 11, p. 220–221 for URLs for popular tagging programs.)

"VIEW AS YOU CREATE" PROGRAMS

These are also called WYSIWYG (what you see is what you get) programs. They allow you to see what your page will look like using a Web browser as you create an HTML document. Some programs add tags to a document and display the text as seen through a browser, other programs provide you with pre-tagged Web page templates that you fill out and then view.

Just like tagging programs, there are lots of "view as you create" programs available for free via FTP or for purchase at your local computer store. Newer and better programs are being created all the time. As we write this book, the most popular Windows programs are: HoTMetaL (Softquad), HotDog, Internet Assistant (Microsoft) and Internet Publisher (Novell). The most popular Macintosh programs are PageMill (Adobe) and HTML Editor. Check Web indexes like Yahoo to find additional programs. (See also Chapter 11, p. 220–221 for URLs for popular WYSIWYG programs.)

HTML CONVERSION PROGRAMS

Using HTML conversion programs, you can use your familiar word-processing program to create documents and then let "convertors" change your documents into HTML files. One of the main advantages to using a conversion program is that don't have to type in or even select HTML tags for text, the programs do that for you. Conversion programs almost entirely eliminate typos and errors in tagging.

One of the disadvantages of using a conversion program is that they don't always convert files correctly. You often must go into a converted document and "tweak" the tagging to make it look right. (Kind of hard to do if you don't know a lot of HTML tagging because your conversion program does it for you.) Another disadvantage is that you have to keep two files up to date instead of one (the word-processed file and the HTML-converted file). This can be quite a headache if you update files often.

There are "conversion" programs for most popular word-processing programs. As we write this book the most popular programs for Windows PCs are: Internet Assistant (Microsoft) and Internet Publisher (WordPerfect). New conversion programs are being created all the time. Check a Web index like Yahoo for other conversion programs. (See also Chapter 11. p. 220–221 for URLs for popular conversion programs.)

8 QUALITY CONTROL— TESTING, MAINTAINING AND UPDATING YOUR WEB SITE

TESTING YOUR WEB SITE

This section explains how to do staff and patron testing and provides you with sample testing questions.

After you've designed and authored your Web site you will want to test it thoroughly. As a rule, test your Web site at least 10 percent of the total number of hours you spent planning and building it. Both staff and patrons should test your Web site. Each group will provide you with unique feedback on whether your Web includes the information and/or services they want and need.

You will want testers to provide you with well thought out answers and fresh observations. Therefore, set a time limit on how much time you want your testers to spend in your Web site. (If volunteers spend more than one hour testing, they become too familiar with your site to give you fresh responses.) Keep testing time under one hour also to encourage many patrons and staff to give you input. Since your Web site should be primarily patron-centered, do extensive testing with staff and patrons but incorporate as many patron ideas and suggestions as possible.

There are various types of tests you can run. You can test to make sure that

- Web pages display correctly using various types of browser software.
- your Web can be accessed through your local area- or wide-area network.
- internal navigation links between your Web pages work correctly.
- external links connect to live sites.
- information you provide for patrons and/or staff is organized effectively, that text is easy to read, that graphics are relevant, and that important information is easy to locate.

Checking to make sure that your Web site meets the informational needs of patrons is by far the most complex and varied process. Below we list the major topics testers should respond to. Under each topic we provide you with selected questions you might want to ask them. The questions are appropriate to both staff and patron testing, therefore they are included in this section rather than in the staff or patron testing sections later in this chapter.

We have been careful to provide you with questions that begin with "how," "which," "what," or "why." Questions that begin with these words can't easily be answered with a simple "yes" or "no" response. Whenever possible avoid "are" and "can" questions which elicit mostly yes or no responses. Make sure that questions are followed up with requests for ways to improve your Web. Test questions can

- provide you with alternative wordings for weak, vague, or overly complex text.
- suggest how you can improve graphics.
- suggest different arrangements of information.
- suggest new links, enhanced help files, or easier-to-use comment forms.

SAMPLE TEST QUESTIONS

Arrangement/organization

- How long did it take you to figure out the arrangement or organization of information?

- What do you the like most/least about the arrangement or organization of information?

- What can we do to make the arrangement or organization better?

- How long did you have to search for important information?

- What important information was where you expected it to be?

- What important information was not where you expected it to be? (tell us what it is and where we should move it)

- What is the most important piece of information on each Web page?

- What important information is missing? (Tell us what it is.)

- If using a text-based browser, does any information display badly? (If so tell us what it is and where we can find it.)

Textual style and textual errors

- What typos or spelling errors did you find? (Tell us what they are and where we can find them.)

- What grammatical errors did you find? (Tell us what they are and where we can find them.)

- Which sentences or phrases are too vague? (Help us by suggesting a better wording.)

- Which sentences or phrases are too wordy? (Help us by suggesting a better wording.)

- Which sentences or phrases are too technical? (Help us by suggesting a better wording.)

- Which sentences or phrases are in the passive voice? (Tell us what they are where to find them.)

- Which sentences or phrases are worded too complexly for the intended patron group? (Tell us what they are and where to find them.)

- Which sentences or phrases are too simple for the intended patron group? (Tell us what they are and where to find them.)

- If using a text-based browser does any text display awkwardly, or because of its placement, seem unclear? (Tell us what and where to find it.)

Pictures

- How do pictures relate to the surrounding text?

- Which pictures provide important information?

- Which pictures, if any, are unnecessary and should be eliminated? (Tell us which pictures and where to find them.)

- How does the size of graphics relate to the page content? (e.g., Are any too large or too small?)

- Which pictures are missing? (Give us specific suggestions.)

- Which graphics took a while to understand/figure out? (Tell us which ones and where they are located.)

- Which graphics, if any, are low quality? (Tell us which ones and where we can find them.)

- Which graphics are especially attractive? (Tell us why you like them.)

- Which graphics, if any, are unattractive? (Tell us how we can make them more attractive.)

- On average, how long did it take for most pictures to display? (Estimate in minutes or seconds.)

- Which pictures took too long to display? (Tell us which ones and where they are located.)

- Which pictures load fast enough? (Tell us the speed of your Internet connection if you know it.)

- If using a text-based browser, which text descriptions of pictures are best? (Tell us which ones and where they are located.)

- If using a text-based browser, which text descriptions confuse more than illuminate? (Tell us which ones and where they are located.)

Navigating between pages

- How easy is it to locate text or graphic links to other Web pages?

- Where is the best place for navigation links to be placed on a page? (e.g., top, bottom, along with graphics)

- How consistent is the placement of navigation links from page to page?

- Which navigation graphics or text phrases are difficult/easy to understand? (Tell us which ones and where to locate them.)

- Which pages would you like to "jump" to, but there is no convenient link to them? (Tell us which page has no link and where you would like to "jump.")

- If using a text-based browser, which navigation text links are clear and which are unclear? (Tell us which and where they are located.)

Internal and external links

- Which links, if any, don't work when you select them? (Tell us which and where to locate them.)

- Which text links are hard to understand? (Help us by suggesting a better wording.)

- Which links are too brief to understand easily? (Help us by suggesting a better wording.)

- If using a text-based browser, which links display incorrectly? (Tell us which and where they are located.)

Help information

- In general, how helpful is the "help" information?

- Which help files did you look at and why?

- Which help information did you find easily?

- Which help information did you find difficult to locate? (Tell us which information and where to find it.)

- What information could we add to make "help" better?

- Which pages need help files? (Tell us which pages and what the help file should focus on.)

- Which pages that have help files, don't need them? (Tell us which pages and which help files are not needed.)

- How often will you use the help files once our Web site is available?

- Which help files will you use most/least? (Tell us which and why.)

- If using a text-based browser, which help files display most clearly or provide you with the best format? (Tell us which and where we can locate them.)

Feedback information

- How easy was it to locate places where you could give us your comments and ideas?

- Where on pages should feedback links be located? (e.g., top, bottom)

- What kind of feedback/comments/ideas would you like to regularly provide us? (Give us some samples.)

- How would you like to give us feedback? (Fill out a paper form? Fill out an online form? Write us an e-mail note?)

- Which kinds of feedback would work best as paper or online forms? Which as e-mail notes?

- Which form style do you like best? <this assumes that you provide different styles during testing>

- How can we improve our forms? (Tell us which to improve and give us specific suggestions.)

- How quickly do you expect a response to a comment or idea?

- How would you like us to respond to you?

- What can we do to encourage you and others to provide us with more ideas/feedback?

- What kind of acknowledgement would you like to receive after giving us your feedback/ideas?

- How often do you anticipate filling out forms to give us feedback and ideas?

- If using a text-based browser, how would you like to give us feedback, since your browser probably won't let you fill out forms?

- If using a text-based browser, how well would e-mail response forms fill your needs?

Overall look and feel

- Overall, how well organized is information on our Web site?

- What one feature/page do you like best/least?

- Which graphic/picture do you like best/least?

- What needs to be improved most and why?

- How graphically consistent are pages to one another?

- What one thing can we do to improve our Web's overall look?

- How easy is it to locate important information?

- What two or three pieces of information should we move to make it easier to find? (Tell us what, where it is located now, and where you think it should go.)

- How can we improve the links which help you move around our Web site?

- Which one piece of information do we need to include that is not now a part of our Web site?

- How does our Web site relate to other "community" Web sites?

- What can we do to make our site work better with other "community" Web sites?

Give our Web site an overall grade

Rate each from 1 (low) to 10 (high).

___ It is well organized.
___ It contains valuable information.
___ It is well written.
___ Web text is appropriate to different ages/interests.
___ It contains pictures that provide essential information.
___ Is it easy to move from page to page.
___ It contains easy to understand links.
___ External links meet my information needs.
___ It is easy to locate help files when I need them.
___ It is easy to give you my ideas, comments and feedback.
___ My overall rating is...

STAFF TESTING

It is important that staff take a look at your Web, test it thoroughly, and provide you with lots of feedback before you "go public" with your Web site. In order to plan for, obtain, and review staff feedback, you will need to set up a temporary testing group. This group should include staff from technical and public service areas as well as subject librarians. Group members should be familiar with writing surveys, running surveys, and interpreting survey results.

Staff can test your Web while at their desks, while at a public service point during slow times, or from home if you provide them with dialup access. You can ask staff to check pages while live online, provide them with screen prints of pages, provide them with screen images saved to floppy disk, or send pages to them via e-mail. (Sending pages via e-mail is an excellent way of checking to see how your Web pages will look using a text-based browser.)

Once your testing group gets staff feedback, they need to review all input and make decisions about what will change and what will stay "as is." Good test questions provide them with substantive input as well as specific suggestions for strengthening your Web. Once your testing group has completed its review of staff comments and suggestions, it should inform staff of the changes being made and the reasons for making them. This is also a good time to thank all staff who took part in testing as well as acknowledge staff who did an exceptional job providing suggestions.

PATRON TESTING

Patrons who volunteer to test your Web site can provide you with invaluable input. Be sure to do extensive patron testing, even if it means pushing back your Web's implementation date. Use the same set of questions you used for staff testing and limit testing to one hour per patron. Involve a wide variety of patrons.

- In a school library involve students at all grade levels and with all levels of keyboard/computer experience. Include teachers and school administrators. Be sure to ask English and art teachers to suggest ways to improve your Web's text and graphic look. Consider asking parents, public librarians, and selected board members to test your Web.
- In a college/university library involve all kinds of students, from freshman philosophy majors to graduate engineering students. Make sure that you get a good mix of ages, majors, and computer experience. Ask faculty to help you test your Web, especially the course- and research-related parts. Ask your faculty library committee to help you find faculty testers and get timely responses. Be sure to involve graphic design and English faculty in order to get input on prose style and graphic layout. Involve the appropriate academic department or school in testing subject- centered pages.
- In a public library involve all ages of patrons, from kids to seniors. Involve patrons with various levels of computer experience (e.g., computer user group members, complete beginners) and with different subject interests (e.g., business people, mothers with kids). Ask diverse patrons to test your Web site. Get different groups to look at different

parts of your Web (e.g., kids and parents can look at kid pages, business people can look at commerce- and government-related pages). Involve different ethnic and/or religious groups to make sure that your Web meets their unique needs. Involve school librarians, library trustees, civic officials, and community groups. Find local artists/ designers who will critique your Web. Find local authors/ writers (e.g., local newspaper reporters) who will check your Web prose.

Patrons can test your library's Web while at the library, from their place of business, from campus offices (if they have a Net connection) or from their home/dorm (if you offer dialup access to your site or offer campus network connections to your Web). You can have them sit down and fill out test questionnaires alone or you can have them look at your Web as a group and then gather responses/suggestions using a focus group format.

You can provide patrons, who have network or dialup access to your site, with online versions of test questionnaires so they can send you their responses electronically. You can provide them with floppy disks containing Web page images, provide them with paper printouts, or e-mail selected Web pages to them.

Once patron testing is complete, your testing group should carefully review all comments and suggestions and make decisions about what will change as a result and what will stay "as is." It is important to let patron testers know which of their suggestions you will implement and why. It is equally important to let them know which of their suggestions you can't/won't implement and why. Finally, take the time to thank and acknowledge publicly (via your local newspaper or library newsletter) all the patrons who took the time to help test your Web. You might even consider giving testers a small gift, like a library mug or paper weight, in appreciation for their time and effort.

MAINTAINING AND UPDATING YOUR PAGES

This section provides you with information about who should be involved with keeping your Web site up-to-date.

Once your Web site is tested and ready for local and Net visitors, you need to keep it accurate, up-to-date, timely, and "fresh."

Companies like IBM and Sun Microsystems maintain and update their Web sites daily or weekly. Time-Warner is almost constantly adding interesting and up-to-date information to its Web site. This makes people want to revisit these sites to see what's new. Libraries need to take the same approach to their Web sites. This means getting staff to check current Web links to make sure they are still the best available. It also means that staff must continually look for new Net resources.

- In a school library, involve librarians, library assistants, and maybe even student assistants to help keep your Web up-to-date. If your Web is a district site, involve staff at each location. Assign different pages to various libraries. Ask school computer club members and computing teachers to regularly contribute their latest finds. Make it simple for teachers and students to tell you about important resources you need to add to your Web site, or to alert you to resources that you need to review and possibly remove from your site.

- In a college/university library, rewrite selector, subject specialist, or collection development job descriptions to include keeping selected pages on your Web up-to-date. Set quantifiable performance goals related to this activity. Encourage all staff to actively use the Web. Encourage staff to look at both interesting new Web sites and existing sites. Encourage both faculty and students to let their library liaisons know of valuable Web resources as they hear about them from colleagues or other students. Ask student computer groups and technologically savvy faculty and staff to regularly contribute their newest finds. Make it simple for everyone to submit suggestions via e-mail, Web forms, or paper.

- In a public library make each staff member responsible for a different part of your Web site. Write this new responsibility into each job description and set quantifiable performance goals related to maintaining and updating sections of your Web. Encourage student library assistants and volunteers to alert you to relevant new Web sites or to let you know when an already-linked Web site should be reviewed (and maybe removed). Find community volunteers, like PC user groups and local computer experts, willing to alert you to the newest and best URLs they find. Make it simple for patrons to suggest new Web resources by providing them with simple e-mail, online, or paper forms. Consider receiving suggestions via phone mail.

MAINTAINING VS. UPDATING YOUR SITE

Maintaining your Web site involves checking current hyperlinks to make sure they work correctly. Web sites wax and wane and sometimes disappear totally for no apparent reason. Therefore staff should check important external links weekly and other external links monthly. Luckily there are software packages that automate some of the link checking process. (See Chapter 11, p. 222–223 for link checker software URLs).

Maintaining your Web site also involves checking to see that Web pages contain links to the best available resources. Web resources are often considered the best only until a better one comes along. Review resource links every couple of months to ensure that you provide your patrons with the best of the Net. If you divide up responsibility for different parts of your Web, staff may only have to spend one or two hours a week on these tasks. (This, of course, depends on the size and complexity of your Web as well as the size and complexity of your staff.)

Updating your Web involves searching for and locating new external Web resources to which you can link. There are literally thousands of new Web sites added each day. Most are of little interest to libraries, but there are hundreds of relevant sites added each week. Check other library Web sites for new Web resources to add to your Web site. Join the WEB4LIB Listserv (listerv@ library.berkeley.edu) to pick up new URLs and great ideas on how to improve your library Web pages.

Updating your Web site also involves creating new and different local Web pages for patrons. There are lots of creative ways to present information to patrons through local Web pages. For instance, children's and school librarians may create a single "kids page" for your initial Web, but later develop and add "homework helper" pages or "just for fun" pages. Staff should check other library Web sites for page ideas to "borrow." If you divide up responsibility for different parts of your Web, solicit, and receive suggestions from patrons, staff may only have to spend two to four hours per week on both tasks (depending on your Web and staff size).

Once your staff starts maintaining and updating your Web site you will need to have a group to oversee the process and make final decisions about what to add/not add to your Web site. We recommend you set up a permanent Web "editorial board." Members should represent both staff and patrons. The group should include your head of collection development or acquisitions, an administrator, a staff member, and one or two patrons. Keeping the group small will help speed discussions and decisions as well as make it (hopefully) easier to set up weekly or bi-weekly meetings.

Your editorial board should be responsible for

- setting up procedures for soliciting recommendations and comments;
- writing a Web acquisitions policy;
- writing a Web "style manual";
- reviewing all recommendations and comments;
- making decisions on what goes, what stays, and what gets added to your Web site;
- setting up procedures for recording and keeping track of changes to each Web page; and
- conducting ongoing staff training sessions on how to improve individual Web pages.

LETTING PATRONS KNOW WHAT'S NEW AND DIFFERENT

It's important that you tell patrons what you have added or changed on your Web site so that they will want to visit it often to see what's new. Many libraries create a "what's new and different" page and update is as often as possible (at least every two weeks). Some libraries temporarily add new resources to this page (which acts like a virtual new book shelf). Other libraries temporarily add "current interest" information to this page (e.g., The World Series, Mardi Gras). Keep information on your "what's new" page no longer than a month before either moving it to a permanent location or deleting it.

Getting patrons involved in helping you maintain and update your Web site is often easy. Just asking them for suggestions (and reminding them every once in a while) is all you'll probably need to do to get lots of input. To help, you can

- provide patrons with paper suggestion forms by Web workstations in your library;
- teach patrons to use online suggestion forms and "mailto" links;
- create handouts explaining how to send e-mail suggestions to Web editorial board members, hold periodic focus group sessions to get ideas for new and different local Web pages and
- create short, focused surveys to get feedback on proposed new local Web pages or groups of links.

Be sure to quickly acknowledge patron suggestions with a simple note or e-mail message. This will let patrons know you value their input and it will encourage them to continue to contribute their suggestions and comments.

9 LETTING THE WORLD KNOW—PUBLICIZING YOUR WEB SITE

GETTING THE WORD OUT LOCALLY

This section explains how to let your primary patrons and "community" know your Web site is ready for them to visit.

Once you have spent so much time and effort planning and implementing your Web site it would be a shame if you didn't also spend some time thinking about and doing something to let your patrons know that your Web site exists.

A lot of us have negative feelings about the term "advertising." Most librarians cringe when thinking about using both "advertising" and "libraries" in the same sentence. That's because we're constantly bombarded by mass advertising on TV, radio, and in the print media. You can compare mass advertising to squirting a large number of people with a fire hose, hoping that there will be a few who like to get wet. (Most of us don't like to get wet except when we choose to, hence our negative reaction to most mass advertising pitches.) The good news is that publicizing your Web site is totally different.

Publicizing your Web site is built on the "if you build it they will come" principle. It is a non-intrusive approach to advertising that most libraries can feel comfortable with. You let people know that your Web site exists, tell them how to find it, and then invite people to visit and explore it. Using a water analogy, it's like building a swimming pool and inviting people over to take a dip. They decide if and when they will come over, and most importantly how deep they want to swim once they're in the water.

The hardest part of "if you build it..." advertising is identifying who "they" are. Once you decide who "they" are, you then need to decide why "they" may want to visit your Web site. If you did your planning well and wrote objectives for specific patron groups, all you need to do is review your library vision statement and objectives; then get together a group of outgoing individuals to start writing customized patron invitations to your Web site.

The group of people you assign to publicize your Web site

should include a least one administrator, one public service librarian, one or more staff members who have extensive "community" contacts, and one or more patrons representing your largest patron groups. If you have a community-based Web site you will also want to include members from each Web partner group. Your publicity group should be willing to have fun, get lots of feedback from community groups and individuals, and be willing to stick their collective neck out to ask for help from community groups in advertising your Web site. Done correctly, publicizing your Web site can be the easiest, most rewarding, and fun staff job assignment ever.

The first thing you will need to decide is when to start publicizing your Web site. It's best not to start publicizing your site until you have a *firm* date when it will be available to patrons. Even better, don't publicize it until your site is fully tested and actually running. (In a Web environment, one of the worst things you can do is invite people to explore your site and not have it available.) Once you have your Web site up, you need to decide which patron groups to target first. You should set realistic time frames for each targeted group and work with community groups to get both staff and/or financial support for your marketing efforts.

Publicizing your Web site should be viewed as a ongoing task (just like keeping your Web site up-to-date). Your publicity group should come up with

- ways to let patrons know about new information added to your Web site;
- ways to let patrons know about unique local resources on your Web site;
- ways to attract new patrons to your Web site;
- ways to keep current patrons coming back to your Web site;
- ways to let patrons know about Web-based and library-based services;
- ways to enhance your library's image;
- ways to do Web-based library outreach;
- ways that Web-based information can save patrons time and money; and
- ways to get patron feedback.

LIBRARY-BASED PUBLICITY

School libraries can have student reporters write feature articles (or a regular "Cool Web Stuff" column) for your school newspaper. You can hold class open-houses, where teachers and students can visit your library and do a little hands-on Web surfing. You can create monthly lists of new fun, interesting, and interactive

Web sites for kids to visit (e.g., science fair idea sites, homework helper sites, Nintendo and Sega hints sites) and post them by Web workstations and on school bulletin boards. You can hold Web "scavenger hunts" and run all sorts of after-school Web-based projects.

College/university libraries can create subject-based "netographies" for student researchers and advertise them in campus newspapers. You can hold introductory "brown bag" sessions for undergrads, grads, and faculty/staff. You can set up "open office hours" for interested faculty or students to get one-on-one Web training and questions answered.

Public libraries can hold a "Web-day" celebration and invite officials and the whole community. You can get your local paper to write a series of Sunday feature articles on the Internet, your library, and your Web site. You can write a series of patron-centered "netographies" (e.g., recipes on the Web, travel and airlines on the Web, tax information and forms on the Web) and post them near Web workstations, and include them with regular patron mailings.

"COMMUNITY"-BASED PUBLICITY

If you're working in a school library, you can host a district-level event to showcase your new library Web site. You can offer to talk to PTA groups and community groups about your new Web site and what it can do for students. You can also organize evening or weekend Web classes for parents and interested community members. You can hold a Web open house in conjunction with parent-teacher conferences. You can write a regular column on "professional/teaching Web resources" in the staff newsletter, or work with teachers to co-sponsor a Web project or event. You can advertise your Web site to other school librarians and teachers by posting an announcement to K-12 and library Listservs, listing it in local Web index sites, and sending press releases to professional journals and newsletters.

Public librarians can volunteer to write a regular "What's New on the Web" column for the local paper. You can ask local community groups to advertise your Web site in their newsletters and invite library staff to speak (and demo. the Web) at their meetings. You can advertise your Web site to other public librarians by posting an announcement to public library Listservs and local Web index sites, as well as sending press releases to public library journals and newsletters.

College or university library staff can sponsor a campus-wide "Internet Day" when staff, students, and faculty can come and explore your Web site, ask questions, and attend subject-specific

Web training sessions. You can offer classes on how to access your Web site from home or the dorm. You can offer to do "on-site" subject-specific Web sessions for different academic departments. Finally, you can advertise your Web site to other colleges and libraries by posting an announcement to college and academic Listservs and local Web index sites as well as sending press releases to academic/library journals and newsletters.

GETTING YOUR URL KNOWN

One of the best ways of getting patrons to visit your Web site is to make your Web site's URL easy to find (and easy to remember). You can do this by including it on

- your library stationary;
- staff business cards;
- all recall and overdue notices;
- all library flyers and posters;
- any mailings you regularly send to patrons;
- advertisements in local newspapers and newsletters;
- your library yellow page listing; and
- staff or library e-mail signature files.

GETTING THE WORD OUT ON THE NET

This section explains how to let Net citizens know your Web is ready for them to visit.

At the same time as you are letting local and community-based patrons know that your Web site exists, you also should let Net citizens know your site is up and ready to visit. Advertising to patrons who can be located anywhere on the planet is really quite simple. There are various Web and e-mail tools to help you spread the word.

WEB INDEXES

General Web indexes like Yahoo, Galaxy, or Open Market may index your Web site at no cost to your library. All you have to do is submit your URL online to the index site along with a short description of your Web site and some key words describing your site. Each site's team of indexers will review your submission and make a decision to index your site or not. (Many indexes include library Web sites, so there is a good chance that yours will be included.) Once indexed, patrons can find your Web site by using either the index's structure or by doing a key word search using either the terms you supplied or they indexed it by. (See a list of Web indexes in Chapter 11, p. 211–212.)

WEB SEARCHERS

You can also let a Web search engine (also called a Web spider) know that your Web exists. Web searcher programs wander around the Net looking for sites to key word index. In order to make sure that a Web search program like WebCrawler, Excite, or Lycos finds your site quickly (there are lots of sites for them to look at and index) you can submit your URL and a short description of your Web site to them, so they can then go take a look and index your site. Be sure and include lots of good key words on your homepage. You can also include key words in comment tags in your HTML documents since some searcher programs look at both text and HTML tag contents for key words to index. (See a list of Web searcher programs in Chapter 11, p. 211–212.)

WEB ANNOUNCEMENT SERVICES

In addition to Web indexes and searchers, there are Web sites dedicated to getting your Web site known by others. They vary from very well known sites like "NCSA's What's New" site http://www.ncsa.uiuc.edu/SDG/Software/Mosaic/Docs/whats-new.html to lesser-known sites that focus on different types of Web sites (e.g., personal pages, games pages, "techie pages"). See the Yahoo index under Announcement Services or see Chapter 11, p. 223–235 for some sample announcement sites.

There are also Web pages that list library Web sites. School libraries can get their Web site listed on Web66 or the Hotlist of K-12 School Sites. Public libraries can get their site listed on the St. Joseph County Public Library list of Web sites or the Library Webs page at the University of California, Berkeley. In addition, the Bookwire index, provides links to all types of library Web sites, including special library sites. (See p. 223–225 for all the URLs listed above.)

USENET NEWSGROUPS

There are also newsgroups set up exclusively to announce your Web site. *comp.infosystems.www.announce* focuses solely on Web announcements including announcements of new Web sites. *comp.internet.net-happenings* focuses on Internet announcements and can include new Web site announcements. You can also post announcements of your Web site to library, school, and academic newsgroups, being careful to only post to newsgroups that would be interested in your site. (You can also ask local Bulletin Board System (BBS) operators to post an announcement message about your Web site to members.)

E-MAIL DISCUSSION GROUPS

There are lots of library-related e-mail discussion groups to which you can send announcements of your Web site. WEB4LIB (@library.berkeley.edu) discusses the use of the Web in libraries. Rather than sending a general announcement about your Web site, you might want to send an announcement of unique information you make available on your Web or ask for feedback on your Web site's design, organization, and content. Public libraries might want to send a focused announcement to PUBLIB or PUBLIB-NET (@nysernet.org). School libraries might want to send a focused announcement to LM-NET (@syvm.acs.syr.edu). You can send general announcements to PACS-L (@uhupvm1.uh.edu). Special libraries should send announcements to their respective discussion groups. You can also send announcements of your Web site to K-12 and academic discussion groups and selected regional discussion groups of interest to your patrons. For instance, school libraries might want to post Web site announcements to WWWEDU (@k12.cnidr.org).

There are lots of subject-related discussion groups where you can announce particular parts of your Web site. For instance, sending a message to senior citizen discussion groups announcing your library's senior page will get lots of seniors visiting your Web site. Likewise sending a message to Latino discussion groups announcing your library's Spanish language pages will result in more visitors to these pages.

BOOKS AND MAGAZINES

One of the easiest ways to let other libraries know your Web site is up and available is to send out a press release to local, state, national, and association library newsletters and journals. Many of them will print your press release if you explain what your Web site contains, especially if it contains interesting patron-centered pages or local information of wider interest. You can also send Web site press releases to "Yellow Page" publications (See p. 210) or to magazines that list new and interesting Web sites (e.g., NetGuide and The Net).

GETTING OTHER LIBRARIES OR GROUPS TO LINK TO YOUR SITE

Another way that Net patrons can find out about your site is to have your library linked on another library's Web site. Many libraries belong to local, state, or national consortia or organizations (e.g., NOLA Regional Library System, Association of Research Libraries). These groups often have Webs which provide links to all member Web sites. Libraries in local or small consortia will often create links to all other member sites. Be sure and inform library and educational groups and individual consortium members of your URL so they can create a link to your Web site if they wish.

MEASURING HOW SUCCESSFUL YOUR WEB SITE IS

This section explains how you can evaluate use of your site.

If you have a dedicated Net connection, you can use either your Web server's transaction logs or special statistical software (like WWWSTAT or GWSTAT) to get an idea of who is visiting your Web site. You can easily count the number of times your Web site is accessed. This can tell you at least how good of job you've done advertising your Web site. However, counts can be inaccurate. Web pages with inline graphics often are counted as multiple accesses. Sometimes Web pages don't get counted when they should. (e.g., When your Web page is stored in a remote computer's memory and re-accessed by using that browser's "history" feature.)

Web logs or statistical software can tell you the Internet address of the computer that is accessing your Web site, not the name of the person who is using the computer. (Of course, you can ask Net patrons to sign a Web "guest book" or fill out a form which will provide you with this information.)

If you have software that counts the number of times individual pages are accessed, you can see which pages are the most popular and which are the most ignored. You can use this information to make under-utilized pages more interesting and to make popular pages even better (or know to update them more often). Transaction logs and statistical software also can tell you where your page is linked (e.g., someone's personal Web page, a Web index, or a list of library Web links).

Analyzing Web statistics on how long a person is connected to your Web site or individual pages can also be misleading. You really can't tell if a person is reading a Web page carefully or is taking a coffee break or talking on the phone while connected to your site.

One valuable way you can use rough statistics is to see how well Web-based response forms or "mailto" links work. Using statistics, you can see which forms are filled out most frequently. (You can also roughly calculate the percentage of users that stop to fill out forms when they visit your Web site.) You can vary the placement of forms/response links on different pages to see which works best. You can also vary how you organize Web response form information, and use statistics to help you select the form that patrons like and respond to most often.

The whole topic of collecting and using Web statistics could, and hopefully soon will, fill a book. It's best to work with a knowledgeable computer person to get your Web site's statistics. Use statistics to get a broad idea how your Web site is being used, but don't rely too heavily on their accuracy. Consider purchasing a good Web statistical package to provide you with more detailed and accurate statistics. Good free or inexpensive programs are GWSTAT and WWWSTAT; their URLs are listed below. Bring in a computer consultant familiar with computer-generated statistics to help you select the best program.

TO LEARN MORE...

See Chapter 11 for complete bibliographic definitions. Also refer to Chapter 11 for additional print and Web resources.

For more information on publicizing your Web site read and connect to:

- *World Wide Web Marketing* by J. Sterne
- *GWSTAT* http://dis.cs.umass.edu/stats/gwstat.html
- *How to Announce Your New Web Site* http://ep.com/faq/webannounce.html
- *Library Webs* http://sunsite.berkeley.edu/LibWeb/
- *Public Libraries with WWW Servers* http://sjcpl.lib.in.us/homepage/PublicLibraries/
- *Places to List Your Web Page* http://www.ntg-campus.com/ntg/public.html
- *World Wide Web Library* Directory http://www.albany.net/~ms0669/cra/libs/libs.html
- *WWWSTAT* http://www.ics.uci.edu/WebSoft/wwwstat/

10 USER-FRIENDLY WEB DEFINITIONS

This glossary contains many of the Web and Internet terms used in this book. We purposely use non-technical words when defining the terms. We find that many of the books on the Web and Net contain definitions that are so technical they are almost impossible for anyone but a computer "techie" to understand. We hope these more friendly definitions will help you understand Web and Net jargon better.

Anchor

Anchors in an HTML document indicate where a link is located. Anchors show both the start and end of a hypertext link.

ASCII (American Standard Code for Information Interchange)

A coding scheme that translates text files in various formats into a common format. ASCII text can be transferred to and from different computers and then re-translated back into "native" forms of text for each computer.

Attribute

A unique quality that an HTML tag can take on. Attributes are added to HTML tags and specify special conditions for that tag.

Bookmark

A Web site saved by your Web browser software that you can access again whenever you want.

Browser

A Web client program that accesses and displays Web documents. Common Web browsers are Netscape, Mosaic, and Lynx.

Bulleted List

A non-numerical list in an HTML document, each item of which is preceded by a graphical dot or asterisk.

CERN (European Lab for Particle Physics)

Place in Switzerland where the World Wide Web project originated and the Web was developed.

CGI (Common Gateway Interface)

A program that links an external program and a Web server. CGIs are often written in C, Perl, or Applescript languages. They are commonly used to process Web-based image maps and forms.

Client, Web

A program running on your computer that makes it possible to connect to a Web site, Gopher, e-mail, or FTP server. Clients customize the way these Internet tools both look and work.

CSU/DSU (Channel Service Unit/Data Service Unit)

A device, used with a dedicated Net connection, that allows your computer to talk to other computers over a digital phone line.

Dedicated Connection

A type of Internet connection that provides twenty-four hour-a-day, seven-day-a-week access to the Internet.

Dialup IP Connection

A type of dialup connection in which you load TCP/IP, SLIP, or PPP software, and various types of client software onto your computer. Dialup IP connections allow you to use graphical client software, such as Netscape, to browse the Web.

Dialup Shell Connection

The most basic of Internet connections that is restricted to text-based access.

DNS (Domain Name System)

The system of linking a numerical Internet address (e.g., 199.28.159.1) to a pseudonym name (e.g., iage.com). When using the Web, you will get a DNS error if your browser can't locate the pseudonym name for the computer you request.

Document, HTML

A document that displays on your browser as a Web page. An HTML document is one that contains tags which advise your browser software how to display it.

Download

The process of transferring ASCII texts or binary programs to your local computer.

Element

The basic unit of an HTML document. Elements are displayed inside tag pairs or followed by single tags (e.g., <title>Library Web Page</title>)

FAQ (Frequently Asked Questions)

A document in question and answer format that addresses commonly asked questions related to software, hardware, or a Net/Web tool.

Firewall

A security program or hardware/software combination that protects a computer or LAN from unwanted external intrusion by those not part of the LAN, or not lawfully having access to a computer.

Forms

Information tagged so that the finished document, as seen through a graphical browser, looks like a form that you can fill out. Forms are used for such things as key word searching, suggesting book purchases, or providing patron feedback.

404 Not Found

When using graphical browser software you may get a response from your browser that it was unable to locate the URL you typed in. When getting a "404" message be sure to check that you typed in the URL correctly. Often when URLs change you will also get this message.

FTP (File Transfer Protocol)

An Internet function that enables you to transfer files from one computer to another.

Gateway

A system/program that makes it possible to transfer information between incompatable networks or applications.

GIF (Graphics Interchange Format)

A color graphic file format developed by CompuServe for storing images. GIF files are often found on the Web because they are a common Web graphic format. They can be identified by the .gif file extension.

Gopher

A tool developed at the University of Minnesota that provides simple, menu-based access to Internet resources. Gophers access texts stored both locally and remotely. They enable you to search Gopher menus using key word tools named Veronica and Jughead.

Graphical Browser

A browser program capable of displaying graphics, video, sounds, etc. in addition to text. Graphical browsers, such as Netscape, enable you to navigate the Web and the rest of the Internet using a mouse or other pointing device.

Graphics File

A file, in any of several graphic formats, that you can view using a graphical browser and/or additional helper-application software.

GUI (Graphical User Interface)

Software that hides the technical stuff. GUIs make using a computer application a matter of pulling down a menu or clicking on an icon. Windows is a common graphical user interface that hides complex DOS routines and makes running application software like word processors simple. Netscape and Mosaic are common Web graphical user interfaces that hide HTML tags, hypertext link structures, and make cruising the Web simple.

Header

A type of HTML tag that makes text larger or bolder in order to set selected text apart from regular text. There are different levels of headers that display in different sizes, etc. so that you can create various levels of main- and sub-heads in a document.

Helper Applications

Software (in addition to browser software) that you load on your computer. Helper software lets you view graphics, videos and hear sounds. Browsers launch helper-applications when you ask them to display files they can't handle themselves.

History List

A list of Web sites you have visited during your current Web browser session.

Home page

1) The primary page of a Web site. 2) The place where you start exploring the Web when you start up your browser software.

HotJava

A Web browser capable of accessing HTML and downloading and running executable program simultaneously. HotJava was developed by Sun Microsystems for use on UNIX workstations.

HTML (Hypertext Markup Language)

A system of tags used to describe and create World Wide Web

documents and display them using browser programs. HTML consists of text and tags which assign text special meanings, formatting instructions, and hypertext links. HTML is a subset of SGML.

HTML Editing Program

A program that simplifies the creation of HTML documents. HTML editors provide you with menu item or button choices for inserting HTML tags into text. They eliminate the need for you to type in HTML tags manually.

HTTP (HyperText Transfer Protocol)

A program that enables your browser to communicate with a Web server, get a response from the server, and transfer the data requested back to your computer.

Hypertext (Hypermedia)

Text formatted with links that enable you to jump from one place on the Web to another.

Hypertext/media Link

Text containing HTML commands to connect you to the requested text, graphic, or audio information.

Image Map

Graphics that represent HTML documents which have hypertext/media links imbedded in them. By clicking on a spot on an image map you select a link, ask your browser to make the connection for you, and display the information you request.

Inline Image

Graphics that are part of a Web document and its HTML tagging. When you ask your browser to display a Web page that contains an inline image, it loads right along with the Web page text.

Internet

An international network of computer networks that communicate with each other using a common communication language (protocol) called TCP/IP.

Internet Access Provider

A company that provides or sells you an Internet connection.

Internet Address

The address of a computer on the Internet. Internet addresses can be expressed as numerals, called an IP address (e.g., 129.22.4.2) or as a series of letters, called an pseudonym address (e.g., po.cwru.edu).

Intranet

An internal, institutional network that uses TCP/IP and Internet tools . . . a private Internet.

IP Address

A numerical expression of an Internet address (e.g., 199.18.159.1).

ISDN (Integrated Services Digital Network)

A type of phone line service. With an ISDN connection, your regular phone line, which has been switched to ISDN service, can carry both digital (computer) and analog (voice) signals.

Java

An object-orientated program language developed by Sun Microsystems for use on UNIX workstations.

JPEG (Joint Photographic Experts Group)

A graphics file format and compression technique developed by the committee for which it is named. JPEG reduces the size of a graphics file by as much as 96 percent. They can be identified by the .jpeg file extension.

LAN (Local Area Network)

A group of computers connected together and managed by a server computer. LAN-connected computers can share information, programming, e-mail, and Internet connectivity.

Line-Mode Browser

A short name for the CERN Line-Mode Browser that connects dumb terminals to the Net and Web.

Link, Hypertext

A connection to another Web site or another part of the same site. Links appear on Web pages as differently colored, underlined, or highlighted text. Links can also be represented by a graphic button, picture, or be imbedded in an image map.

Lynx

A text-based Web browser developed at the University of Kansas. Lynx is most often used with dialup shell Internet accounts.

MBONE (Multimedia Backbone)

An international multimedia network-within-a-network that

makes it possible for users to exchange real time or prerecorded video and audio.

MIME (Multipurpose Internet Mail Extensions)

A set of rules for sending and receiving multimedia electronic mail, such as word processing files.

Mirror Site, Web

A "carbon copy" Web site that contains the same information as a popular site. Mirror sites help Web users access popular information by providing them with an alternative connection site.

Modem

A device for connecting a computer to a phone line, so that you can transmit data.

Mosaic

Short for NCSA Mosaic, the first Web browser to support graphics, sound, and video in addition to text. Mosaic requires that you have either a dedicated Internet connection, a SLIP/PPP/ISDN connection, or a program to make a dialup shell connection act like a SLIP/PPP connection.

MPEG (Motion Picture Experts Group)

A video file compression format developed by the group for which it is named. To run MPEG videos, your browser may need to launch helper-application software. They can be identified by the .mpeg file extension.

Multimedia

A term that describes a Web document which integrates text, graphics, sound, video, etc.

Navigation

A term for getting around the Web (or moving from link to link).

NCSA (National Center for Supercomputing Applications)

An organization, based at the University of Illinois Urbana-Champaign, that developed NCSA Mosaic, the first graphical browser.

Netscape

A popular Web browser that supports graphics, sound, and video in addition to text. Netscape requires that you have a dedicated Internet connection, a SLIP/PPP/ISDN connection, or a program to make a dialup shell connection act like a SLIP/PPP connection.

Node

A single computer, a network, or a computer system connected to the Internet.

Numbered List

A list of items in an HTML document, arranged hierarchically by number.

Online Service

A commercial network that offers subscribers both locally loaded databases and a gateway to the Internet.

Page, Web

A Web document that is displayed by your browser. Single Web pages are linked together to form a Web presence or Web site.

Player (Viewer)

Players/viewers are helper-application programs that let you play videos or hear sounds while viewing a Web page.

Port Number

A number that identifies where you can find specific Internet application programs on a server (e.g., gopher://riceinfo.rice.edu:70 or http://guaraldi.cs.colostate.edu:2000). Port numbers in URLs let computers know where to find and access a particular resource.

Postscript

A page description language used to save and print both text and graphics.

PPP (Point-to-Point Protocol)

The most popular type of direct Internet connection. With a PPP connection your computer has TCP/IP loaded on it, its own Internet address, and is directly connected to the Internet. Having a PPP connection means that you can use a graphical browser, like Netscape, to access media in addition to text.

Protocol

Specific rules (e.g., TCP/IP) that define how computers respond when communicating with each other and pass data to and from each other. If two computer use the same protocol then can "talk." If not, they can't.

RFC (Request for Comments)

A document written by committees involved with Internet policy or development that answers questions or explains established or proposed Internet standards.

Router

A telecommunication device, used with a dedicated net connection, that makes decisions about the path that incoming and outgoing Internet traffic will take.

Search Engine, Web

A program that searches the Web using key words supplied by you. WebCrawler, Lycos, and Excite are well-known Web search engines.

Server

1) A computer that runs server software. 2) The software that allows one computer to offer services to another computer.

SGML (Standard Generalized Markup Language)

A standard for creating tagged documents that describes text, graphics, and other aspects of a document. HTML is a subset of SGML.

SLIP (Serial Line Internet Protocol)

The first popular type of direct Internet connection. With a SLIP connection, your computer has TCP/IP loaded on it, its own Internet address and is directly connected to the Net. Having a SLIP connection means that you can use a graphical browser, like Netscape, to access media in addition to text.

Sound File

A computer file that contains digitized sound. Sound files can be heard by launching "helper-application" programs along with your graphical browser.

Tag

HTML Instructions placed around regular text to indicate how Web browsers should display the text (e.g., Oh Boy!).

TCP/IP (Transmission Control Protocol/Internet Protocol)

The protocol, or common "language," of the Internet that allows different computers and computer systems to communicate with each other.

Telnet

An Internet function that allows your computer to log-in to a remote computer and view its resources. You can telnet to Net resources using a Web browser, but you are restricted to viewing text.

Text-Based Browser

A browser program that does not display graphics or provide multimedia access. Typically text-based browsers are used mostly with dialup shell Internet connections.

Title

The title of a single Web page, as named by the HTML author. The words you use in the title become the words that are saved by and displayed as bookmarks.

URL (Uniform Resource Locator)

1) An Internet address expressed so that any Web browser can understand it. 2) What you type to get your Web browser to search for, connect to, and display a Web site (or other Net tool). 3) The information imbedded into a hypertext link that tells your browser which computer to connect to and which information to request from the server computer. 4) A way of citing a Web or other Internet resource.

URN (Uniform Resource Name)

A possible future standard of identifying a Web site. Unlike a URL, which indicates the resource's location, a URN names the resource regardless of its location.

Usenet

A worldwide network for distributing and viewing messages. It is available through many Internet service providers, mainframe computers, and many Web browsers.

Video File

A computer file composed of digitized video. To view a video file, you may need to launch a helper-application program along with your graphical browser.

Viewer

A separate helper-application program you store on your computer along with your Web browser program. Viewers help browsers display graphics, video, and multimedia. Some newer browsers come with selected viewers included as part of the browser software package.

Web Browser

Another name for a Web client. Browsers contact Web servers, request information from them, and display that information to you in the way you want to see it.

Web Client

Another name for a Web browser. Web clients contact Web servers, request information from them, and display that information to you in the way you want to see it.

Web Index

A Web site that categorizes Web resources into groups or disciplines so you can find and access them. Most Web indexes can be key word searched. Yahoo and Galaxy are well-known Web indexes.

Web Server

A computer that houses Web documents and that runs HTTP software in order to communicate and share information with Web clients.

Web Site, Web Presence

A series of organized Web pages, created by libraries, businesses, government agencies, groups, or individuals.

Webmaster, WebWeaver

The person in charge of the technical aspects of a Web site.

WinSock

Software that makes it possible for a Windows-based computer to perform Internet functions using Windows.

World Wide Web (The Web, WWW, W3)

A worldwide network of computers that provides hypertext/media links to a wide variety of Internet resources.

11 LEARN MORE ABOUT IT—A BIBLIOGRAPHY OF PRINT AND NET RESOURCES

IN THE BEGINNING—WEB BASICS

PRINT

December, John and Neil Randall. *The World-Wide Web Unleashed.* 2nd ed. Indianapolis, IN: Sams.net, 1995.

Ford, Andrew. *Spinning the Web.* New York: Van Nostrand Reinhold, 1994.

Internet and the World Wide Web Simplified. Foster City, CA: IDG, 1995.

Pfaffenberger, Bryan. *World Wide Web Bible.* New York: MIS, 1995.

Stout, Rick. *The World Wide Web Complete Reference.* Berkeley, CA: Osborne McGraw-Hill, 1996.

Vaugn-Nichols, Steven, et al. *Inside the World Wide Web.* Indianapolis, IN: New Riders, 1995.

WebWeek. Westport, CT: Mecklermedia, 1995-.

URLS

Beginners Guide to Uniform Resource Locators
http://www.ncsa.uiuc.edu/demoweb/url-primer.html

Entering the World-Wide Web (K. Hughes)
http://www.eit.com/web/www.guide/guide.toc.html

FAQ: WWW (T. Boutell)
http://www.boutell.com/faq/

Usenet Newsgroups
news:comp.infosystcms.www.misc
news:comp.infosystems.www.advocacy

Web Review (ezine)
http://gnn.com/wr

Web Success (ezine)
http://www.kdcol.com/~ray/index.html

Yahoo: WWW
http://www.yahoo.com/Computers/World_Wide_Web/

WEB BROWSERS

PRINT

Angell, David. *Mosaic for Dummies.* Windows ed. San Mateo, CA: IDG, 1995.

Ernst, Warren. *Using Netscape.* Indianapolis, IN: QUE, 1995.

Grimes, Galen. *Ten Minute Guide to Netscape for Windows 95.* Indianapolis, IN: QUE, 1995.

Gunn, Angela. *Plug-n-Play Mosaic for Windows.* Indianapolis, IN: Sams, 1994.

———— and Joe Kraynak. *Plug-n-Play Netscape for Windows.* Indianapolis, IN: Sams, 1995.

Hoffman, Paul. *Netscape and the World Wide Web for Dummies.* Foster City, CA: IDG, 1995.

Keeler, Elissa and Robert Miller. *Netscape Virtuoso.* New York: MIS, 1996.

Pfaffenberger, Bryan. *Mosaic User's Guide.* New York: MIS, 1994.

Reiss, Levi and Joseph Radin. *Open Computing Guide to Mosaic.* Berkeley, CA: Osborne McGraw-Hill, 1995.

Tauber, David. *Surfing the Internet with Netscape.* San Francisco, CA: Sybex, 1995.

URLS

CERN Line-Mode Browser
http://www.w3.org/pub/WWW/LineMode/

Enhanced Mosaic (Spyglass)
http://www.spyglass.com/

Internet Explorer (Microsoft)
http://www.microsoft.com/

Lynx
ftp://ftp2.cc.ukans.edu/pub/

Lynx User's Guide
http://www.cc.ukans.edu/lynx_help/Lynx_users_guide.html

NCSA Mosaic
http://www.ncsa.uiuc.edu/SDG/Software/Mosaic/
 NCSAMosaicHome.html

NCSA Mosaic for Macintosh User's Guide
http://www.ncsa.uiuc.edu/SDG/Software/Mac_Mosaic/Docs/
 MacMosa.0.html

NCSA Mosaic for Windows User's Guide
http://www.ncsa.uiuc.edu/SDG/Software/WinMosaic/Docs/
 Docs.html

Netscape
http://www.netscape.com/

Oracle
http://www.oracle.com/

SlipKnot
http://www.interport.net/slipknot/slipknot.html

Sprynet Mosaic
http://www.spry.com/tools/browsers/index.html

Usenet Newsgroups
news:comp.infosystems.www.browsers.mac
news:comp.infosystems.www.browsers.ms-windows
news:comp.infosystems.www.browsers.x
news:comp.infosystems.www.browsers.misc

Web Explorer (IBM)
http://www.ibm.com/

Yahoo: WWW Browsers
http://www.yahoo.com/Computers/World_Wide_Web/Browsers/

WWW Clients
http://www.w3.org/pub/WWW/Clients.html

HELPER APPLICATIONS

URLS

Graphical and Internet Viewers
http://fox.nstn.ca/~nstn2879/viewers.html

Macintosh Helper Software
http://wwwhost.ots.utexas.edu/mac/main.html

RealAudio (Progressive Network)
http://www.realaudio.com/

Setting Your Web Reader Properly
http://sunsite.unc.edu/wm/about/tech.html

Streamworks (Xing Technologies)
http://www.xingtech.com/

Windows Helper Software
ftp://ftp.ncsa.uiuc.edu/Mosaic/Windows/

MEDIA

URLS

Audio File Formats Guide
http://cuiwww.unige.ch/OSG/AudioFormats/

FAQ: JPEG (T. Lane)
ftp://rtfm.mit.edu/pub/usenet-by-group/comp.graphics.misc/
   JPEG_image_compression_FAQ%2C_part_1_2

FAQ: MPEG (L. Filippini)
http://www.crs4.it/~luigi/MPEG/

Index to Multimedia
http://viswiz.gmd.de/Multimediainfo/

Internet Clip Art
http://www.eff.org/pub/Graphics

Rob's Multimedia Lab
http://www.acm.uiuc.edu/rml/

Quicktime Continuum (Apple Computer Inc.)
http://quicktime.apple.com/

Sites with Audio Clips
http://www.eecs.nwu.edu/~jmyers/other-sounds.html

Vincent Voice Library
http://web.msu.edu/vincent/index.html

THINK BIG—LOOK AT THE ISSUES FOR LIBRARIES

PRINT

Benson, Allen and Linda Fodemski. *Connecting Kids and the Internet: A Handbook for Librarians, Teachers and Parents.* New York: Neal-Schuman, 1996.

Chrobak, Kimberly. "Build a WWW Homepage for Your School." *School Library Media Activity Monthly* (May 1995): 39+.

Cisler, Steve. "Library Web Sites." *Library Journal* (November 15, 1995): 24+.

Ensor, Pat L. "The Wonderful World of the Web in the Library..." *Technicalities* (March 1995): 6-7.

Fredette, Kevin. "Building a Better Beast: Designing a WWW Home Page for Government Resources." *Documents to the People* (June 1995): 111-14.

Garlock, Kristen and Sherry Piontek. *Building the Service-Based Library Web Site.* Chicago, IL: ALA, 1996.

Goldberg, Beverly. "Virtual Patrons Flock Into the Internet Public Library." *American Libraries* (May 1995): 387-88.

Healy, Paul D. "Untangling the Web: the World Wide Web as a Reference Tool." *RQ* (Summer 1995): 441-4.

Lester, Daniel W. "The Web Goes Prime Time: Libraries Can Too." *Technicalities* (April 1995): 6-7.

"Spokane PL Create Web Page Just for Kids." *School Library Journal* (November 1995): 12-13.

Thompsen, Elizabeth. *Reference and Collection Development on the Internet.* New York: Neal-Schuman, 1996.

Valauskas, Edward and Monica Ertel. *The Internet for Teachers and School Library Media Specialists.* New York: Neal-Schuman, 1996.

Van Brakel, Pieter. "Some Guidelines for Creating World Wide Web Home Page Files." *The Electronic Library* (August 1995): 383-88.

URLS

American Association of Law Libraries
http://lawlib.wuacc.edu/aallnet/aallnet.html

American Association of School Librarians (AASL)
http://ericir.syr.edu/ICONN/AASL/aasl.html

American Library Association (ALA)
http://www.ala.org/

Art Libraries Society of North America (ARLIS-NA)
http://web.syr.edu/%7Edcstam/

Association of Research Libraries (ARL)
http://arl.cni.org/

Canadian Library Association (CLA)
http://www.ncf.carleton.ca/freeport/prof.assoc/cla/menu

CAUSE
http://cause-www.colorado.edu/cause.html

Coalition for Networked Information (CNI)
http://www.cni.org/CNI.homepage.html

*Coalition for Networked Information Discovery and Retrieval
 (CNIDR)*
http://cnidr.org/welcome.html

Consortium for School Networking (CoSN)
http://cosn.org/

Educom
http://www.educom.edu/

Electronic Freedom Foundation (EFF)
http://www.eff.org/

International Society for Technology in Education (ISTE)
ISTE@Oregon.uoregon.edu

Internet Society (ISOC)
http://info.isoc.org/home.html

InterNic
http://www.internic.net/

Medical Library Association (MLA)
http://www.kumc.edu/MLA

Music Library Association (MLA)
http://www.music.indiana.edu/tech_s/mla/index.htm

National Center for Supercomputing Applications (NCSA)
http://www.ncsa.uiuc.edu/

National Public Telecomputing Network (NPTN)
http://www.nptn.org/

Public Library Association
http://pla.org/

Research Libraries Group (RLG)
http://www.rlg.stanford.edu/welcome.html

Special Libraries Association (SLA)
http://ils.unc.edu/SLA/

GOING ONLINE—GETTING AN INTERNET CONNECTION AND WEB SERVER

LANS/NETWORKING/MODEMS

Print

Gibbons, Dave et al. *Using Your Modem*. Indianapolis, IN: QUE, 1995.

Jenkins, Neil and Stan Schatt. *Understanding Local Area Networks*. Indianapolis, IN: Sams, 1995.

Kee, Eddie. *Networking Illustrated*. Indianapolis, IN: QUE, 1994.

Lowe, Doug. *Client/Server Computing for Dummies*. Foster City CA: IDG, 1995.

————. *Networking for Dummies*. San Mateo, CA: IDG, 1994.

Rathbone, Tina. *Modems for Dummies*. San Mateo, CA: IDG, 1994.

URLs

Curt's High Speed Modem Page
http://www.teleport.com/~curt/modems.html

FAQ: Data Communication Cables
http://www.cis.ohio-state.edu/hypertext/faq/usenet/LANs/cabling-faq/faq.html

FAQ: ISDN
http://www.cis.ohio-state.edu/hypertext/faq/usenet/isdn-faq/faq.html

FAQ: LANs/Ethernet
http://www.cis.ohio-state.edu/hypertext/faq/usenet/LANs/ethernet-faq/faq.html

Usenet Newsgroups
bit.listserv.big-lan
comp.dcom.isdn
comp.dcom.lans.ethernet
comp.dcom.modems
comp.sys.ibm.pc.hardware.com

INTERNET CONNECTIONS

Print

Abraham, Ralph et al. *The Web Empowerment Book: An Introduction and Connection Guide to the Internet and the World Wide Web.* Santa Clara, CA: TELOS, 1995.

Angell, David. *ISDN for Dummies.* Foster City, CA: IDG, 1995.

Derfler, Frank. *PC Magazine Guide to Connectivity.* Emeryville, CA: Ziff-Davis, 1995.

Estrada, Susan. *Connecting To the Internet: A Buyer's Guide.* Sebastopol, CA: O'Reilly, 1993.

Internet Connections: A Librarian's Guide to Dial-up Access and Use. Chicago, IL: Library and Information Technology Association, 1995.

Gilster, Paul. *The SLIP/PPP Connection: The Essential Guide to Graphical Internet Access.* New York: J. Wiley and Sons, 1995.

Schneider, Karen G. *The Internet Access Cookbook: A Librarian's Comprehensive Guide to Low-Cost Connections.* New York: Neal-Schuman, 1995.

Wilensky, Marshall and Candace Leiden. *TCP/IP for Dummies.* Foster City, CA: IDG, 1995.

URLs

Internet Access Guide
ftp://nic.merit.edu/introducing.the.internet/access.guide

POCIA (Providers of Commerical Internet Access)
http://www.celestin.com/pocia/index.html

Service Provider Web Servers
http://www.eit.com/web/www.servers/networkservice.html

SlipKnot (software that emulates a SLIP connection)
http://www.interport.net/slipknot/slipknot.html

The LIST
http://thelist.com/

TIA (software that emulates a SLIP connection)
http://marketplace.com/tia/tiahome.html

Yahoo: Access Providers
http://www.yahoo.com/Business/Corporations/
  Internet_Access_Providers/

WEB SERVERS

Print

Chandler, David M. *Running a Perfect Web Site*. Indianapolis,
  IN: QUE, 1995.
Magid, Jonathan et al. *The Web Server Book*. Chapel Hill, NC:
  Ventana, 1995.
Net.Genesis and Deva Hall. *Build a Web Site*. Rocklin, CA:
  Prima, 1995.
Stein, Lincoln. *How to Set Up and Maintain a World Wide Web
  Site*. Reading, MA: Addison-Wesley, 1995.
Tilton, Eric et al. *Web Weaving: Designing and Managing an
  Effective Web Site*. Reading, MA: Addison-Wesley, 1996.
Web Developer. Westport, CT: Mecklermedia, 1996-.
WebSmith. Seattle, WA: SCC, 1995-.

URLs

Building Web Servers
http://www.sybergroup.com/

Usenet Newsgroups
news:comp.infosystems.www.servers.mac
news:comp.infosystems.www.servers.ms-windows
news:comp.infosystems.www.servers.unix
news:comp.infosystems.www.servers.misc

Web Server Primer (N. Torkington)
http://www.vuw.ac.nz/who/Nathan.Torkington/ideas/www-
  servers.html

Web66: Internet Server Cookbook
http://web66.coled.umn.edu/Cookbook/contents.html

WebMaster Magazine
http://www.cio.com/WebMaster/

Webmaster's Reference Library
http://www.webreference.com/

Webmaster's Starter Kit
http://wsk.eit.com/wsk/doc/

Webster (ezine)
http://www.tgc.com/webster.html

SECURITY

Print

Cohen, Frederick. *Protection and Security on the Information Superhighway.* New York: J. Wiley and Sons, 1995.

Weiss, Aaron. *The Complete Idiot's Guide to Protecting Yourself on the Internet.* Indianapolis, IN: QUE, 1995.

URLs

FAQ: WWW Security
http://www-genome.wi.mit.edu/WWW/faqs/www-security-faq.html

Site Security Handbook
ftp://nic.merit.edu/documents/fyi/fyi_08.txt

ONCE YOU ARE CONNECTED— LEARNING AND TEACHING THE WEB

TRAINING

Print

Brandt, D. Scott. "Teaching the World Wide Web With a Text-Based Browser." *Computers in Libraries* (April 1995): 49-51.

Burke, John. *Learning the Internet: A Workbook for Beginners.* New York: Neal-Schuman, 1995.

Clement, Gail. *Science and Technology on the Internet: An Instructional Guide.* Berkeley, CA: Library Solutions, 1995.

Jaffe, Lee. *Introducing the Internet: A Trainer's Workshop.* Berkeley, CA: Library Solutions, 1994.

Junion-Metz, Gail. *K-12 Resources on the Internet: An Instructional Guide.* Berkeley, CA: Library Solutions, 1996.

Kovacs, Diane. *The Internet Training Guide.* New York: Van Nostrand Reinhold, 1995.

Peete, Gary. *Business Resources on the Internet: An Instructional Guide.* Berkeley, CA: Library Solutions, 1995.

Robison, David. *All About Internet FTP: Learning and Teaching To Transfer Files on the Internet.* Berkeley, CA: Library Solutions, 1994.

Ryan, Steve. "Training With the Web: Internet Training in an Academic Library Environment." *Australian Library Journal* (February 1995): 22-26.

Schiller, Nancy. "Internet Training and Support: Academic Libraries and Computer Centers..." *Internet Research* (Summer 1994): 35-47.

Tennant, Roy et al. *Crossing the Internet Threshold: An Instructional Handbook.* Berkeley, CA: Library Solutions, 1995.

URLs

Commonly Asked Questions When Conducting Internet Training
http://www.sir.arizona.edu/rick/conduct.html

IETF Training Materials Catalogue
http://coolabah.itd.adelaide.edu.au/TrainMat/catalogue.html

Information Technology Training Initiative
http://info.mcc.ac.uk/CGU/ITTI/ITTI.html

Internet Training Resources
http://www.brandou.ca/~ennsnr/Resources/Welcome.html

Nerd World: Internet Training
http://www.nerdworld.com/nw155.html

Net Etiquette Guide (A. Rinaldi)
http://www.fau.edu/rinaldi/netiquette.html

Nettrain
listserv@ubvm.cc.buffalo.edu

Nettrain Archive
ftp://ubvm.cc.buffalo.edu/nettrain/

Resources for Internet Trainers
http://lcweb.loc.gov/global/internet/trainers.html

Trainmat
http://mailbase.ac.uk:7070/11/

Trainpack
ftp://ftp.ncl.ac.uk/pub/network-training/

DOING RESEARCH USING THE NET/WEB

Print

Boehning, Julie C. "Web Site Rating Directories Increase." *Library Journal* (October 1, 1995): 14+.

Campbell, Dave and Mary Campbell. *The Student's Guide to Doing Research on the Internet.* Reading, MA: Addison-Wesley, 1995.

Li, Xia and Nancy Crane. *The Official Internet World Guide to Electronic Styles: A Handbook To Citing Electronic Information.* Westport, CT: Mecklermedia, 1996.

Maxymuk, John. *Finding Government Information on the Internet: A How-To-Do-It Manual.* New York: Neal-Schuman, 1995.

Morville, Peter et al. *The Internet Searcher's Book: Locating Information, People and Software.* New York: Neal-Schuman, 1996.

Pfaffenberger, Bryan. *Web Search Strategies.* New York: MIS, 1994.

Rowland, Robin and Dave Kinnaman. *Researching on the Internet.* Rocklin, CA: Prima, 1995.

WEB DIRECTORIES

Print

Eager, Bill. *Using the World Wide Web.* Indianapolis, IN: QUE, 1994.

Internet World WWW Yellow Pages. Foster City, CA: IDG, 1996.

Jamsa, Kris and Ken Cope. *World Wide Web Directory.* Las Vegas, NV: Jamsa, 1995.

New Rider's Official World Wide Web Yellow Pages. Indianapolis, IN: New Riders, 1996.

Point Communications. *World Wide Web Top 1000.* Indianapolis, IN: New Riders, 1996.

Powell, Bob and Karen Wickre. *Atlas to the World Wide Web.* Emeryville, CA: Ziff-Davis, 1995.

Richardson, Robert. *Web.Guide.* San Francisco, CA: SYBEX, 1995.

Turlington, Shannon. *Walking The World Wide Web.* Chapel Hill, NC: Ventana, 1995.

Waltz, Mitzi. *The Internet International Directory.* Emeryville, CA: Ziff-Davis, 1995.

WEB INDEXES AND SEARCH ENGINES

CD ROM

Filo, David and Jerry Yang. *Yahoo! Unplugged: Your Discovery Guide to the Web.* Foster City, CA: IDG, 1995.

URLs

Aliweb
http://web.nexor.co.uk/public/aliweb/search/doc/form.html

Alta Vista
http://www.altavista.digital.com/

All-in-One Search Page
http://www.albany.net/allinone/

Archieplex
http://cuiwww.unige.ch/archieplexform.html

CUI WWW Catalog
http://cuiwww.unige.ch/cgi-bin/w3catalog/

CUSI
http://www.usask.ca/cusi/cusi.html

DejaNews
http://www.dejanews.com/forms/dnquery.html

Excite
http://www.excite.com/

Galaxy
http://galaxy.tradewave.com/galaxy.html

InfoSeek
http://home.netscape.com/home/internet-search.html

Inktomi
http://inktomi.berkeley.edu/query.html

Lycos
http://lycos.cs.cmu.edu/

MetaCrawler
http://metacrawler.cs.washington.edu:8080/

Netnews
http://harvest.cs.colorado.edu/Harvest/brokers/Usenet

Open Text
http://www.opentext.com/

Savvy Search
http://guaraldi.cs.colostate.edu:2000/form

Starting Point
http://www.stpt.com/

WANDEX
http://wandex.netgen.com/cgi/wandex

WebCrawler
http://webcrawler.com/

Searching Page
http://www.oise.on.ca/webstuff/general-docs/searching.html

World Wide Web Worm
http://wwww.cs.colorado.edu/home/mybryan/WWWW.html

WWW Search Engines (A Nedashkovsky)
http://ugweb.cs.ualberta.ca/%7Ementor02/search/search-
  all.html

WWW Spiders
http://info.webcrawler.com/mak/projects/robots/robots.html

WWW Virtual Library
http://www.w3.org/hypertext/DataSources/bySubject/
  Overview.html

WWW Wanderer
http://netgen.com/cgi-bin/wendex/index/

Yahoo
http://www.yahoo.com/search.html

SELECTED REFERENCE

URLs

Campus Newspapers on the Internet
http://beacon-www.asa.utk.edu/resources/papers.html

CityLink
http://banzai.neosoft.com/citylink/

CWIS Web
http://www.rpi.edu/dept/library/html/cwis/cwis.html

Federal Web Locator
http://www.law.vill.edu/fed-agency/fedwebloc.html

Free-Nets Homepage
http://herald.usask.ca/~scottp/free.html

Legal Information Institute
http:/www.law.cornell.edu/

Library Resources on the Internet
http://www.library.nwu.edu/.nul/libresources.html

Master Listserv List
http://www.tile.net/tile/listserv/index.html

Michigan Clearinghouse Guides to the Internet
http://www.lib.umich.edu/chhome.html

Nonprofit Organizations on the Internet
http://www.ai.mit.edu/people/ellens/non.html

Online Books
http://www.cs.cmu.edu/Web/books.html

Online Journals
http://www.lib.cmu.edu/bySubject/CS+ECE/lib/journals.html

Reference Resources via the WWW
http://vm.cfsan.fda.gov/reference.html

Taxing Times
http://www.scubed.com/tax/index.html

Virtual Tourist
http://www.tourist.com/

World Map
http://pubweb.parc.xerox.com/map

Yahoo: Reference
http://www.yahoo.com/Reference/

DIVERSITY RESOURCES, GENERAL

URLs

Galaxy: Cultures
http://galaxy.tradewave.com/Community/Culture.html

Guide to Diversity Resources
gopher://una.hh.lib.umich.edu:70/00/inetdirsstacks/
    diversity%3Aheise

RiceInfo Gopher: Anthropology and Culture
gopher://riceinfo.rice.edu:70/11/Subject/Anth/

Yahoo: Society and Culture
http://www.yahoo.com/Society_and_Culture/Cultures

SELECTED SPECIFIC RESOURCES

URLs

A-Z of Jewish and Israel Related Resources
http://www.ort.org/anjy/a-z/

African American Haven
http://www.auc.edu/~tpearson/haven.html

AfriNET
http://www.afrinet.net/

Aging Research Centre
http://www.hookup.net:80/mall/aging/agesit59.html

Berit's Kids Sites
http://www.cochran.com/theosite/Ksites.html

Canadian Kids Homepage
http://www.onramp.ca/~lowens/107kids.htm

Chicano/LatinoNet
http://latino.sscnet.ucla.edu/

China Connections
http://www.eel.ufl.edu/~wli/china.html

Chinese Historical and Cultural Project
http://www.dnai.com/~rutledge/CHCP_home.html

Chinese Internet Directory
http://www.ceas.rochester.edu:8080/ee/users/yeung/main.html

Cybermuslim Information Collective
http://www.uoknor.edu/cybermuslim

El Mundo Latino
http://www.mundolatino.org/

Felipe's Things Latino Page
http://edb518ea.edb.utexas.edu/html/latinos.html

Fun Kid Links
http://www.ucalgary.ca/~darmstro/kid_links.html

Gay and Lesbian Resources
http://users.aol.com/chilibn/

Gay, Lesbian, Bisexual Links
http://txdirect.net/~slakjr/glb/

Guide to Aging Resources
http://astro.ocis.temple.edu/~pgcmed/post.html

Guide to Bisexual Resources
gopher://una.hh.lib.umich.edu:70/00/inetdirsstacks/
    bisexual%3Ahamilton

Guide to Black/African Resources
http://www.sas.upenn.edu/African_Studies/Home_Page/
    mcgee.html

Guide to Islamic Resources
gopher://una.hh.lib.umich.edu:70/00/inetdirsstacks/
    muslim%3Acajee

Hmong Homepage
http://www.stolaf.edu/people/cdr/hmong/

Interesting Places for Kids
http://www.crc.ricoh.com/people/steve/kids.html

Japan Resource Page
http://www.culturewave.com/culturewave/jrp/jrp.html

JapanStation
http://www-leland.stanford.edu/~december/japan.html

Japan Window (for kids)
http://jw.stanford.edu/KIDS/kids_home.html

Judaica Web World
http://www.nauticom.net/users/rafie/judaica-world.html

The Kids on the Web
http://www.zen.org/~brendan/kids.html

Kids Page
http://www.clark.net/pub/journalism/kid.html

KidsWeb
http://www.npac.syr.edu/textbook/kidsweb/

Kwanzaa Information Center
http://www.melanet.com/melanet/kwanzaa/kwanzaa.html

LatinoLink
http://www.latinolink.com/

Latino Web
http://www.catalog.com/favision/latnoweb

Native American Resources
http://www.ota.gov/nativea.html

Native Web
http://kuhttp.cc.ukans.edu/~marc/native_main.html

Page for Chinese
http://www.geopages.com/SiliconValley/1250/

The Peoples Homepage
http://www.cris.com/~nlthomas/

Seniors Site
http://seniors-site.com/

T n T: Daily Cool Stuff for Kids
http://www.polar7.com/tnt/

Uncle Bob's Kids' Page
http://gagme.wwa.com/~boba/kids.html

Universal Black Pages
http://www.gatech.edu/bgsa/blackpages.html

VietWeb
http://vweb.net/vietweb

PLANNING AND DESIGNING YOUR WEB SITE

PRINT

Albertson, Rick et al. *Designer's Guide to the Internet.* Indianapolis, IN: Hayden, 1995.

Digital Publishing Design Graphics. Ferny Creek, Victoria, Australia. 1994-.

Fahey, Mary Jo. *Web Publishers' Design Guide for Macintosh.* Scottsdale, AZ: Coriolis, 1995.

—— and Jeffrey Brown. *Web Publishers' Design Guide for Windows.* Scottsdale, AZ: Coriolis, 1995.

Horton, William. *Designing and Writing Online Documentation.* New York: J. Wiley and Sons, 1994.

—— et al. *The Web Page Design Cookbook.* New York: J. Wiley and Sons, 1996.

Marcus, Aaron et al. *The Cross-GUI Handbook: For Multiplatform User Interface Design.* Reading, MA: Addison-Wesley, 1995.

McClements, Nancy and Cheryl Becker. "Writing Web Page Standards." *C&RL News* (January 1996): 16-17.

Schneider, Karen. "Five Steps To a Home Page on the World Wide Web." *American Libraries* (October 1995): 918+.

Tilton, Eric et al. *Web Weaving: Designing and Managing an Effective Web Site.* Reading, MA: Addison-Wesley, 1996.

Valauskas, Edward and Nancy John. *The Internet Initiative: Libraries Providing Internet Services and How They Plan, Pay, and Manage.* Chicago, IL: ALA, 1995.

Weinman, Lynda. *Designing Web Graphics.* Indianapolis, IN: New Riders, 1996.

Wilson, Stephen. *World Wide Web Design Guide.* Indianapolis, IN: Hayden, 1995.

URLS

Guide To Web Style
http://www.sun.com/styleguide/

HTML Design Notebook (D. Connolly)
http://www.w3/org/pub/WWW/People/Connolly/drafts/html-
design.html

Web Design Guidelines for Public Libraries
http://www.tiac.net/users/mpl/guidelines.html

Web Page Design
http://www.unc.edu/~mikey/web.htm

Web Style Manual (P. Lynch)
http://info.med.yale.edu/caim/StyleManual_Top.HTML

WWW Weavers
http://www.nas.nasa.gov/NAS/WebWeavers/

GENERAL POLICIES

URLs

Acceptable Use Policies (ERIC)
gopher://ericir.syr.edu:70/11/Guides/Agreements

Acceptable Use Policies (EFF)
gopher://gopher.eff.org:70/11/CAF/library

Acceptable Use Policies (NSLS)
gopher://nslsilus.org:70/11/int_resources/policies

Acceptable Use Policies (Rice)
gopher://riceinfo.rice.edu:1170/00/More/Acceptable

Acceptable Use Policy Definition (B. Manning)
gopher://riceinfo.rice.edu:1170/00/More/Acceptable/bmanning

Bill of Rights and Responsibilities for Electronic Learners
gopher://riceinfo.rice.edu:1170/00/More/Acceptable/brrec

Developing a School or District AUP (C. Wolf)
gopher://inspire.ospi.wednet.edu:70/00/Accept_Use_Policies/
IN_policies.txt

Freedom Pages
http://www.bluehighways.com/freedom/

SCHOOL, DISTRICT, AND PUBLIC LIBRARY POLICIES

URLs

Aberhart High School
gopher://ericir.syr.edu:70/00/Guides/Agreements/Wm.Aberhart

Berkeley Public Library
http://www.ci.berkeley.ca.us/bpl/files/usepolicy.html

Boulder Valley School District
gopher://ericir.syr.edu:70/00/Guides/Agreements/BVSD

California Dept. of Education
gopher://goldmine.cde.ca.gov:70/00/C_D_E_Info/Technology/
    Acceptable_Use/Policy

Common Knowledge (Pittsburgh)
gopher://ericir.syr.edu:70/00/Guides/Agreements/Pittsburgh

Lawrence Public Library
http://www.databank.com/~lawrlibr/iag.html

Montgomery-Floyd Regional Library
http://www.bluehighways.com/freedom/polmfrl.html

NuevaNet
gopher://riceinfo.rice.edu:1170/00/More/Acceptable/nueva

Oceanside High School
gopher://ericir.syr.edu:70/00/Guides/Agreements/Oceanside

Queens Borough Public Library
http://www.bluehighways.com/freedom/polqbpl.html

St. Joseph County Public Library
http://sjcpl.lib.in.us/homepage/SJCPLDisclaimer.html

Virginia Public Education Network
gopher://riceinfo.rice.edu:1170/00/More/Acceptable/pen

GETTING DOWN TO IT—AUTHORING YOUR WEB SITE

HTML

Print

Aronson, Larry. *HTML 3 Manual of Style*. Emeryville, CA: Ziff-Davis, 1995.

December, John and Mark Ginsburg. *HTML and CGI Unleashed*. Indianapolis, IN: Sams.net, 1995.

Ford, Andrew. *Spinning the Web*. New York: Van Nostrand Reinhold, 1995.

Graham, Ian. *HTML Sourcebook*. New York: J. Wiley and Sons, 1995.

Heslop, Brent and David Holzgang. *HTML Publishing on the Internet for Macintosh*. Chapel Hill, NC: Ventana, 1995.

Holden, Greg. *Publishing on the World Wide Web for Macintosh*. Indianapolis, IN: Hayden, 1995.

Lemay, Laura. *More Teach Yourself Web Publishing with HTML in a Week*. Indianapolis, IN: Sams.net, 1995

———. *Teach Yourself Web Publishing with HTML in a Week*. Indianapolis, IN: Sams.net, 1995.

———. *Teach Yourself Web Publishing with HTML 3.0 in a Week*. Indianapolis, IN: Sams.net, 1996.

Morris, Mary. *HTML Authoring for Fun and Profit*. New York: Prentice Hall, 1995.

Randall, Neil. *Using HTML*. Indianapolis, IN: QUE, 1996.

Scharf, Dean. *HTML Visual Quick Reference*. Indianapolis, IN: QUE, 1995.

Shafran, Andy and Don Doherty. *Creating Your Own Netscape Web Pages*. Indianapolis, IN: QUE, 1995.

Taylor, Dave. *Creating Cool Web Pages with HTML*. Foster City, CA: IDG, 1995.

Tittel, Ed and Steve James. *HTML for Dummies*. Foster City, CA: IDG, 1995.

URLS

A Beginner's Guide to HTML
http://www.ncsa.uiuc.edu/General/Internet/WWW/HTMLPrimer.html

Guide to HTML (I. Graham)
http://www.utirc.utoronto.ca/HTMLdocs/NewHTML/htmlindex.html

HTML
http://www.w3.org/pub/WWW/MarkUp/

HTML Bad Style Guide
http://www.earth.com/bad-style/

HTML Quick Reference
http://www.ncsa.uiuc.edu/General/Internet/WWW/
    HTMLQuickRef.html

HTML Style Guide
http://www.york.ac.uk~risw100/hobby/style.html

Usenet Newsgroups
news:alt.hypertext
news:comp.infosystems.www.authoring.html
news:comp.infosystems.www.authoring.misc

Web Publishing Guide
http://www.cl.cam.ac.uk/users/gdr11/publish.html

WWW and HTML Tools
http://www.w3.org/hypertext/WWW/Tools/

HTML EDITORS

Print

Kidder, Gayle and Stuart Kidder. *HTML Publishing with Internet Assistant*. Chapel Hill, NC: Ventana, 1995.

URLs

HotDog
http://www.sausage.com/

HoTMetaL for Windows (SoftQuad)
http://www.sq.com/

HTML Assistant for Windows
http://www.microsoft.com/

HTML Easy!
http://www.seed.net.tw/~milkylin/

HTML.edit
http://ogogpogo.nttc.edu/tools/HTMLedit/HTMLedit.html

HTML Editor for Macintosh (R. Giles)
http://dragon.acadiau.ca:1667/~giles/HTML_Editor/

Internet Assistant (Microsoft)
http://www.microsoft.com/msoffice/freestuf/msword/download/
    ia/default.htm

Internet Publisher (Novell)
http://wp.novell.com/elecpub/intpub.htm

List of Editors and Converters
http://www.w3.org/hypertext/WWW/Tools/

PageMill (Adobe)
http://www.adobe.com/Apps/PageMill/

WebEdit
http://www.nesbitt.com/

Yahoo: HTML Editors
http://www.yahoo.com/Computers/World_Wide_Web/
   HTML_Editors/

GRAPHICS FOR WEB PAGES

URLs

Anthony's WWW Images
http://www.cit.gu.edu.au/images/Images.html

FAQ: Backgrounds
http://www.sci.kun.nl/thalia/guide/color/faq.html

HTML Goodies Page
http://www.cs.bgsu.edu/~jburns/gifs.html

Terry Gould's Graphics
http://www.netaccess.on.ca/~kestrel/list.html

Usenet Newsgroup
news:comp.infosystems.www.authoring.images

Yahoo: Backgrounds
http://www.yahoo.com/Computers_and_Internet/
   World_Wide_Web/Page_Design_and_Layout/
   Color_Information/

Yahoo: Icons
http://www.yahoo.com/Computers_and_Internet/Internet/
   World_Wide_Web/Programming/Icons/

Yahoo: Transparent Backgrounds
http://www.yahoo.com/Computers_and Internet/Internet/
   World_Wide_Web/Programming/Transparent Images/

CGI AND IMAGE MAPS

URLs

Carlos' Forms Tutorial
http://robot0.ge.uiuc.edu/~carlosp/cs317/cft.html

Common Gateway Interface
http://hoohoo.ncsa.uiuc.edu/cgi/overview.html

Graphical Information Map Tutorial
http://wintermute.ncsa.uiuc.edu:8080/map-tutorial/image-
maps.html

Imagemap Guide & Tutorial Sites
http://www.cris.com/~automata/tutorial.shtml

Imagemap Help Page
http://www.hway.net/ihip

Imagemap Tutorial (NCSA)
http://hoohoo.ncsa.uiuc.edu/docs/tutorials/imagemapping.html

*An Instantaneous Introduction to CGI Scripts and HTML
Forms*
http://kuhttp.cc.ukans.edu/info/forms/forms-intro.html

Usenet Newsgroup
news:comp.infosystems.www.authoring.cgi

QUALITY CONTROL—TESTING AND UPDATING YOUR WEB SITE

URLS

Checker
http://www.ugrad.cs.ubc.edu/spider/q7f192/branch/checker.html

Doctor HTML
http://www.imagiware.com/RxHTML.cgi

HTML Analyzer
http://www.w3.org/hypertext/WWW/Tools/Pitcow/
Overview.html

HTML Validation Service
http://www.webtechs.com/html-val-svc/

Htmlcheck
http://uts.cc.utexas.edu/~churchh/htmlchek.html

Ivrfy
http://www.cs.dartmouth.edu/~crow/Ivrfy.html

URL-minder
http://www.netmind.com/URL-minder/example.html

Verify Links
http://wsk.eit.com/wsk/dist/doc/admin/webtest/verify_links.html

Viewer Test Page
http://www-dsed.llnl.gov/documents/WWWtest.html

Weblint
http://www.unipress.com/weblint

Yahoo: Validation/Checkers
http://www.yahoo.com/Computers_and_Internet/Software/
 Data_Formats/HTML/Validations_Checkers.

LETTING THE WORLD KNOW— PUBLICIZING YOUR WEB SITE

PRINT

Cisler, Steve. "Promoting the Internet in Your Library." *Library Journal* (June 15, 1995): 26+.

Ellsworth, Jill and Matthew Ellsworth. *Marketing on the Internet.* New York: J. Wiley and Sons, 1995.

Sterne, Jim. *World Wide Web Marketing.* New York: J. Wiley, 1995.

WebConnect. Boca Raton: Worldata, 1996-.

URLS

Announcement Archives
http://cair-archive.kaist.ac.kr:80/Archive/Announce/

Bookwire Index: Canadian Libraries
http://www.bookwire.com/index/Canadian-Libraries.html

Bookwire Index: Special Libraries
http://www.bookwire.com/index/Special-Libraries.html

Bookwire Index: US Libraries
http://www.bookwire.com/index/US-Libraries.html

Canadian Libraries on the WWW
http://library.usask.ca/~scottp/canlib.html

GWSTAT
htp://dis.cs.umass.edu/stats/gwstat.html

Hotlist of K-12 School Sites
http://sendit.sendit.NoDak.edu/k12/

How To Announce Your New Web Site
http://ep.com/faq/webannounce.html

Library Webs
http://sunsite.berkeley.edu/Libweb/

NCSA's What's New
http://www.ncsa.uiuc.edu/SDG/Software/Mosaic/Docs/whats-
new.html

New Sites Gopher
gopher://liberty.uc.wlu.edu/11/internet/new_internet

Open Market Directory
http://www.directory.net/

Places to List Your Web Page
http://www.ntg-campus.com/ntg/public.htm

Promoting Your Page
http://www.orst.edu/aw/stygui/propag.htm

Public Libraries with WWW Servers
http://sjcpl.lib.in.us/homepage/PublicLibraries/
PublicLibraryServers.html

Scout Report
http://rs.internic.net/scout_report-index.html

State Library Gopher and Web Listing
http://www.state.wi.us/agencies/dpi/www/statelib.html

Usenet Newsgroups
news:comp.infosystems.www.announce
news:comp.internet.net-happenings

US Public Libraries on the Web
http://www.tiac.net/users/mpl/public.libraries.html

Web66 School List
http://web66.coled.umn.edu/schools.html

What's New Lists
http://www.clark.net/pub/global/new.html

What's New Metalist
http://www.seas.upenn.edu/~mengwong/whatsnew.list.html

What's New Too!
http://newtoo.manifest.com/WhatsNewToo/submit.html

World Wide Web Library Directory
http://www.albany.net/~ms0669/cra/libs/libs.html

WWWSTAT
http://www.ics.uci.edu/WebSoft/wwwstat/

Yahoo: Announcement Services
http://www.yahoo.com/Computers_and_Internet/Internet/
    World_Wide_Web/Announcement_Services/

APPENDIX: SAMPLE WEB PAGES

For descriptions of individual pages, see the list of figures on pp. v–viii.

Serving Cornell University's College of Agriculture and Life Sciences, College of Human Ecology, Division of Biological Sciences, and Division of Nutritional Sciences

Welcome

The Mann Library Gateway is now on the Web, making it possible to offer more features and provide access to more databases and library services on the network:

Gateway

List of the library's print holdings, plus direct access to hundreds of databases -- references, statistics, and full text.

What's New

- Announcements (updated 3/1/96)
- New Books
- New Databases

Instructional Support

- Course Materials
  Course support materials -- tests, handouts, etc.
- Technologies for Learning Center (TLC)
  Instructional technology -- use and consultation.
- Workshops and Tutorials: Spring '96
  Information technology and access -- learning opportunities.

Information

- User Guides and Helper Applications
- About Mann Library

Send your questions or comments to Mann Library Reference at mann_ref@cornell.edu or phone us at (607) 255-5406.

★ ★ ★ ★ Recipient of 4-star rating for ease of use from McKinley's Internet Directory

This page was last updated Saturday, 1/13/96.

Mann Library Home Page : New Books Page

Requesting a Book From the New Book Shelf

To place a hold on a book, we'll need your name, ID #, and e-mail address.

Name:

E-mail address:

Cornell ID number:

Select any title you'd like to charge out. You will be notified when the titles are available.

- ☐ American food habits in historical perspective
- ☐ Cancer and self-help : bridging the troubled waters of childhood illness
- ☐ Flowering plant origin, evolution & phylogeny
- ☐ Generation on hold : coming of age in the late twentieth century
- ☐ Individualization in childhood and adolescence
- ☐ Land, custom and practice in the South Pacific
- ☐ Old southern apples
- ☐ Patient self-determination in long-term care : implementing the PSDA in medical decisions
- ☐ Storm over a mountain island : conservation biology and the Mt. Graham affair
- ☐ The family Trichodoridae : stubby root and virus vector nematodes
- ☐ The future of play theory : a multidisciplinary inquiry into the contributions of Brian Sutton-Smith
- ☐ The loch : a year in the life of a Scottish loch
- ☐ The neonatal pig : development and survival
- ☐ Treating the changing family : handling normative and unusual events

You will receive notification when the book is available to be checked out.

[Mail This] [Clear Form]

Document Access Unit, Albert R. Mann Library, Cornell University, (807) 255-3298
This page was last updated on Tuesday, February 27, 1996 8:17:38 AM

<u>Mann Library Home Page</u>

User Guides

GENERAL GATEWAY INFORMATION

- <u>World Wide Web: How to Use Netscape</u>: Learn about the Internet and how to use the Netscape browser to search the Gateway. Also includes information on how to find for other interesting and useful WWW resources.

- <u>BearAccess</u>: Instructions to connect to the WWW version of the Gateway, how to configure helper applications, how to print and download files.

DATABASE GUIDES

The database guides that include information about the search software are available on the database description pages. Use the <u>Gateway Catalog</u> (subject, title, or keyword) to find the database you are interested in. After you click on the database title, you will be prompted with a short description of the file, including its content, producer, update frequency, etc. This is the database description page. For help on how to search the database, click on the help icon that is on the right margin following the title of the database.

Enter the title of the database in the following box to go to the database description page:

Database Title: [_____] [Go] [Clear]

In addition to the above method, you can also locate user guides by referring to the **Database Guides List**.

- <u>Go to the Database Guides List</u>

Crossroads...from here you can:

Go back to:
- o <u>Mann Library Home Page</u>

Direct questions to Mann Library Reference: <u>mann_ref@cornell.edu</u>, (607) 255-5406.
This page was generated on September 12, 1995.

New!

Request for a subscription to the

Mann Gateway Announcements Mailing List

Subscribe to this service and keep up with what's happening on the Mann Gateway!

The Mann Gateway Announcements Mailing List is an automated email list. After you have registered, you will automatically receive news about Mann's Gateway. Whenever we put news items on Mann's Web "Announcements" page, we will also send them to you via email (two or three messages per week).

Your name:

Your affiliation:

Your email address:

eg. xyz9@cornell.edu

Send request   Clear Form

Crossroads...from here you can go to:

Announcements Page

New Books

New Databases

Gateway Catalog

Mann Library

Albert R. Mann Library
Cornell University, Ithaca, NY 14853

Send your questions or comments to Mann Library Reference at mann_ref@cornell.edu or phone us at (607) 255-5406.

The Rochester Hills Public Library

I RHPL Home Page I Community Information I Internet Resources I

The Rochester Hills Public Library is an award-winning building located on the banks of the Paint Creek in downtown Rochester, Michigan. The library was dedicated on November 1, 1992, the newest building in the seventy-year history of Rochester libraries.

About 8,000 people a week are served by the staff at RHPL. The library contains more than 166,231 books, 300 magazine subscriptions, 12,000 cassettes, compact discs, Books on Tape, and videos, and access to a world of information through the Internet. Recent circulation statistics show that 909,630 items were checked out from the library in the past year.

The library is governed by a Board of Trustees and the library director is Christine Lind Hage.

Library Information

- RHPL Online Catalog
- Location, Hours, Telephone Numbers
- Information about Library Cards and Borrowing Policies
- Departments and Services: Circulation, Adult, Youth, Outreach
- Internet Access
- Local History Room
- Friends of the Library
- The *Almanac*, a quarterly publication of library news and events
- Five-year Plan
- Annual Report for 1994-95
- RHPL FAQ, Frequently Asked Questions about RHPL, such as „ How big is the aquarium?‰

I RHPL Home Page I Community Information I Internet Resources I

The Greater Rochester Community
| RHPL Home Page | Library Information | Internet Resources |

The City of Rochester, the City of Rochester Hills, and Oakland Township make up the Greater Rochester Community. About 77,000 people live in this historic and beautiful part of southeast Michigan.

Community Information

- City of Rochester
- City of Rochester Hills
  - Press Release
  - Text of Mayor Ken Snell's Inaugural Speech, November 20, 1995
- Oakland Township
- Rochester Community Schools
  - Global Village Project - Adams High School
  - Rochester High School Interact Club
- Important community telephone numbers, provided by the Greater Rochester Chamber of Commerce
- "Getting in Touch" - how to contact elected officials

| RHPL Home Page | Library Information | Internet Resources |

Internet Resource Lists
We have found these lists to be very helpful in finding information on the Internet.
Please direct any comments to matscosa@metronet.lib.mi.us.

**from
Rochester Hills
Public Library**

| Library Information |
| Community Information |
| RHPL Home Page |

- Getting Started on the Internet
- Government Resources Page
- **Internet Reference Desk**
- Job Search Page
- Just for Kids Page
- Legal Resources Page

- Michigan Internet Sites
- Readers' Services Page
- Selected Business Resources
- Special Services Page
- **Useful Sites by Subject**

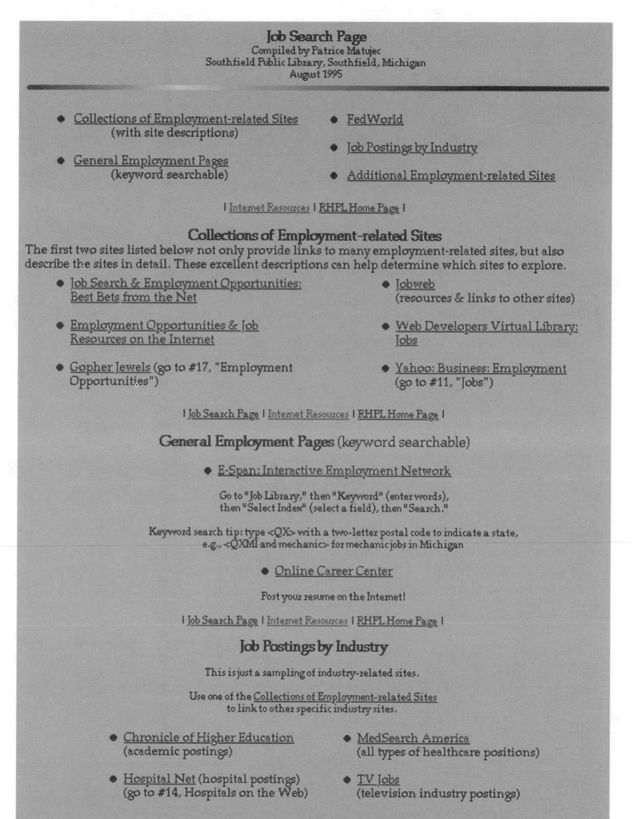

Job Search Page
Compiled by Patrice Matujec
Southfield Public Library, Southfield, Michigan
August 1995

- Collections of Employment-related Sites
  (with site descriptions)
- General Employment Pages
  (keyword searchable)
- FedWorld
- Job Postings by Industry
- Additional Employment-related Sites

| Internet Resources | RHPL Home Page |

Collections of Employment-related Sites

The first two sites listed below not only provide links to many employment-related sites, but also describe the sites in detail. These excellent descriptions can help determine which sites to explore.

- Job Search & Employment Opportunities: Best Bets from the Net
- Employment Opportunities & Job Resources on the Internet
- Gopher Jewels (go to #17, "Employment Opportunities")
- Jobweb (resources & links to other sites)
- Web Developers Virtual Library: Jobs
- Yahoo: Business: Employment (go to #11, "Jobs")

| Job Search Page | Internet Resources | RHPL Home Page |

General Employment Pages (keyword searchable)

- E-Span: Interactive Employment Network

  Go to "Job Library," then "Keyword" (enter words), then "Select Index" (select a field), then "Search."

  Keyword search tip: type <QX> with a two-letter postal code to indicate a state, e.g., <QXMI and mechanic> for mechanic jobs in Michigan

- Online Career Center

  Post your resume on the Internet!

| Job Search Page | Internet Resources | RHPL Home Page |

Job Postings by Industry

This is just a sampling of industry-related sites.

Use one of the Collections of Employment-related Sites to link to other specific industry sites.

- Chronicle of Higher Education
  (academic postings)
- Hospital Net (hospital postings)
  (go to #14, Hospitals on the Web)
- MedSearch America
  (all types of healthcare positions)
- TV Jobs
  (television industry postings)

| Job Search Page | Internet Resources | RHPL Home Page |

I Help/Search I Your Comments I About the Libraries I Collections & Resources I Library Catalogs I
I Map of the Libraries I UC Berkeley I Digital Library SunSITE I

UC Berkeley Library Web   HELP/SEARCH   CATALOGS   COMMENTS   HOME

Description of the Library | Library Hours | Library Services | Staff Materials

Library Service Points

Anthropology Library
Architecture Slide Library
Art History/Classics Graduate Service
Asian American Studies Library
Astronomy/Mathematics/Statistics Library
Bancroft Library
Biosciences and Natural Resources Library
Business and Economics Library
California Indian Library Collections
Carl G. Rosberg International Studies Library
Center for Chinese Studies Library
Chemistry Library
Chicano Studies Library
Circulation Services
Continuing Education of the Bar
Earth Sciences and Map Library
Earthquake Engineering Research Center
East Asian Library
Education/Psychology Library
Engineering Library
Environmental Design Library
General Reference Service
Giannini Foundation
Government and Social Science Information
Health Sciences Information Service

Information Desk
Institute of Governmental Studies
Institute of Industrial Relations
Institute of Transportation Studies
InterLibrary Services
Law Library
Media Resources Center
Moffitt Library
Morrison Library
Music Library
Native American Studies Library
Newspapers & Microforms
Optometry Library
Periodicals Circulation
Physics Library
Public Health Library
Social Welfare Library
South/Southeast Asia Library Service
Teaching Library
Water Resources Center Archive

HELP/SEARCH   CATALOGS   COMMENTS   HOME

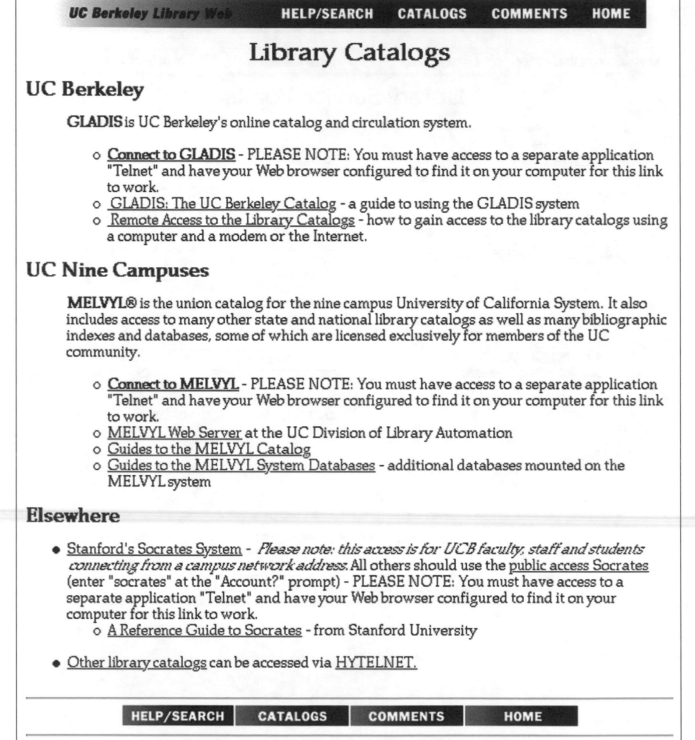

UC Berkeley Library Web   HELP/SEARCH   CATALOGS   COMMENTS   HOME

Library Catalogs

UC Berkeley

GLADIS is UC Berkeley's online catalog and circulation system.

- o **Connect to GLADIS** - PLEASE NOTE: You must have access to a separate application "Telnet" and have your Web browser configured to find it on your computer for this link to work.
- o GLADIS: The UC Berkeley Catalog - a guide to using the GLADIS system
- o Remote Access to the Library Catalogs - how to gain access to the library catalogs using a computer and a modem or the Internet.

UC Nine Campuses

MELVYL® is the union catalog for the nine campus University of California System. It also includes access to many other state and national library catalogs as well as many bibliographic indexes and databases, some of which are licensed exclusively for members of the UC community.

- o **Connect to MELVYL** - PLEASE NOTE: You must have access to a separate application "Telnet" and have your Web browser configured to find it on your computer for this link to work.
- o MELVYL Web Server at the UC Division of Library Automation
- o Guides to the MELVYL Catalog
- o Guides to the MELVYL System Databases - additional databases mounted on the MELVYL system

Elsewhere

- • Stanford's Socrates System - *Please note: this access is for UCB faculty, staff and students connecting from a campus network address.* All others should use the public access Socrates (enter "socrates" at the "Account?" prompt) - PLEASE NOTE: You must have access to a separate application "Telnet" and have your Web browser configured to find it on your computer for this link to work.
  - o A Reference Guide to Socrates - from Stanford University

- • Other library catalogs can be accessed via HYTELNET.

HELP/SEARCH   CATALOGS   COMMENTS   HOME

| *UC Berkeley Library Web* | HELP/SEARCH | CATALOGS | COMMENTS | HOME |

UC Berkeley Library Staff Materials

The following materials are meant primarily for use by the staff of the UC Berkeley Library. If you would like to find a particular staff member, you may wish to use the **Library Staff Directory: By Name**.

Contents and Links:

- Administrative Planning and Projects
- Staff Manuals
- Committees, Task Forces, and Discussion Groups
- Support Units
- Publications and Directories
- News and Information
- Librarian's Association of the University of California (LAUC)
- Library Resources on the Internet
- Staff Gopher

Administrative Planning and Projects

- Organization Charts
- Special Projects
- Access and Academic Services Explained
- Access Services
    - Strategic Plan - Draft 9/15/95
    - Annual Plan - Draft 11/9/95
    - Access Services Organization Chart
- Academic Services
    - Academic Services Planning Group, An Introduction - July 26, 1995
    - Updates
        - June 30, 1995
        - August 29, 1995
        - October 18, 1995
        - December 8, 1995
    - Report of the Academic Services Planning Group - December 8, 1995
- Administrative Services
    - Progress Report - January 12, 1996
- Financial Planning and Administration
    - Organization Chart
- Technical Services
    - Organization Chart
- "Reality Checks" Documents

Library Staff Manuals

- Automated Circulation User's Manual
- Library Orientation Manual
- Public Service Manual

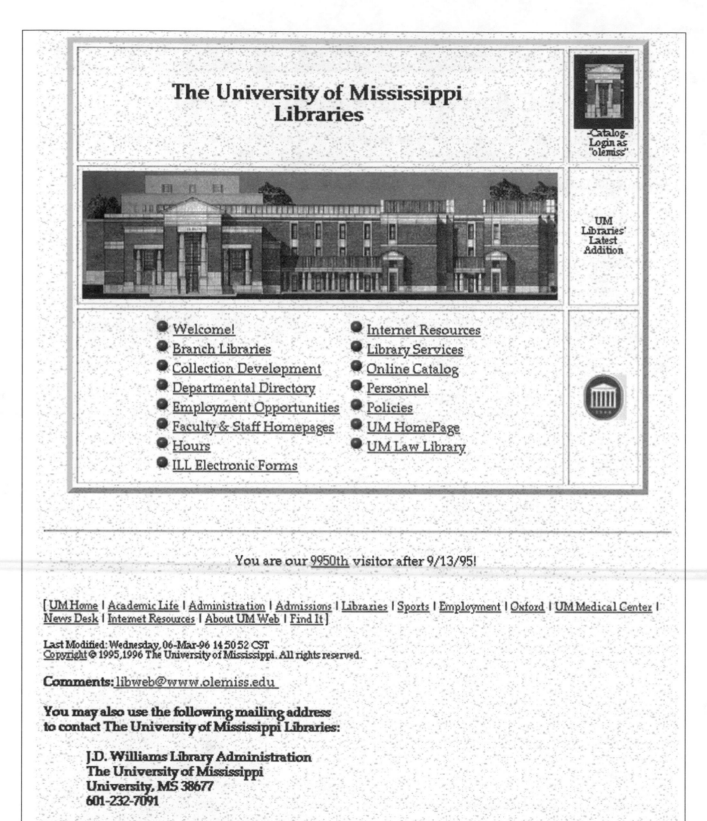

The University of Mississippi Libraries

-Catalog-
Login as
"olemiss"

UM
Libraries'
Latest
Addition

- Welcome!
- Branch Libraries
- Collection Development
- Departmental Directory
- Employment Opportunities
- Faculty & Staff Homepages
- Hours
- ILL Electronic Forms

- Internet Resources
- Library Services
- Online Catalog
- Personnel
- Policies
- UM HomePage
- UM Law Library

You are our 9950th visitor after 9/13/95!

[UM Home | Academic Life | Administration | Admissions | Libraries | Sports | Employment | Oxford | UM Medical Center | News Desk | Internet Resources | About UM Web | Find It]

Last Modified: Wednesday, 06-Mar-96 14 50 52 CST
Copyright © 1995, 1996 The University of Mississippi. All rights reserved.

Comments: libweb@www.olemiss.edu

**You may also use the following mailing address
to contact The University of Mississippi Libraries:**

J.D. Williams Library Administration
The University of Mississippi
University, MS 38677
601-232-7091

Thank you for visiting our Library WebPage.

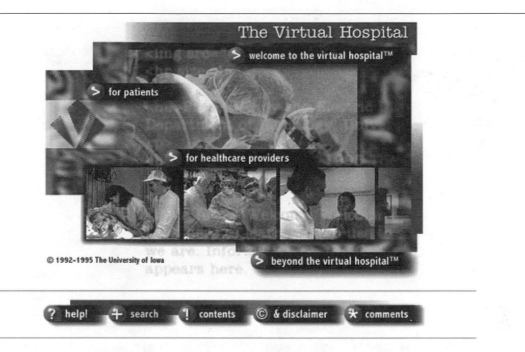

© 1992-1995 The University of Iowa

? help!   + search   ! contents   © & disclaimer   * comments

The Virtual Hospital (tm) is the Apprentice's Assistant (tm)

Presented by the Electric Differential Multimedia Laboratory, Department of Radiology, University of Iowa College of Medicine, Iowa City, Iowa

Copyright © 1992-1996 The University of Iowa

- Welcome to the Virtual Hospital
  Look here to learn how to use the Virtual Hospital, find out what's new, and discover who we are. Information on the College of Medicine and University of Iowa Hospitals & Clinics appears here.

- For Patients
  Look here for the Iowa Health Book and information about University of Iowa Hospitals & Clinics services and staff.

- For Healthcare Providers
  Look here for multimedia textbooks, teaching files, clinical guidelines and assorted publications.

- Beyond the Virtual Hospital
  Look here for information about the University of Iowa, its Health Sciences Colleges, Hardin Library for the Health Sciences, and links to other Internet health science resources.

Help is available. Search the Virtual Hospital. View an outline of the contents. Please read the attached copyright and disclaimer notice. We welcome your comments and suggestions.

librarian@vh.radiology.uiowa.edu

Electric Differential Multimedia Lab

Return to the Virtual Hospital Home Page

Queen's Library Home Page | Queen's University Home Page | **About QTECH**

QUEEN'S UNIVERSITY LIBRARIES
QTECH Web

Serving the Technical Services Units of Queen's University Libraries, Kingston, Ontario, Canada

▶ Services & Organization

▶ Technical Services Resources

General

● Library Catalogues: QLINE & Other Libraries ● Library Utilities & System Vendors ● NOTIS Documentation ● National Library of Canada. CEBEC. Cataloguing & Bibliographic Services ● Other Library Technical Services Web Sites ● General Reference Tools ● Conservation ● Technical Services & Related Discussion Lists

Acquisitions Tools

● Currency Converter ● Serials Acquisition ● Vendors and Publishers ● Discussion Lists

Cataloguing Tools

● Cutter Tables ● ISM Catss Procedures ● U.S. Library of Congress resources ● U.S. National Library of Medicine resources ● MARC Documentation ● Cataloguing Electronic Pubs. ● Discussion Lists

---

Note on Navigating the Web. All QTECH pages will return you to the QTECH Contents Page or QTECH Home Page through hypertext links at the top of each page. To return to QTECH from another Internet site, press the "BACK" button on your browser's button bar (top left corner in Netscape or Mosaic)

If you have any questions, comments or suggestions, please contact me by [E-mail ▦] .

Sam Kalb
Queen's University at Kingston
613-545-2830
kalbs@post.queensu.ca

Queen's Library Home Page | Queen's University Home Page

Page maintained by Sam Kalb. Created: 6/21/95 Updated: 1/10/96
URL: http://stauffer.queensu.ca/techserv/qtechweb.html OR
URL: http://130.15.161.74/techserv/qtechweb.html

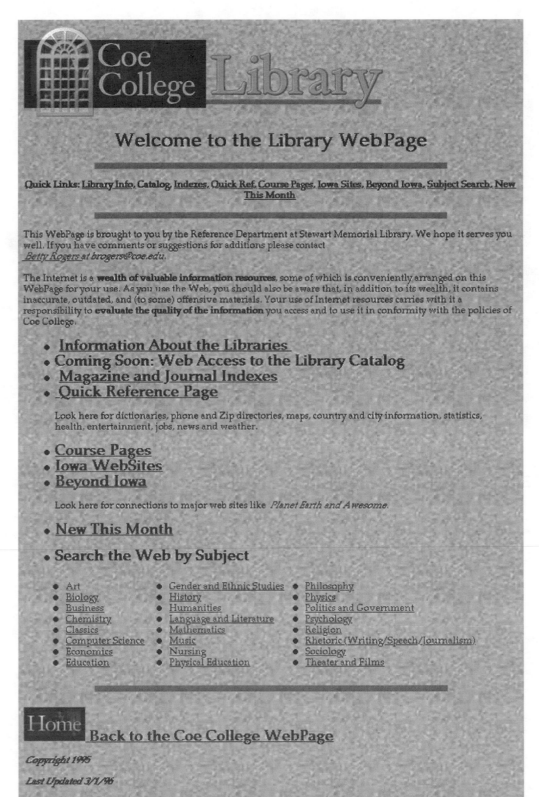

Coe College Library

Welcome to the Library WebPage

Quick Links: Library Info, Catalog, Indexes, Quick Ref, Course Pages, Iowa Sites, Beyond Iowa, Subject Search, New This Month

This WebPage is brought to you by the Reference Department at Stewart Memorial Library. We hope it serves you well. If you have comments or suggestions for additions please contact *Betty Rogers at brogers@coe.edu.*

The Internet is a **wealth of valuable information resources**, some of which is conveniently arranged on this WebPage for your use. As you use the Web, you should also be aware that, in addition to its wealth, it contains inaccurate, outdated, and (to some) offensive materials. Your use of Internet resources carries with it a responsibility to **evaluate the quality of the information** you access and to use it in conformity with the policies of Coe College.

- **Information About the Libraries**
- **Coming Soon: Web Access to the Library Catalog**
- **Magazine and Journal Indexes**
- **Quick Reference Page**

  Look here for dictionaries, phone and Zip directories, maps, country and city information, statistics, health, entertainment, jobs, news and weather.

- **Course Pages**
- **Iowa WebSites**
- **Beyond Iowa**

  Look here for connections to major web sites like *Planet Earth and Awesome.*

- **New This Month**

- **Search the Web by Subject**

  - Art
  - Biology
  - Business
  - Chemistry
  - Classics
  - Computer Science
  - Economics
  - Education

  - Gender and Ethnic Studies
  - History
  - Humanities
  - Language and Literature
  - Mathematics
  - Music
  - Nursing
  - Physical Education

  - Philosophy
  - Physics
  - Politics and Government
  - Psychology
  - Religion
  - Rhetoric (Writing/Speech/Journalism)
  - Sociology
  - Theater and Films

Home Back to the Coe College WebPage

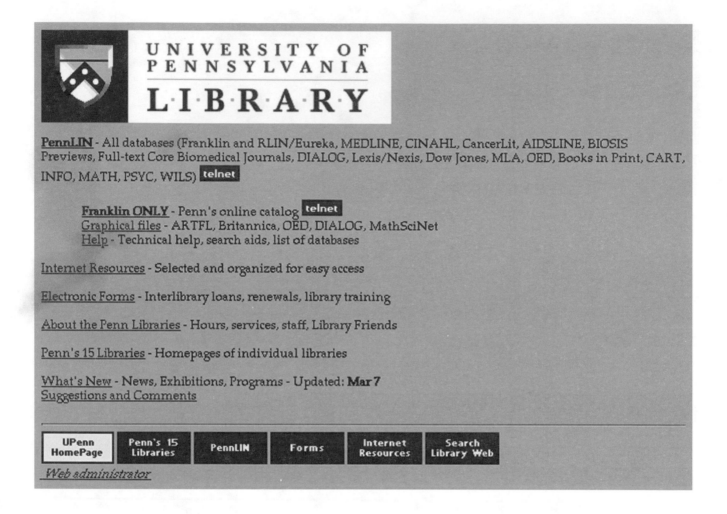

PENN LIBRARY

Penn's 15 Libraries

Library Hours

- Annenberg School for Communication Library
- Biddle Law Library
- Center for Judaic Studies Library
- Chemistry Library
- Engineering and Applied Science Library
- Fisher Fine Arts Library
- Health Sciences Libraries - Biomedical, Dental, and Veterinary Library
- Lippincott Library of the Wharton School
- Mathematics-Physics-Astronomy Library
- Museum Library
- Music Library
- Special Collections Library
- Van Pelt Library

- Map of Campus Libraries

| Penn Library HomePage | Penn's 15 Libraries | PennLIN | Forms | Internet Resources | Search Library Web |

Last update: Friday, 29-Dec-95 05:48:06 EST
Send mail concerning this page to: pennlin@pobox.upenn.edu

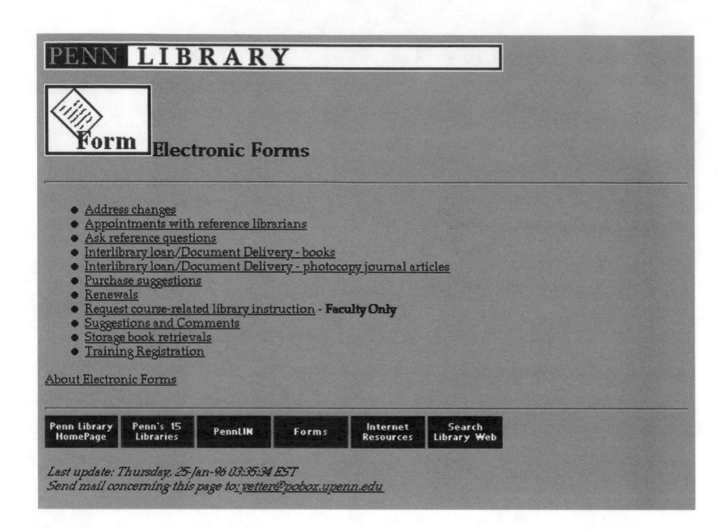

PENN LIBRARY

Form Electronic Forms

- Address changes
- Appointments with reference librarians
- Ask reference questions
- Interlibrary loan/Document Delivery - books
- Interlibrary loan/Document Delivery - photocopy journal articles
- Purchase suggestions
- Renewals
- Request course-related library instruction - **Faculty Only**
- Suggestions and Comments
- Storage book retrievals
- Training Registration

About Electronic Forms

| Penn Library HomePage | Penn's 15 Libraries | PennLIN | Forms | Internet Resources | Search Library Web |

Last update: Thursday, 25-Jan-96 03:35:34 EST
Send mail concerning this page to: yetter@pobox.upenn.edu

PENN LIBRARY

Form Ask a Reference Question

Further information on asking reference questions.

To reply to your question, we need the following information:

- Your Name: [   ]
- E-mail or Mail Address: [   ]
- Phone#: [   ]

Optional:

- Department or School: [   ]
- Status: [(Choose a status)   ▼]
- Forward question to: [Van Pelt (or choose another library)   ▼]

Type Reference Question:

[   ]
[   ]
[   ]
[   ]
[   ]
[   ]

☐   Check if you would like the opportunity to print your
     completed form after sending your request

[Send request]
[Clear request]

| Penn Library HomePage | Penn's 15 Libraries | PennLIN | Forms | Internet Resources | Search Library Web |

Last update: Thursday, 23-Nov-95 08:55:21 EST
Send mail concerning this page to: pennlin@pobox.upenn.edu

PENN LIBRARY

Form Make an Appointment with a Reference Librarian

Meet with a reference or departmental librarian, by appointment, to discuss your particular research needs.

To reply to your request, we need the following:

- Your Name: _____
- E-mail Address: _____
- Phone #: _____
- Forward request to: (Choose a library) ▼

To expedite your request, please fill in the following:

- Preferred Dates and Times:
  _____

- School/Department/Status:
  _____

- Please describe your topic:
  _____
  _____
  _____
  _____
  _____

☐ Check if you would like the opportunity to print your completed form after sending your request

[Send request]
[Clear request]

| Penn Library HomePage | Penn's 15 Libraries | PennLIN | Forms | Internet Resources | Search Library Web |

Last update: Thursday, 23-Nov-95 08:55:10 EST
Send mail concerning this page to: pennlin@pobox.upenn.edu

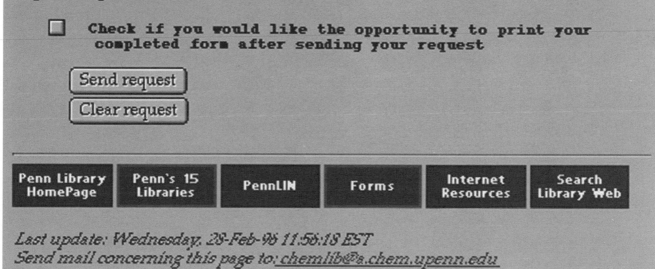

PENN LIBRARY

Register for DIALOG Training

Register below to attend a one-hour training session on searching the DIALOG Science and Engineering Databases. The sessions are held in 225 Moore Building.

Faculty may also fill out a form to request course-related instruction.

To facilitate your request, please provide the following information:

- Your Name:
- E-mail Address:
- Phone#:
- Department or School:
- Status: (Choose a Status) ▼
- Spring 1996 training sessions: (Choose date/time) ▼

Description of the Training Sessions: These sessions provide an introduction to basic commands and search features, as well as an overview of the DIALOG science and engineering databases available at Penn.

☐ **Check if you would like the opportunity to print your completed form after sending your request**

Send request

Clear request

Penn Library HomePage	Penn's 15 Libraries	PennLIN	Forms	Internet Resources	Search Library Web

Last update: Wednesday, 28-Feb-96 11:56:18 EST
Send mail concerning this page to: chemlib@a.chem.upenn.edu

Multnomah County LIBRARY KidsPage

Welcome to the Multnomah County Library KidsPage!

It's the official Web page for Multnomah County Library Youth Services. We're here for everyone from birth to age 18, for every family with kids, and for everyone who works with kids. We want every child to discover the joys of language, literature, and culture... to learn and have fun! Select your choice:

- Multnomah County Library family program & activity calendar.
- We bring Books 2 U! --or rather, we send our book-loving volunteers out to tell 3rd-5th grade students what's good to read...
- Ramona is here! Visit Portland's new Beverly Cleary Sculpture Garden for Children!
- Teen Corner for middle school and high school students.
- Readers' Choice: new & favorite books for all ages.
- Parents' Page: stuff from the library and the Internet that can help you as a parent.
- Educator Info: library and Internet resources for teachers and others in education.
- Cool spots on the Web: visit other Web pages for kids of all ages.

Joke of the Month:

When a librarian eats dinner, what does she eat from?
ANSWER

Ellen Fader is Coordinator of Youth Services for Multnomah County Library.
She welcomes your comments and suggestions at ellenf@nethost.multnomah.lib.or.us.

This web page was created by
Walter Minkel, Gresham Youth Librarian, walterm@nethost.multnomah.lib.or.us,
with the help of the Youth Services staff of the Multnomah County Library System.
Your feedback on the KidsPage is welcome!
This page was last updated on 3/6/96.
Back to the Library Web Page

WELCOME TO THE NMSU Library

NEW MEXICO STATE UNIVERSITY

The NMSU Library

Access to the online catalog and information about Library programs and services

NMSU Information

Access to other NMSU departments & services

Internet Gateway

Access to resources around the world

New Mexico State University Library
Box 30006, Dept. 3475
Las Cruces, NM 88003-8006
(505) 646-6928
library@lib.nmsu.edu
Last revised November 17, 1995

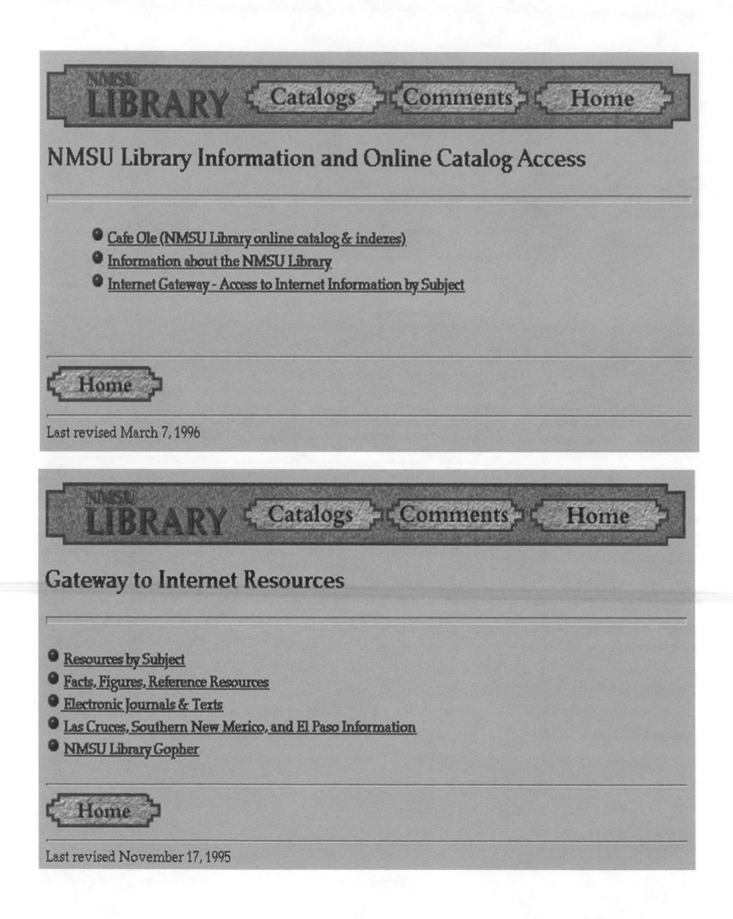

NMSU LIBRARY · Catalogs · Comments · Home

NMSU Library Information and Online Catalog Access

- Cafe Ole (NMSU Library online catalog & indexes)
- Information about the NMSU Library
- Internet Gateway – Access to Internet Information by Subject

Home

Last revised March 7, 1996

NMSU LIBRARY · Catalogs · Comments · Home

Gateway to Internet Resources

- Resources by Subject
- Facts, Figures, Reference Resources
- Electronic Journals & Texts
- Las Cruces, Southern New Mexico, and El Paso Information
- NMSU Library Gopher

Home

Last revised November 17, 1995

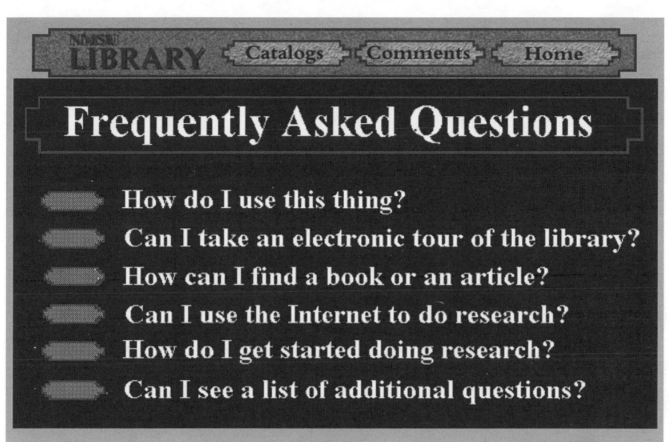

How do I use this thing? | Can I take an electronic tour of the NMSU Library? | How do I find a book or an article? | Can I use the Internet to do research? | How do I get started doing research? | Can I see a list of additional frequently asked questions?

You can return to the NMSU Library Homepage or the NMSU Homepage if you wish.

Comments?

answers@lib.nmsu.eduLast updated 1/96

UNDERGRADUATE LIBRARY

Undergraduate Library, General Libraries, University of Texas at Austin

- **Location Information**

    Find out where we are located on campus.

- **UGL Virtual Tour**

    Take a tour of our three floors and learn about the services we offer.

- **UGL Electronic Information Center** NEW

    Our lab will be re-opening soon with new equipment for information searching.

- **Ten New Books for the Month**

    Browse some of our newest additions to our collection--covers and all.

- **Calendar of Electronic Information Classes**

    Calendar of Internet and electronic information classes offered by the General Libraries.

- **Universal Times: Electronic Newspaper**

    Read articles collected from the ClariNet Electronic News Service.
    Currently the Newspaper is being updated to include new newsgroups. Check again soon.

- **UGL Suggestion Box**

    Please leave us questions, comments and suggestions about UGL services and facilities.

Boolean **AND, OR, NOT**, as well as **truncation** ('form*' finds 'forms', 'formed', and 'formal') may be used in your search. Searches are not **case sensitive**.

[_____] [Search this Server]

Last updated: 12 January, 1996
Created by: Elizabeth Dupuis
Please send comments to: beth@mail.utexas.edu

UT Library Online | UT Austin Web Central | www@lib.utexas.edu

ELECTRONIC INFORMATION CLASSES

March 1996

Sunday	Monday	Tuesday	Wednesday	Thursday	Friday	Saturday
					1	2
3	4	5	6	7	8	9
10	11	12	13	14	15	16
17	18	19	20	21	22	23
24	25	26	27	28	29	30
31						

- Classes on March 8, 1996
- Class Schedule for this session
- List of Classes taught by the General Libraries

February   April

Classes offered on March 6, 1996 :

Wednesday March 6
   9:00-10:30 Hands-on Internet Basics: Using the World Wide Web
   FAC 227, Student Microcomputer Facility Training Room, Undergraduate Library
   2:00-3:30 Hands-on Finding Art Information on the Internet
   FAB 3.200 Fine Arts Library, Micrcomputer Lab (FAML)

⤶ Current Month

The General Libraries | *UT Austin Central Server* | *www@lib.utexas.edu*
Last Modified:

ClariNet Electronic Newspaper

An Electronic Newspaper From the Undergraduate Library, The University of Texas at Austin
Compiled from the ClariNet Electronic News Service

Sections

- Top Stories
- U.S. National News
- Texas and Campus News
- Local News From Around the U.S.
- World News
- General News
- Issues in the News
- Groups in the News
- Business, Economic, and Industry News
- Lifestyle
- Arts and Entertainment
- Sports
- Computers
- Science and Technology
- ClariNet Features and Columns
- News From the San Francisco Bay Area

For a brief explanation of this newspaper service, see the About section.

The General Libraries | *UT Austin Central Server* | *www@lib.utexas.edu*
Last Modified: *Thursday, 18-Jan-96 15:22:00*

UGL Suggestion Box

If your browser does not support forms you can send us e-mail to: ann.neville@mail.utexas.edu.

We welcome your comments and suggestions concerning services provided by the Undergraduate Library. We do not answer questions concerning the Student Microcomputer Facility (SMF), questions about other General Libraries units or reference questions.

We will answer your comments as promptly as possible. Selected comments and the replies will be posted on the Suggestion Board mounted in the lobby of UGL. Thank you for your input.

E-mail Address: (Required)

Name: (Optional)

Subject:

Comments:

[Send Your Comment] [Clear This Form]

Kids' Home Page

Welcome to Spokane Public Library's Kids' Page, a resource list of Internet sites for youth, parents, guardians, and educators.

You are visitor 0000396 to access this page
Since February 12, 1996.

The Library's Youth Services staff has designed this page to help youth find age-appropriate sites on the Internet. We have included a large of selection of sites, some of which will be more appropriate for younger readers, while others will appeal to young adults. We invite you to explore any or all of these excellent sites. If you can't find exactly what you need, a Children's Librarian will be happy to assist you. We hope you enjoy using this page as much as we have enjoyed putting it together. If you discover a site that you think we should include in this list of resources, let us know about it.

Click on one of the following topics at a time:

- *For sites by topic for youth of all ages*
- *For great general starting points for youth of all ages*
- *For useful sites for parents, guardians, educators*

Favorite Books - click on a topic for wonderful books to read:

- If you like *Goosebumps*
- If you like *Mystery*
- If you like *Fantasy/Time Travel*
- If you like *Humor*
- If you like *Animal Stories*
- If you like *Sports*
- If you like *Baby-Sitters Club*
- If you like *Historical Fiction*
- If you like *Adventure/Survival Stories*
- If you like *Chapter Books*
- Vote for your favorite *Washington Children's Choice Picture Book, 1996 Nominees*
- View a list *Washington Children's Choice Picture Book, Award Winners*
- Vote for your favorite *Children's Choice, 1996 Nominees*
- View a list *Children's Choice Award Winners*

SPOKANE
PUBLIC
LIBRARY

Youth Services Coordinator, nledeboer@spokpl.lib.wa.us

| SPL Home Page | Online Catalog |

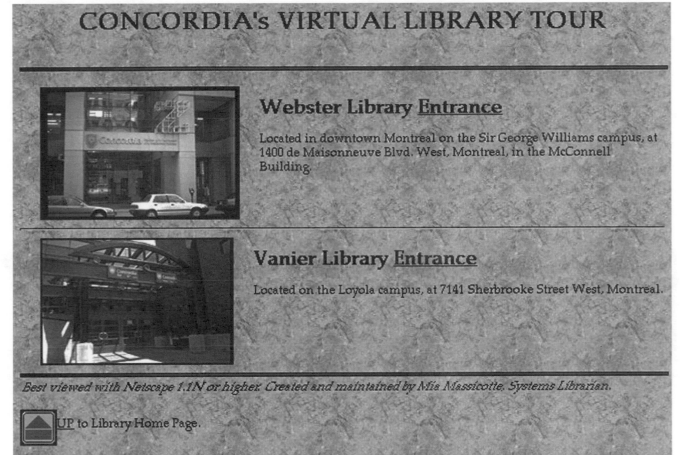

CONCORDIA's VIRTUAL LIBRARY TOUR

Webster Library Entrance

Located in downtown Montreal on the Sir George Williams campus, at 1400 de Maisonneuve Blvd. West, Montreal, in the McConnell Building.

Vanier Library Entrance

Located on the Loyola campus, at 7141 Sherbrooke Street West, Montreal.

Best viewed with Netscape 1.1N or higher. Created and maintained by Mia Massicotte, Systems Librarian.

UP to Library Home Page.

Last modified by MM on 05-oct-1995.

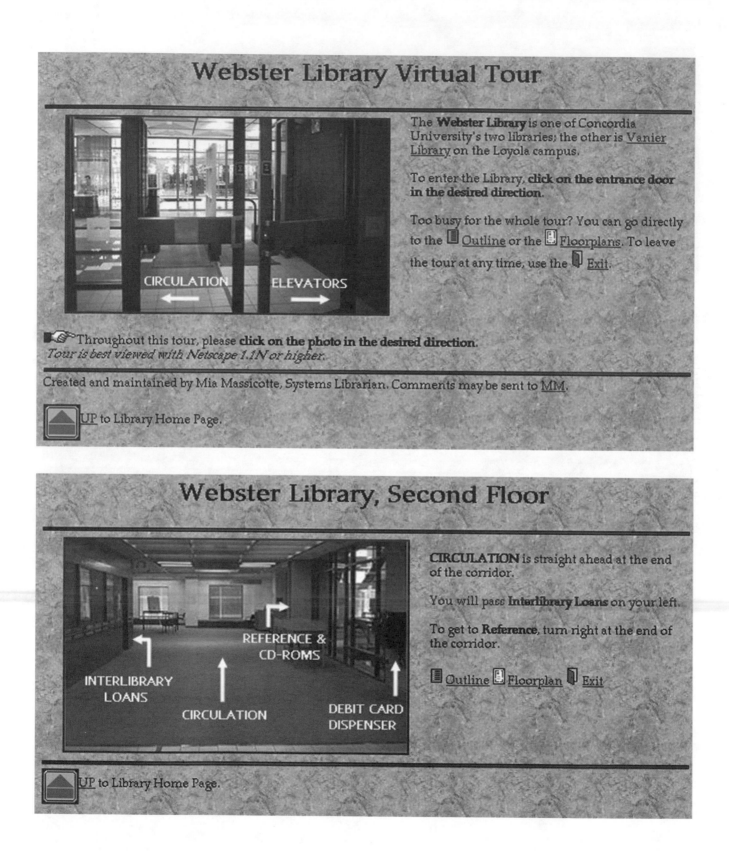

Webster Library Virtual Tour

The **Webster Library** is one of Concordia University's two libraries; the other is Vanier Library on the Loyola campus.

To enter the Library, **click on the entrance door in the desired direction.**

Too busy for the whole tour? You can go directly to the 🖾 Outline or the 🖾 Floorplans. To leave the tour at any time, use the 🚪 Exit.

CIRCULATION ← ELEVATORS →

☞ Throughout this tour, please **click on the photo in the desired direction.**
Tour is best viewed with Netscape 1.1N or higher.

Created and maintained by Mia Massicotte, Systems Librarian. Comments may be sent to MM.

🔼 UP to Library Home Page.

Webster Library, Second Floor

CIRCULATION is straight ahead at the end of the corridor.

You will pass **Interlibrary Loans** on your left.

To get to **Reference**, turn right at the end of the corridor.

🖾 Outline 🖾 Floorplan 🚪 Exit

INTERLIBRARY LOANS
REFERENCE & CD-ROMS
CIRCULATION
DEBIT CARD DISPENSER

🔼 UP to Library Home Page.

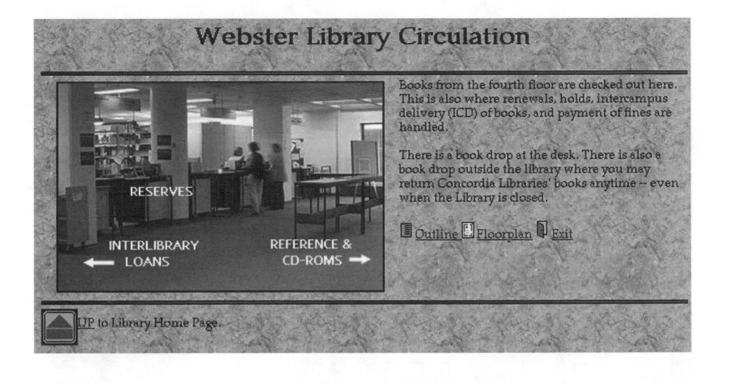

Webster Library Circulation

RESERVES

INTERLIBRARY LOANS

REFERENCE & CD-ROMS

Books from the fourth floor are checked out here. This is also where renewals, holds, intercampus delivery (ICD) of books, and payment of fines are handled.

There is a book drop at the desk. There is also a book drop outside the library where you may return Concordia Libraries' books anytime -- even when the Library is closed.

Outline Floorplan Exit

UP to Library Home Page.

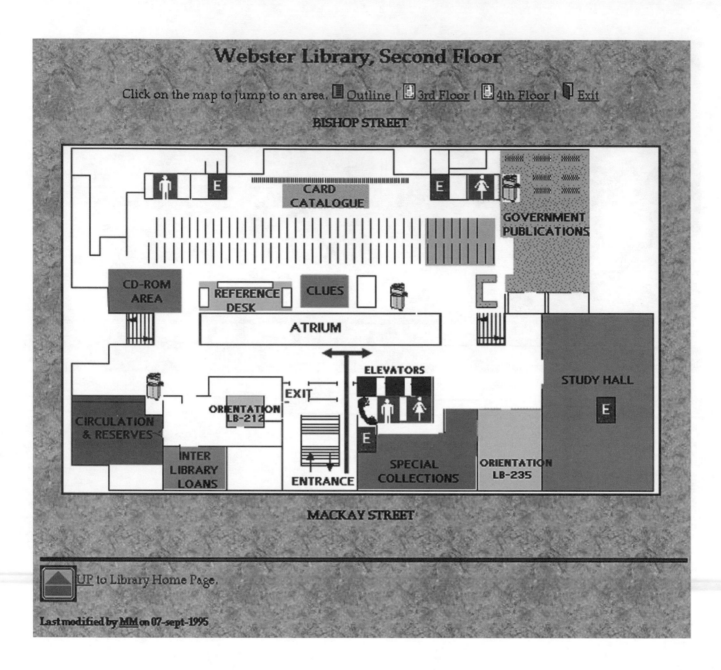

INDEX

COLOPHON

Ray E. Metz is Interim Director of University Library at Case Western Reserve University. He is responsible for overseeing Internet training on campus as well as managing the library's Web presence. Ray has given presentations on the Net at both CAUSE and Educom and has written numerous articles on the subject of information technology for professional journals. Ray has worked at the University of Rochester as Head of Library Systems and at Northern Michigan University.

Gail Junion-Metz is President of Information Age Consultants of Cleveland, OH. She is a librarian and Net trainer. She is the author of *K-12 Resources on the Internet* published by Library Solutions Press (1996) in addition to numerous journal articles. She is the "Surf For" columnist for *School Library Journal*, and has presented Internet workshops around the country and in Canada. Gail has worked at Cleveland State University, the University of Rochester, Bowling Green State University, and Indiana University, Bloomington.

Additional Titles of Interest in the *Neal-Schuman NetGuide* Series

THE COMPLETE INTERNET COMPANION FOR LIBRARIANS
by Allen C. Benson

"An effective road map for new drivers on the information superhighway, teaching not only the rules of the road but also showing how to deal with roadblocks and detours." *Library Journal*

1-55570-178-7. 1995. 8 1/2 x 11. 405 pp. $49.95.

LEARNING THE INTERNET:
A Workbook for Beginners
by John Burke

"A short, practical introduction to the Internet, for beginning Internet users. For classroom, workshop, or home use." *Reference and Research Book News*

" . . . unlike many recent Internet titles, is designed to serve as a hands-on tutorial . . . recommended . . . as a clear, concise, practical introduction to the Internet." *Library Journal*

1-55570-248-1. 1996. 8 1/2 x 11. 150 pp. $29.95.

THE INTERNET COMPENDIUM: GUIDES TO RESOURCES BY SUBJECT
By Louis Rosenfeld, Joseph Janes, and Martha Vander Kolk

This unique series compiled by a team from the acclaimed University of Michigan Internet Clearinghouse, provides direct location access to a virtual mall of over ten thousand Internet addresses in hundreds of subjects.

Subject Guides to Humanities Resources
1-55570-218-X. 1995. 8 1/2 x 11. 368 pp. $75.00.

Subject Guides to Health and Science Resources
1-55570-219-8. 1995. 8 1/2 x 11. 529 pp. $75.00.

Subject Guides to Social Sciences, Business & Law
1-55570-220-1. 1995. 8 1/2 x 11. 424 pp. $75.00.

Buy all three subject guides for $175
1-55570-188-4.

"While indexing the ever-changing environment of the Internet may seem an impossible job, this series makes an excellent start and will be valuable on the reference shelf for both librarians and patrons." *Library Journal*

CONNECTING KIDS AND THE INTERNET:
A Handbook for Librarians, Teachers, and Parents
By Allen C. Benson and Linda Fodemski

At last, an Internet guide that teaches school media specialists, teachers, and parents how to navigate the Net—and provides sample lesson plans that will enable kids to learn too. It also contains a guide to the best educational and recreational resources for kids.

1-55570-244-9. 1996. 8 1/2 x 11. 300 pp. $35.00.

THE INTERNET FOR TEACHERS AND SCHOOL LIBRARY MEDIA SPECIALISTS:
Today's Applications, Tomorrow's Prospects
Edited by Edward J. Valauskas and Monica Ertel

Wondering how other schools incorporate the Internet into their curricula? Look here for successful Internet programs used in elementary, middle, and high schools to teach math, science, history, literature, music, and more. Program descriptions are written by the faculty members and/or school library media specialists involved. Each contains goals and results; budget, technical, and curricular information.

1-55570-239-2. 1996. 6 x 9. 231 pp. $35.00.

THE INTERNET SEARCHER'S HANDBOOK
Locating Information, People, and Software
by Peter Morville, Louis Rosenfeld, and Joseph Janes

Novice or advanced Internet searchers can use this handy resource to conduct comprehensive research investigations—and find the answers to quick reference queries. The book provides in-depth coverage on virtual libraries, Internet directories, communities of people, and Internet search tools, plus examples of real searches for each resource.

1-55570-243-0. 1996. 8 1/2 x 11. 240 pp. $35.00.

REFERENCE & COLLECTION DEVELOPMENT ON THE INTERNET:
A How-To-Do-It Manual for Librarians
By Elizabeth Thomsen

Here is a cutting-edge manual that evaluates and gives librarians the tools to find thousands of different Internet resources that offer guidance in collection development and reference services. It explains how and where to benefit from online communities, email professional interest groups, Usenet newsgroups, literary groups, FAQs, and electronic texts.

1-55570-243-0. 1996. 8 1/2 x 11. 240 pp. $45.00.

THE INTERNET ACCESS COOKBOOK:
A Librarian's Commonsense Guide to Low-Cost Connections
by Karen G. Schneider

"What distinguishes this title from the glut of Internet books in print is its ability to empower a computer novice with the knowledge and confidence to successfully plan and connect to the Internet. Schneider, *American Libraries*' 'Internet Librarian' columnist . . . covers everything. This is recommended. Bon appetit!" *Library Journal*

1-55570-235-X. 1996. 6 x 9. 322 pp. $24.95.

FINDING GOVERNMENT INFORMATION ON THE INTERNET:
A How-To-Do-It Manual
Edited by John Maxymuk

"For librarians and anyone else with interest in government information policy, this book offers the most comprehensive overview available of government information on the Internet . . . thorough and well-documented . . ." *Library Journal*

1-55570-228-7. 1996. 8 1/2 x 11. 175 pp. $45.00.

USING THE INTERNET, ONLINE SERVICES, AND CD-ROMs FOR WRITING RESEARCH AND TERM PAPERS
Edited by Charles Harmon

This unique guide is a basic, comprehensive manual for high school and college students that does for electronic resources what Turabian does for print. Includes MLA and APA citation formats for Internet and CD-ROM sources.

1-55570-238-4. 1996. 6 x 9. 170 pp. $29.95.

Publication dates, prices, and number of pages for new titles may be estimates and are subject to change.

To order or request further information, contact:
Neal-Schuman Publishers
100 Varick Street, New York, NY 10013
212-925-8650
or fax toll free—1-800-584-2414